SUPPLY CHAIN MANAGEMENT
in the Retail Industry

SUPPLY CHAIN MANAGEMENT

in the Retail Industry

MICHAEL HUGOS

CHRIS THOMAS

WILEY

JOHN WILEY & SONS, INC.

Library of Congress Cataloging-in-Publication Data

Hugos, Michael H.
    Supply chain management in the retail industry / Michael Hugos, Chris Thomas.
        p.   cm.
    Includes index.
    ISBN-13: 978-0-471-72319-6 (pbk.)
    ISBN-10: 0-471-72319-3 (pbk.)
    1. Business logistics. 2. Retail trade—Management. I. Thomas, Chris. II. Title.
    HD38.5.H86 2006
    658.8'7—dc22

                                                            2005019108

Printed in the United States of America

10 9 8 7 6 5 4 3 2 1

CONTENTS

CHAPTER **3**
SUPPLY CHAIN OPERATIONS: PLANNING 45

CHAPTER **4**
SUPPLY CHAIN OPERATIONS: SOURCING MATERIALS AND MAKING PRODUCTS 69

CHAPTER **5**
SUPPLY CHAIN OPERATIONS: DELIVERIES AND RETURNS 93

CHAPTER **6**

TECHNOLOGY AND SUPPLY CHAIN COORDINATION 113

CHAPTER **7**

MEASURING PERFORMANCE: SUPPLY CHAIN METRICS 137

CHAPTER **8**

DEFINING SUPPLY CHAIN OPPORTUNITIES 159

PREFACE

It's always a challenge for an author to take a subject like supply chain management (SCM) and make it meaningful to students who may (understandably) be saying something like, "Give me a break—I just want a good job at the mall! Why in the world do I need to know all this?"

The interesting thing about SCM is how pervasive it is. It's one of those topics like health or taxes that impacts our lives in ways we often don't even notice. Like the colonies of ants discussed in Steven Johnson's book *Emergence: The Connected Lives of Ants, Brains, Cities, and Software* (Scribner, 2002), which we discuss in Chapter 10, supply chains are hard at work every minute of every day, largely behind the scenes. They make and move and store and price and sell every item we purchase as consumers. And, like ants, when someone carelessly steps in the middle of the anthill or the pest control company shows up, things change rather quickly when supply chains are disrupted.

Here are a couple of examples that have made news headlines in a single month (April 2005):

- In Savar, Bangladesh, a boiler exploded in a clothing factory and brought the whole building down with it. The collapse killed 21 people, injured 92, and at the time of the initial news report, an estimated 200 workers were still buried in the rubble.
- The following week, General Motors announced a recall of 2.1 million vehicles, the majority of them sport utility vehicles and pickup trucks, for a variety of problems that range from seat belt malfunctions to overheating of fuel pump wires.

■ Also in the news in spring 2005 is a Securities and Exchange Commission case that bears watching because its outcome and aftermath could change the entire supply chain profit picture for retailers. The SEC has scrutinized the accounting practices of one particular national department store chain, and the way it bills its suppliers for unsold merchandise, a practice known as collecting "chargebacks" or "markdown money."

A little background on the last bullet point: The big retailers have become even bigger in recent years, with buyouts and mergers. They've consolidated partly to compete with Wal-Mart, but partly to exercise more overall clout in their negotiations with suppliers. Since the 1980s, it's become the norm in negotiations for retailers to ask for, and receive, some money from manufacturers if goods didn't arrive on time, or if they just didn't sell well and have to be marked down in price to clear them out of inventory.

But now some of the manufacturers are rethinking these standard arrangements. They say they're being taken advantage of; that stores have demanded money for reasons the manufacturers did not agree to; and that retailers are, in fact, forcing them to guarantee a profit with the payment of markdown money.

How do you feel about that? Your view may change as you read this book. Chapters 1 and 2 introduce supply chains and distribution channels, highly collaborative groups of businesses that are required for today's retailers—large and small—to get their products into the stores for sale. Chapters 3, 4, and 5 take readers through the major operational and logistical decisions that are made in the five-step process of getting goods to market. These are based on the Supply-Chain Operations Reference (SCOR) model of the Supply-Chain Council, a nonprofit organization made up of almost 1,000 member companies worldwide (www.supply-chain.org):

■ Planning (forecasting and determining what and how much to sell)
■ Sourcing (finding the suppliers of these goods, negotiating with them, exchanging money for the goods)
■ Making (designing a good product and scheduling its production)
■ Delivering (importing, warehousing, and physically moving the goods through the supply chain)
■ Returns (handling customer service and complaints, and determining what to do with returned merchandise)

Chapter 6 introduces the theory and practice of collaboration between supply chain members, as well as the types of information they must learn to share in order to work together efficiently and profitably. This "sharing," as you will note, is difficult when companies naturally feel competitive, or when some are better funded or better organized than others. Chapter 7 continues the discussion with an in-depth look at metrics, measurements of market conditions that supply chain members must constantly monitor to determine whether their plans are on track and mutually beneficial, or whether changes are in order.

Chapters 8 and 9 cover a topic that may frustrate retail management students who don't see how it applies to them: the step-by-step creation of a large-scale systems improvement project. These major undertakings cost companies a great deal of time and money, but they are often necessary in order to synchronize data with supply chain partners, to streamline ordering processes, to get an eCommerce Web site up and running, and so forth. This information is included in the book because it is a huge part of supply chain cooperation, and because any good retail manager will want to have as much input as possible into the purchase, or design and implementation, of systems that his or her department will have to use.

Finally, Chapter 10 looks at several important technological developments in the business world and how they have opened the doors to new partnerships as well as vast new opportunities for multichannel distribution and sales. Two facts are of interest to would-be retailers here—first, that each opportunity brings with it formidable new challenges; and second, that no matter how technologically advanced we become, retailing is still about people. The interaction of human beings in supply chains is just as critical to their success as the interaction of software systems. Perhaps more so.

Your customers are people, not companies and not computers. A recent newspaper article about the chargeback controversy reinforced this point with an interesting sidelight from America's Research Group, a consumer research firm in Charleston, South Carolina: Less than 12 percent of American shoppers say they are "willing to pay full price" for clothing. That's down from 24 percent just five years ago.

You might say bargain-conscious consumers are stepping on the anthill—which should make the study of supply chain management even more important for the next generation of retail managers.

AN INTRODUCTION TO SUPPLY CHAIN MANAGEMENT

When a retailer sells a new suit to a satisfied customer, the supply chain has done its job. A **supply chain** encompasses every step that was taken to get that suit into the hands of that customer—a combination of the companies and the business activities needed to design, make, deliver, and use a product or service. In some types of retail, the supply chain also includes follow-up services: the purchase of that suit, for instance, may include tailoring services, or credit services from the bank or store credit department responsible for accepting the customer's monthly payments.

Businesses depend on their supply chains to provide them with what they need to survive and thrive. For retailers, of course, this means their very lifeblood—the goods that they sell to consumers—but every business fits into one or more supply chains and has a role to play in each of them.

After reading this chapter, you will be able to

- Explain and appreciate what a supply chain is, and what it does.
- Define the different organizations that participate in any supply chain.
- Discuss ways that companies align their supply chains with their business strategy.
- Recognize supply chain management issues in retail businesses.

The pace of change and the uncertainty about how markets will evolve has made it increasingly important for companies to be aware of the supply chains they participate in and to understand the roles that they play. Companies that learn how to build and participate in strong supply chains do so to create a substantial competitive advantage in their markets.

THE EVOLUTION OF THE SUPPLY CHAIN

The practice of supply chain management is guided by some basic underlying concepts that have not changed much over the centuries. Several hundred years ago, Napoleon made the remark, "An army marches on its stomach." Napoleon was a master strategist and a skillful general, and this remark shows his clear understanding of the importance of what we would now call an efficient supply chain—that is, unless the soldiers are fed, the army cannot move. Getting them fed required a supply chain in the late 1700s . . . and would still require one today.

Another pertinent saying is, "Amateurs talk strategy; professionals talk logistics." People can discuss all sorts of impressive maneuvers and grand victories, but none of that will be possible without first figuring out how to meet the day-to-day demands of providing an army with fuel, spare parts, food, shelter, and ammunition. It is the seemingly mundane (but not always simple) activities of the quartermaster and the supply sergeants that often determine an army's success.

WHAT MADE ALEXANDER SO GREAT? SUPPLY CHAIN MANAGEMENT!

Alexander the Great based his strategies and campaigns on his army's unique capabilities—and he was a master of effective supply chain management.

In the spirit of the saying, "Amateurs talk strategy and professionals talk logistics," let's look at the campaigns of Alexander the Great. For those who think his greatness was due to his ability to dream up bold moves and cut a dashing figure in the saddle, think again.

The authors from Greek and Roman times who recorded his deeds had little to say about something so apparently unglamorous as how he secured supplies for his army. Yet, from these same sources, many little details can be pieced together to show the overall supply chain picture and how Alexander managed it.

A modern historian, Donald Engels, investigated this topic in *Alexander the Great and the Logistics of the Macedonian Army* (University of California Press, Los Angeles, California, 1978). Engels observes that, given the conditions of Alexander's time, his strategy and tactics had to be very closely tied to his ability to get supplies and to run a lean, efficient organization. The only way to transport large amounts of material over long distances was by ocean-going ships or by barges on rivers and canals. Away from rivers and sea coasts, an army had to be able to live off the land as it traveled. Diminishing returns set in quickly using pack animals and carts to haul supplies—the animals themselves had to eat, and would soon consume all the food and water they were hauling unless they could graze along the way.

In the typical military arrangement of the day, the number of support people and camp followers was often as large as the number of actual fighting soldiers, because armies traveled with huge numbers of carts and pack animals to carry their equipment and provisions, as well as the people needed to tend them. These ancillary workers and pack animals significantly reduced the army's speed and mobility.

In Alexander's Macedonian army, however, the use of carts was severely restricted. Soldiers were trained to carry their own equipment and provisions. The result of this logistical decision was the fastest, lightest, and most mobile army of its time. As its leader, Alexander could use this capability to devise strategies and employ tactics that allowed him to surprise and overwhelm enemies that were numerically much larger.

The picture that emerges of how Alexander managed his supply chain is an interesting one. For instance, time and again the historical sources mention that before he entered a new territory, he would receive the surrender of its ruler and arrange in advance with local officials for the supplies his army would need. If a region did not surrender to him in advance, Alexander would not commit his entire army to a campaign in that land. He would not risk putting his army in a situation where

Continued

it could be crippled or destroyed by a lack of provisions. Instead, he would gather intelligence about the routes, the resources, and the climate of the region and then set off with a small, light force to surprise his opponent. The main army would remain behind at a well-stocked base until Alexander secured adequate supplies for it to follow.

Whenever the army set up a new base camp, it looked for an area that provided easy access to a navigable river or a seaport. Then ships would arrive from other parts of Alexander's empire, bringing in large amounts of supplies. The army always stayed in its winter camp until the first spring harvest of the new year, so that food supplies would be available. When it marched, it avoided dry or uninhabited areas and moved through river valleys and populated regions whenever possible, so the horses could graze and the army could requisition supplies along the route.

Alexander had a deep understanding of the capabilities and limitations of his supply chain. He formulated strategies and tactics based on the unique strengths of his supply chain, and he wisely took measures to compensate for whatever limitations it had as well. His opponents often outnumbered him and were usually fighting on their own home turf—but they were undermined by clumsy and inefficient supply chains that restricted their ability to act, and limited their options for opposing Alexander's moves.

The idea has many analogies in business. The term "supply chain management" arose in the late 1980s and came into widespread use in the 1990s. Prior to that time, businesses used terms such as "logistics" and "operations management" instead. Following are some definitions of a supply chain:

- A supply chain is the alignment of firms that bring products or services to market.[1]
- A supply chain consists of all stages involved, directly or indirectly, in fulfilling a customer request. The supply chain not only includes the manufacturer and suppliers, but also transporters, warehouses, retailers, and customers themselves.[2]
- A supply chain is a network of facilities and distribution options that performs the functions of procurement of materials, transformation of these materials into intermediate and finished products, and the distribution of these finished products to customers.[3]
- The systemic, strategic coordination of the traditional business functions and the tactics across these business functions within a particular company and across businesses within the supply chain, for the purposes of improving the long-term performance of the individual companies and the supply chain as a whole.[4]

In short, supply chain management is the coordination of production, inventory, location, and transportation among the participants in a supply chain to achieve the best mix of responsiveness and efficiency for the market being served. We can further define supply chain management as the things we do to influence the behavior of the supply chain and get the results we want.

What does all this have to do with retail? Consider all the decisions—from the individuals who are responsible for making them to the products and services required to carry them out—that a retail buyer makes when purchasing a single line of clothing. In Figure 1-1, you see four distinct systems or "streams" set into effect by the buyer's decisions. Each of these systems requires a supply chain and, of course, responsive and efficient management of that chain.

Isn't That . . . Logistics?

There are distinct differences between the concepts of supply chain management and traditional logistics. Logistics typically refers to activities that occur within the boundaries of a single organization. Supply chains refer to networks of companies that coordinate their actions to deliver a product to market. Also, traditional logistics focus attention on activities such as procurement, distribution, maintenance, and inventory management. Supply chain management acknowledges all of the traditional logistics, but adds activities such as marketing, new product development, finance, and customer service.

In the wider view of supply chain thinking, these additional activities are now seen as part of the "big picture" of tasks required to fulfill customer requests. Supply chain management views the supply chain and the organizations in it as a single entity. It brings a "systems approach" to understanding and managing the different activities needed to coordinate the flow of products and services to best serve the ultimate customer. The systems approach provides the framework in which to best respond to business requirements that otherwise would seem to be in conflict with each other.

When examined individually, different supply chain requirements often seem to have conflicting needs. For instance, the requirement of maintaining high levels of customer service would probably call for maintaining high levels of inventory, but the requirement to operate efficiently would suggest reducing inventory levels. It is only when these requirements are seen together—as parts of a larger picture—that ways can be found to effectively balance their various demands.

Effective supply chain management requires simultaneous improvements in both customer service levels and the internal operating efficiencies of the companies that make up the supply chain. Customer service at its most basic level means consistently high order fill rates, high on-time delivery rates, and a very low rate of products returned by customers for whatever reason. Internal efficiency means that the organizations in the supply chain get an attractive rate of return on their investments in inventory and other assets, and that they find ways to lower their operating and sales expenses.

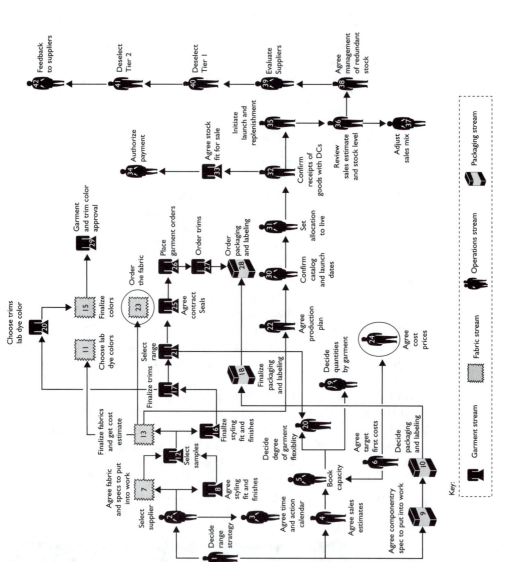

Figure 1-1. Critical decisions in the retail buying process. (A retail buyer's choices set into motion four different streams of goods and services, all of which are parts of a supply chain.) From the report "11 Ways to Make a Difference—For Retailers," © A.T. Kearney, an EDS Company, Chicago, Illinois, 2002. All rights reserved. Reprinted with permission.

There is an underlying pattern to the practice of supply chain management. Each supply chain has its own unique set of market demands and operating challenges, and yet the issues remain essentially the same in every case. Companies in any supply chain must make decisions individually and collectively regarding their actions in five areas, as shown in Figure 1-2 and described here:

1. **Production.** What products does the market want? How much of which products should be produced and by when? This activity includes the creation of master production schedules that take into account plant capacities, workload balancing, quality control, and equipment maintenance.

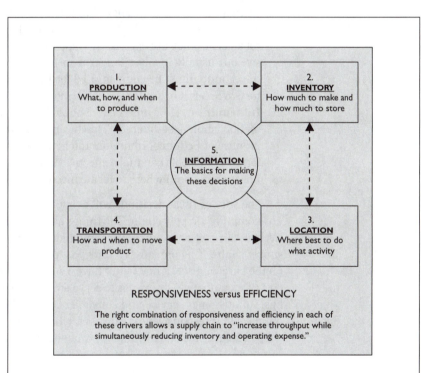

RESPONSIVENESS versus EFFICIENCY

The right combination of responsiveness and efficiency in each of these drivers allows a supply chain to "increase throughput while simultaneously reducing inventory and operating expense."

Each market or group of customers has a specific set of needs. The supply chains that serve different markets need to respond effectively to these needs. Some markets demand and will pay for high levels of responsiveness. Other markets require their supply chains to focus more on efficiency. The overall effect of the decisions made concerning each driver will determine how well the supply chain serves its market and how profitable it is for the participants in that supply chain.

Figure 1-2. The five major supply chain drivers.

2. **Inventory.** What inventory should be stocked at each stage in a supply chain? How much inventory should be held as raw materials, partially finished goods, or finished goods? The primary purpose of inventory is to act as a buffer against uncertainty in the supply chain. However, holding inventory can be expensive, so what are the optimal inventory levels and reorder points?

3. **Location.** Where should facilities for production and inventory storage be located? Where are the most cost-efficient locations for production and for storage of inventory? Should existing facilities be used or new ones built? Once these decisions are made, they determine the possible paths available for product to flow through for delivery to the final consumer.

4. **Transportation.** How should inventory be moved from one location to another in the chain? Air freight and truck delivery are generally fast and reliable, but they are expensive. Shipping by sea or rail is much less expensive but usually involves longer transit times and more uncertainty. This uncertainty must be compensated for by stocking higher levels of inventory. When is it better to use which mode of transportation?

5. **Information.** How much data should be collected, and how much information should be shared? Timely and accurate information holds the promise of better coordination and better decision making. With good information, people can make effective decisions about what to produce and how much, about where to locate inventory and how best to transport it.

The sum of these decisions will define the capabilities and effectiveness of any company's supply chain. The things a company can do, and how competitively it can do them, are all very much dependent on the effectiveness of its supply chain. If a company's strategy is to serve a mass market and compete on the basis of price, it had better have a supply chain that is optimized for low cost. If a company's strategy is to serve a market segment and compete on the basis of customer service and convenience, it had better have a supply chain optimized for responsiveness. In short, what a retailer is and what it can do is shaped in large measure by its supply chain and by the markets it serves.

HOW THE SUPPLY CHAIN WORKS

Great business leaders don't operate in a vacuum, and so it is with the gurus of supply chain management, or "SCM" for short. A couple of the earliest and most influential books that defined the principles and practice of supply chain management are still in use, in updated versions, today:

- *The Goal* was first published in 1984 and is now in its third edition by North River Press (2004). Its author, Dr. Eliyahu ("Eli") M. Goldratt, captured the attention of the business world by describing workplace challenges in the form of a novel. His character, Alex Rogo, is the new manager of a fictitious manufacturing plant who must make some big adjustments or watch the company go under—at the same time Rogo's marriage is faltering. These universal lessons can be applied to almost any business system and, of course, to life in general.

■ *Supply Chain Management: Strategy, Planning, and Operation* by Northwestern University professor Sunil Chopra and alumnus Peter Meindl, both of Northwestern's Kellogg School of Management. A second edition was released in 2003 by Prentice Hall. The book began as Kellogg's second-year MBA course text and focuses on solving supply chain problems with analytical tools.

If more depth is desired on any of the topics covered in this book, especially in the first three chapters, we'll recommend those two to augment our introductory discussions.

According to Dr. Goldratt, the goal or mission of supply chain management can be defined quite simply: "Increase throughput while simultaneously reducing both inventory and operating expense."

Throughput refers to the rate at which sales to the end customer occur. Depending on the market being served, sales or throughput occur for different reasons—in some markets, customers value and will pay for high levels of service; in other markets, they are motivated by the lowest price, and price alone.

As mentioned previously, there are five key areas in which companies can make decisions that will define their supply chain capabilities: production, inventory, location, transportation, and information. Chopra and Meindl define these areas as "performance drivers" that can be managed to produce the capabilities needed for a given supply chain. So the first step in effective supply chain management is to understand each driver and how it operates, because each has the ability to directly affect the supply chain and enable certain capabilities.

The next step is to develop an appreciation for the results that can be obtained by mixing different combinations of drivers. But one thing at a time! Let's start by looking at the drivers individually.

Production

Production refers to the capacity of a supply chain to make and store products. The facilities of production—and retailers are no exception—are factories and warehouses. The fundamental decision that managers face when making production decisions is how to resolve the trade-off between responsiveness and efficiency. If factories and warehouses are built with a lot of excess capacity, they can be very flexible and respond quickly to wide swings in product demand. Facilities where all or almost all capacity is being used are not capable of responding easily to fluctuations in demand. On the other hand, capacity costs money—and excess capacity is idle capacity, since it's not in use and not generating revenue. So the more excess capacity that exists, the less efficient the operation becomes.

Factories can be built to accommodate one of two approaches to manufacturing:

1. **Product focus.** A factory that takes a product focus performs the whole range of different operations that is required to make a given product line. This may include everything from fabrication of the various parts of the product to the assembly of these parts.
2. **Functional focus.** A functional approach concentrates on performing just a few operations, perhaps only making a select group of parts, or only doing assembly. These functions can be applied to making many different kinds of products.

Why does this matter? Because a product approach tends to result in developing expertise about a given set of products at the expense of expertise about any particular function. A functional approach results in expertise about particular functions instead of expertise in a given product. Companies need to decide which approach (or what mix of these two approaches) will give them the capability and expertise they need to best respond to customer demands.

As with factories, warehouses can also be built to accommodate different approaches. There are three main approaches to use in warehousing:

1. **Stock-keeping unit (SKU) storage.** In this traditional approach, all of a given type of product is stored together. This is an efficient and easy-to-understand way to store products.
2. **Job lot storage.** In this approach, all the different products related to the needs of a certain type of customer or related to the needs of a particular job are stored together. This allows for an efficient picking and packing operation but usually requires more storage space than the traditional SKU storage approach.
3. **Cross-docking.** Pioneered by Wal-Mart in its drive to increase efficiencies in its supply chain, in this approach, product is not actually warehoused in the facility. Instead, the facility is used to house a process, in which trucks from suppliers arrive and unload large quantities of different products. These large lots are then broken down into smaller lots. Then, smaller lots of different products are recombined according to the needs of the day and quickly loaded onto outbound trucks that deliver the products to their final destinations—in this case, Wal-Mart stores.

Inventory

Inventory is spread throughout the supply chain and includes everything from raw material, to work in process, to finished goods that are held by the manufacturers, distributors, and retailers in the supply chain. Again, managers must decide where they want to position themselves in the trade-off between responsiveness and efficiency. Holding large amounts of inventory allows a company or an entire supply chain to be very responsive to fluctuations in customer demand. However, the creation and storage of inventory is a cost, and to achieve high levels of efficiency, the cost of inventory should be kept as low as possible.

There are some basic decisions to make regarding the creation and holding of inventory that result in three types of inventory, as follows:

1. **Cycle inventory.** This is the amount of inventory needed to satisfy demand for the product in the period between purchases of the product. Companies tend to produce and to purchase in large lots in order to gain the advantages that economies of scale can bring. However, large lots also mean greater **carrying costs**, the term for what it costs at various places along the chain to store, handle, and insure the inventory. Managers face the trade-off between the reduced cost of ordering and better prices offered by purchasing product in large lots, versus the increased carrying cost of the cycle inventory that comes with purchasing in large lots.

2. **Safety inventory.** Inventory that is held as a buffer against uncertainty. If demand forecasting could be done with perfect accuracy, then the only inventory that would be needed would be cycle inventory. But since every forecast has some degree of uncertainty in it, we cover that uncertainty to a greater or lesser degree by holding additional inventory in case demand is suddenly greater than anticipated. The trade-off here is to weigh the costs of carrying the extra inventory against the costs of losing sales due to insufficient inventory.

3. **Seasonal inventory.** This is inventory built up in anticipation of predictable increases in demand that occur at certain times of the year. For example, it is predictable that demand for antifreeze will increase in the winter. If a company that makes antifreeze has a fixed production rate that is expensive to change, then it will try to manufacture product at a steady rate all year long and build up inventory during periods of low demand to cover for periods of high demand that will exceed its production rate. The alternative to building up seasonal inventory is to invest in flexible manufacturing facilities that can quickly change their rate of production of different products to respond to increases in demand. In this case, the trade-off is between the cost of carrying seasonal inventory and the cost of having more flexible production capabilities.

Location

Location refers to the geographical sites of supply chain facilities. It also includes the decisions related to which activities should be performed in each facility. The responsiveness versus efficiency trade-off here is the decision whether to centralize activities in fewer locations to gain economies of scale (and therefore efficiency), or to decentralize activities in many locations close to customers and suppliers in order for operations to be more responsive—a system that creates a different kind of efficiency.

When making location decisions, managers must consider a range of factors that relate to a given location. These include the cost of facilities, the cost of labor, skills available in the workforce, infrastructure conditions, taxes and tariffs, and proximity to suppliers and customers. Location decisions tend to be very strategic decisions because they commit large amounts of money to long-term plans.

Location decisions have strong impacts on the cost and performance characteristics of a supply chain. Once the size, numbers, and locations of facilities are determined, that also defines the number of possible paths through which products can flow on the way to the final customer. Location decisions reflect a company's basic strategy for building and delivering its products to market.

Transportation

Transportation refers to the movement of everything from raw materials to finished goods between different facilities in a supply chain. In transportation the trade-off between responsiveness and efficiency is manifested in the choice of transport mode. The fastest modes of transport are very responsive but also more costly. Slower modes are cost-efficient but not as responsive. Since transportation costs can be as much as one-third of the operating cost of a supply chain, decisions made here are very important.

There are six basic modes of transport from which a company can choose:

1. *Cargo ships* are very cost-efficient but are also the slowest mode of transport. Of course, shipping by water is also limited to locations situated near to navigable waterways and facilities such as harbors and canals.
2. *Rail* is also very cost-efficient but can be slow. This mode is also restricted to use between locations that are served by rail lines.
3. *Pipelines* can be very efficient but are restricted to liquid and gas commodities, such as water, oil, and natural gas.
4. *Trucks* are a relatively quick and very flexible mode of transport. Trucks can go almost anywhere. The cost of this mode is prone to fluctuations though, as the cost of fuel fluctuates and road and weather conditions vary.
5. *Airplanes* are a fast and responsive mode of transport; however, they are also the most expensive option and are somewhat limited in rural areas by the availability of appropriate airport facilities.
6. *Electronic transport* is the fastest mode, both flexible and cost-efficient, but it can only be used for movement of certain types of products such as electric energy, data, and products composed of data—music, pictures, and

text. Someday technology that allows us to convert matter to energy and back to matter again may completely rewrite the theory and practice of supply chain management ("Beam me up, Scotty . . ."). But for now, hard goods can't be transmitted!

Given these different modes of transportation and the locations of the facilities in a supply chain, managers must design routes and networks for moving products. A **route** is the path through which products move, and **networks** are composed of the collection of the paths and facilities connected by those paths. As a general rule, the higher the value of a product—electronic components or pharmaceuticals, for example—the more its transport network should emphasize responsiveness and the lower the value of a product (say, bulk commodities like grain or lumber), the more its network should emphasize efficiency.

Information

Information is the basis upon which to make decisions regarding the other four supply chain drivers. It is the connection between all the activities and operations in a supply chain. To the extent that this connection is a strong one, (i.e., the data is accurate, timely, and complete), the companies in a supply chain will each be able to make good decisions for their own operations. This will also tend to maximize the profitability of the supply chain as a whole. That is the way that stock markets or other free markets work, and supply chains have many of the same dynamics as markets.

Information is used for two purposes in any supply chain:

1. *Coordinating daily activities* related to the functioning of the other four supply chain drivers: production, inventory, location, and transportation. The members of the supply chain use available data on product supply and demand to decide on weekly production schedules, inventory levels, transportation routes, and stocking locations.
2. *Forecasting and planning* to anticipate and meet future demands. Available information is used to make tactical forecasts to guide the setting of monthly and quarterly production schedules and timetables. Information is also used for strategic forecasts to guide decisions about whether to build new facilities, enter a new market, or exit an existing market.

Within an individual company, the trade-off between responsiveness and efficiency involves weighing the benefits that good information can provide against the cost of acquiring that information. Abundant, accurate information can enable very efficient operating decisions and better forecasts, but the cost of building and installing systems to deliver this information can be very high.

Within the supply chain as a whole, the responsiveness versus efficiency trade-off that companies make is one of deciding how much information to share with the other companies and how much information to keep private. The more information about product supply, customer demand, market forecasts, and production schedules that companies share with each other, the more responsive everyone can be. Balancing this openness, however, are the concerns that each company has about revealing information that could be used against it by a competitor. The potential costs associated with increased competition can hurt the profitability of a company.

THE EVOLVING STRUCTURE OF SUPPLY CHAINS

The participants in a supply chain are continuously making decisions that affect how they manage the five supply chain drivers. Each organization tries to maximize its performance in terms of these drivers, through a combination of outsourcing, partnering, and in-house expertise. In the fast-moving markets of our present economy, a company usually will focus on what it considers to be its "core competencies" in supply chain management—and outsource the rest.

This was not always the case, though. In the slower-moving mass markets of the industrial age, it was common for successful companies to attempt to own much of their supply chain, a theory known as **vertical integration**. The aim of vertical integration was to gain maximum efficiency through economies of scale (see Figure 1-3).

In the first half of the 1900s, Ford Motor Company owned much of what it needed to feed its car factories. It owned and operated iron mines that extracted iron ore, steel mills that turned the ore into steel products, plants that made component car parts, and assembly plants that turned out the finished cars.

In addition, they owned farms where they grew flax to make into linen car tops, and forests that they logged and sawmills where they produced the lumber for making wooden car parts. Ford's famous River Rouge Plant was a monument to vertical integration—iron ore went in at one end and cars came out at the other end. In his 1926 autobiography, Henry Ford boasted that his company could take in iron ore from the mine and put out a car 81 hours later.[5]

This was a profitable way of doing business in the more predictable, one-size-fits-all industrial economy that existed in the early 1900s. Ford and other businesses churned out mass amounts of basic products. But as the markets grew and customers became more particular about the kinds of products and features they wanted, this model began to break down. It could not be responsive enough or produce the variety of products that were being demanded. For instance, when Henry Ford was asked about the number of different colors a customer could request, he is famous for saying, "They can have any color they want—as long as it's black."[6] In the 1920s, Ford's market share was more than 50 percent, but by the 1940s, it had fallen to below 20 percent. Henry Ford's factories still put out dependable vehicles; it's just that focusing on efficiency at

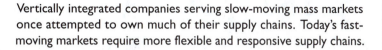

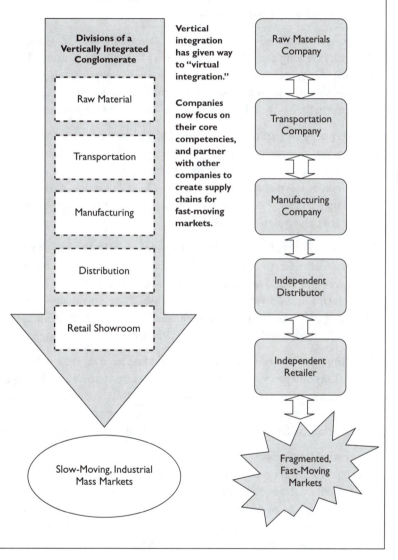

Figure 1-3. Old supply chain versus new.

the expense of being responsive to customer desires was no longer a successful business model.

Globalization, highly competitive markets, and the rapid pace of technological change have driven the modern-day supply chain in which multiple companies work together, with each focusing on the activities that it does best.

SUPPLY CHAIN MANAGEMENT IN ACTION: HOW WAL-MART WORKS

Wal-Mart is a company shaped by its supply chain, and the efficiency of its supply chain has made it a world leader in the markets it serves.

Sam Walton decided to build a company that would serve a mass market and compete on the basis of price by creating one of the world's most efficient supply chains. The entire structure and company operations have been defined by the need to lower costs and increase productivity in order to pass these savings on to its customers in the form of lower prices. In so doing, Wal-Mart introduced concepts that are now industry standards. There are four in particular that relate to its supply chain.

The strategy of expanding around DCs (distribution centers) is central to the way Wal-Mart enters a new geographical market. The company looks for areas that can support a group of new stores, not just a single new store. It then builds a new DC at a central location in the area and opens its first store at the same time. The DC is the supply chain bridgehead into the new territory. It supports the opening of more new stores in the area at a very low additional cost. Those savings are passed along to the customers.

The use of EDI (Electronic Data Interface) with suppliers provides the company two substantial benefits. First, it cuts the transaction costs associated with well-defined, routine processes like ordering products and paying invoices—everything is done electronically, by computer. Second, these electronic links with suppliers allow Wal-Mart a high degree of control and coordination in scheduling and receiving product deliveries. This helps to ensure a steady flow of the right products at the right time, delivered to the right DCs, by all Wal-Mart suppliers.

The "big box" store format allows Wal-Mart to, in effect, combine a store and a warehouse in a single facility and get great operating efficiencies from doing so. The big box is big enough to hold large amounts of inventory like a warehouse. And since this inventory is being held at the same location where the customer buys it, there is no delay or cost that would otherwise be associated with moving products from warehouse to store. Again, these savings are passed along to the customer.

"Everyday low prices" are a way of doing two things—first, telling price-conscious customers that they will always get the best price. They need not look elsewhere or wait for special sales. Second, the effect of this message to customers helps Wal-Mart to accurately forecast product sales. By eliminating special sales and assuring customers of low prices, it smoothes out demand swings for certain products, making demand more steady and predictable. This way, stores are also more likely to have what customers want, when they want it.

Taken individually, these four concepts are each useful—but their real power comes from being used in connection with each other. They combine to form a supply chain that drives a self-reinforcing business process. Each concept builds on the strengths of the others to create a powerful business model for a company that has grown to become the dominant player in the world of retail.

Mining companies focus on mining, timber companies focus on logging and making lumber, and manufacturing companies focus on different types of manufacturing, from making component parts to doing final assembly. This way, people in each company can keep up with rapid rates of change and keep learning the new skills needed to compete in their particular business.

Where companies once routinely ran their own warehouses or operated their own fleets of trucks, they now have to consider whether those operations are really a core competency—or whether it is more cost-effective to outsource those operations to other companies that make logistics the center of their business. To achieve high levels of operating efficiency and to keep up with continuing changes in technology, companies need to focus on their core competencies. It requires this kind of focus to stay competitive.

Instead of vertical integration, companies now practice what some call **virtual integration**. Companies find other companies with whom they can work to perform the activities called for in their supply chains. How a company defines its core competencies—and how it positions itself in the supply chains it serves—are perhaps the most important decisions it can make.

PARTICIPANTS IN THE SUPPLY CHAIN

In its simplest form, a supply chain is composed of a company and the suppliers and customers of that company. This is the basic group of participants that creates a simple supply chain. Extended supply chains contain three additional types of participants:

- First there is the supplier's supplier or the ultimate supplier at the beginning of an extended supply chain.
- Then there is the customer's customer or ultimate customer at the end of an extended supply chain.
- Finally there is a whole category of companies that are service providers to other companies in the supply chain. These are companies that supply services in logistics, finance, marketing, and information technology.

In any given supply chain, there is some combination of companies that perform different functions. There are companies that are producers, distributors or wholesalers, retailers, and companies or individuals who are the customers, the final consumers of a product. Still other firms support these companies as providers of a range of services related to the product lines.

Producers

Producers or manufacturers are organizations that make a product—perhaps raw materials, perhaps finished goods. Producers of raw materials are organizations that mine for minerals, drill for oil and gas, and cut timber. It also includes organizations that farm, raise animals, or catch seafood. Producers of finished goods use the raw materials and subassemblies made by other producers to create their products. Some types of retailers deal with raw materials producers more often than others—supermarkets, for example, in creating private label brands.

Producers can create products that are intangible items such as music, entertainment, software, or designs. A product can also be a service such as mowing a lawn, cleaning an office, performing surgery, or teaching a skill. In many instances, the producers of tangible, industrial products are moving to areas of the world where labor is less costly. Producers who remain in the developed world of North America, Europe, and parts of Asia are increasingly producers of intangible items and services.

Distributors

Distributors are companies that take inventory in bulk from producers and deliver a bundle of related product lines to customers. Distributors are also known as wholesalers. They typically sell to other businesses, and they sell products in larger quantities than an individual consumer would usually buy. Distributors buffer the producers from fluctuations in product demand by stocking inventory and doing much of the sales work to find and service customers. For the customer, distributors fulfill the "time and place" function; they deliver products when and where the customer wants them.

In addition to product promotion and sales, other functions the distributor performs are inventory management, warehouse operations, and product transportation, as well as customer support and post-sales service. Distributors can either buy their wares outright from producers or can simply broker them between the producer and the customer and never take ownership of the products. In both of these cases, as the needs of customers evolve and the range of available products changes, the distributor is the agent that continually tracks customer needs and matches them with products available.

Retailers

Retailers stock inventory and sell in smaller quantities to the general public. Retailers also closely track the preferences and demands of their customers. They place advertising to attract these customers and use some combination of price, product selection, service, and convenience as the primary draws to attract customers for the products they sell. Discount department stores attract customers using price and wide product selection, upscale specialty stores offer a unique line of products and high levels of service, quick-service food restaurants use convenience and low prices as their draw, and so on.

Customers

Customers or consumers are the groups or individuals who purchase the product. Of course, a customer organization may buy the product in order to incorporate it into another product that they, in turn, sell to other customers. Or the customer may be the final end user of a product, buying it in order to consume, wear, or otherwise use it.

Service Providers

These are organizations that provide services to producers, distributors, retailers, and customers. Service providers have developed special expertise or skills that focus on a particular activity needed by a supply chain. Because of this, they are able to perform these services more effectively and probably at better prices than any of the other groups (producers, retailers, and so forth) could do on their own.

Some common service providers in any supply chain are the companies that handle transportation and warehousing services, otherwise known as logistics providers. Another category of service providers delivers financial services—making loans, doing credit analysis, and collecting past-due amounts. This group includes banks, credit rating companies, and collection agencies, to name a few. Still other service providers deliver market research and advertising, product design, engineering services, legal services, management advice, and more. The newest and fastest-growing field in the past decade has been information technology, as companies hire external service providers to choose, program, install, align, and/or service their computer systems—even if they also have their own IT people in-house.

To summarize, supply chains are composed of repeating sets of participants that fall into one or more of these categories. Over time, the needs of the supply chain as a whole remain fairly stable. What is more likely to change is the mix of participants in the chain, or the roles that each participant plays. For example, in some supply chains, there are few service providers—because the other participants perform these services on their own. In other supply chains, very efficient providers of specialized services have evolved and the other participants outsource work to them, instead of doing it themselves. Examples of supply chain structure are shown in Figure 1-4.

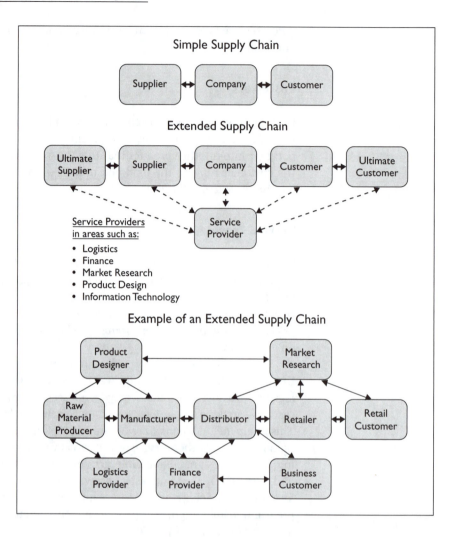

Figure 1-4. Supply chain structure.

ALIGNING THE SUPPLY CHAIN WITH BUSINESS STRATEGY

A company's supply chain is an integral part of its approach to the markets it serves. The supply chain needs to respond to market requirements and do so in a way that supports the company's business strategy. The business strategy a company employs starts with the needs of the customers that the company serves or will serve. Depending on the needs of its customers, a company's supply chain must deliver the appropriate mix of responsiveness and efficiency. A company whose supply chain allows it to more efficiently meet the needs of its customers will gain market share at the expense of other companies in that market and also will be more profitable.

For example, let's consider two retail companies and the requirements they place on their supply chains—7-Eleven and Sam's Club, which is a part of Wal-Mart. The customers who shop at convenience stores like 7-Eleven have a different set of needs and preferences than those who shop at a discount warehouse like Sam's Club. The 7-Eleven customer is looking for convenience and wants the store to be close by and have enough variety of products so that they can pick up small amounts of common household or food items, often needed immediately. Clearly, the supply chain for 7-Eleven needs to emphasize responsiveness, since its customers expect convenience and will pay for it.

Sam's Club customers, on the other hand, are looking for the lowest price. They are not in a hurry and are willing to drive some distance and buy large quantities of limited numbers of items in order to get bargains by purchasing in bulk. The Sam's Club supply chain needs to focus tightly on efficiency, finding every opportunity to reduce costs so that these savings can be passed on to the customers.

Both of these companies' supply chains are well aligned with their business strategies, and because of this, they are each successful in their markets.

There are three steps to use in aligning any retailer's supply chain with its business strategy. The first step is to understand the markets that the retailer serves. The second step is to define the strengths or core competencies of the retailer, and the role it can play in serving its markets. The last step is to develop the needed supply chain capabilities to support the roles the retailer has chosen.

Understanding the Markets a Company Serves

If you were a retail executive, you'd begin by asking questions about your customers. What kind of customer does your company serve? To whom do you sell products? What kind of supply chain is your company a part of? The answers to these questions will tell you whether your supply chain needs to emphasize responsiveness or efficiency. Chopra and Meindl have defined the following attributes that help to clarify requirements for different types of customers:

- **The quantity of the product needed in each lot.** Do your customers want small amounts of products, or will they buy large quantities? A pharmacy customer will no doubt buy in smaller quantities than the customer of a discount store.
- **The response time that customers are willing to tolerate.** Do your customers buy on short notice and expect quick service, or is a longer lead time acceptable? Customers on their lunch hours expect speedy service from a fast-food chain; but customers buying custom machinery would plan the purchase in advance and expect some lead time before the product could be delivered.

- **The variety of products needed.** Are customers looking for a narrow and well-defined bundle of products or a wide selection of different kinds of products? Customers of a fashion boutique expect a narrowly defined group of designer items, while people who buy from a "big box" discount store expect a wider variety.
- **The service level required.** Do customers expect all products to be available for immediate delivery, or will they accept partial deliveries of products and longer lead times? Customers of a music store expect to get the newest CD they want to hear immediately, or they will probably go elsewhere; other types of stores may be able to special-order merchandise for which customers don't mind waiting.
- **The price of the product.** How much are customers willing to pay? We've already discussed the all-important "price or convenience" trade-off.
- **The desired rate of innovation in the product.** How fast are new products introduced, and how long before the existing products become obsolete? In fields such as electronics and computers, customers expect a high rate of innovation. But in hardware or house paint, innovations happen—just not with incredible frequency.

Defining Core Competencies

The next step is to define the role that your company plays (or wants to play) in these supply chains. Yes, retailers are retailers—but some may also be producers, distributors, or service providers, too. What does your company do to enable the supply chains that it is part of? What are the core competencies of the company? How does it make money? The answers to these questions tell you what roles in a supply chain will be the best fit.

Be aware that any company can serve multiple markets and participate in multiple supply chains—in fact, the smartest ones do just that. A company like W.W. Grainger serves several different markets. It sells maintenance, repair, and operating (MRO) supplies to large national customers such as Ford and Boeing, and it also sells these supplies to small businesses and building contractors. Its two very different markets have different requirements.

When you are serving multiple market segments, your company should always be looking for ways to leverage its core competencies. Parts of these supply chains may be unique to the market segment they serve, while other parts can be combined to achieve economies of scale. For example, if manufacturing is a core competency for a company, it can build a whole range of different products in the same production facility. Then, different inventory and transportation options can be used to deliver the products to customers in different market segments. This situation is rare for retailers, but it's worth knowing about as you select suppliers as partners in your supply chain. Who can be the most flexible? Who is "best" at what skills?

Developing Supply Chain Capabilities

Once you know what kind of markets your company serves and the role your company plays in the supply chains of these markets, the last step is to develop the supply chain capabilities needed to support the roles your company plays. This development is guided by the decisions made about the five supply chain drivers. Each of these drivers can be developed and managed to emphasize responsiveness or efficiency, depending on the business requirements. Remember, not all of these examples apply to retail—or do they? See what you think.

1. **Production.** This driver can be made very responsive by building factories that have a lot of excess capacity and that use flexible manufacturing techniques to produce a wide range of items. To be even more responsive, a company could split its production into many, smaller plants that are close to major groups of customers so that delivery times would be shorter. If efficiency is the goal, a company might build factories with very little excess capacity, which produce only a limited range of items—but do it quickly and expertly. Further efficiency could be gained by centralizing production in large central plants to get better economies of scale.

2. **Inventory.** Responsiveness here might mean stocking high levels of inventory for a wide range of products. Additional responsiveness can be gained by stocking products at many locations, so the inventory is close to customers and available to them almost immediately. Efficiency might mean reducing inventory levels of all items, especially those items that do not sell as frequently. Also, inventory could be stocked in only a few central locations to reduce costs.

3. **Location.** Responsiveness means opening many locations, to be physically close to the customer base. McDonald's is a great example of responsive use of location. Efficiency, on the other hand, can be achieved by operating from only a few locations and centralizing activities in common locations. An example of this is the way computer manufacturer/retailer Dell serves large geographical markets from only a few locations that perform a wide range of activities.

4. **Transportation.** Responsiveness in transportation means "fast and flexible." Many companies that sell products by mail-order catalogs or over the Internet are able to offer high levels of responsiveness by using "rush" forms of transportation (like Federal Express) to deliver their products, often within 24 hours, if customers are willing to pay for it. Efficiency means transporting products in larger batches, and doing it less often, using ship or rail transport. It can be even more efficient if the transportation originates from a central hub facility instead of from many branch locations.

5. **Information.** The power of this driver grows stronger by the minute as computer technology becomes more sophisticated, but easier to use and

TWO COMPANIES, TWO TYPES OF SUPPLY CHAIN: WAL-MART AND DELL

Sunil Chopra is the IBM Distinguished Professor of Operations Management at Northwestern University's Kellogg School of Management, and a director of the Masters of Management in Manufacturing program. He is also coauthor of *Supply Chain Management: Strategy, Planning, and Operation,* a widely recognized source book in the field.

Professor Chopra agreed to share his thoughts here about two companies that both have risen to prominence by offering low prices as key selling points to customers. This strategy requires a highly efficient supply chain in order to generate cost savings while still making a profit. Professor Chopra offers his analysis of how each company has aligned its supply chain to support its business strategies.

WAL-MART: To begin with, Wal-Mart's competitors opened stores in ones and twos and used demographic data to select store sites. Wal-Mart took a supply chain approach and would not even open a store in an area unless it determined that the area could support a distribution center (DC) and a sufficient number of stores to gain scale economies at the DC. Then they targeted specific business operations from which to get efficiencies.

"Wal-Mart said, 'We are going to replenish our stores much more efficiently,' Chopra explains. "They began to replenish stores two times a week, where their competition was replenishing two times a month. What this meant was that a Wal-Mart manager only had to forecast for half a week, and an equally capable store manager elsewhere had to forecast sales and inventory needs for half a month—they couldn't do as well.

"Since they were replenishing more often, they pioneered the cross-docking technique, in order to reduce the cost of small lot replenishment. They also said that they would own and control their own trucks and their computer systems, because these were the two assets that they used to make their supply chain so efficient. They invested heavily in information technology and trucks—they bought a fleet of trucks. They made these into core competencies of the company."

DELL: "When I look at Dell," says Chopra, "I see a company that was able to live through and learn from a big mistake they made early on. Their roots were as a direct sales company—but then in the early 90s, they tried to sell through retail stores and almost went broke. That drove them back to the direct model and they have not strayed since.

"PCs are now much like cars; it is more of a replacement market than a growth market. Customers know what they want and they also want a good price. Dell's message to the market is customization and great prices. They can support this strategy because they enjoy economies of scale and postpone assembly. They use a few large facilities to assemble PCs, and they assemble to order and not to stock, so inventory is kept very low. In a high-change technology market, they do not get stuck with obsolete inventory. Their shipping costs are high but there is enough profit margin to cover that."

But what would happen if the PC market suddenly changed? "Dell and its competitors all use many of the same components to build their machines. If the market no longer values customization and simply wants the best price on a standard machine, then the Dell model doesn't work as well. [In that case,] build to stock and position inventory close to the customers via retail stores becomes a better model."

In short, there is no one "right model" for a supply chain. Markets change, and as they do, retailers must reevaluate their business model and their strategy. As Professor Chopra puts it, "Since a company's supply chain has a great impact on its ability to execute its business model successfully, that supply chain must always be adjusted as the business strategy changes."

less expensive. Like money, information is a useful commodity because it can be applied directly, to enhance the performance of the other four supply chain drivers. High levels of responsiveness are achieved when companies collect and share accurate and timely data generated by the operations of the other four drivers. Where efficiency is the focus, less information about fewer activities can be collected—too much data that isn't especially useful isn't really necessary. Companies may also elect to share less information among themselves so as not to risk having that information used against them.

Please note, however, that these information efficiencies are *only* efficiencies in the short term. They become less efficient over time, because the cost of information continues to drop, while the costs of the other four drivers usually continue to rise. Over the longer term, those companies and supply chains that learn how to maximize the use of information to get optimal performance from the other drivers will gain the most market share and be the most profitable.

CHAPTER SUMMARY

Every retailer is part of at least one supply chain, and often many different supply chains. A supply chain is composed of all the companies involved in the design, production, and delivery of a product to market.

Supply chain management is the coordination of production, inventory, location, and transportation among the participants in a supply chain to achieve the best mix of responsiveness and efficiency for the market being served. The goal of supply chain management is to increase sales of goods and services to the final end user or customer, while at the same time reducing both inventory and operating expenses.

The business model of vertical integration that came out of the industrial economy of the last century has given way to today's "virtual integration" of companies in a supply chain with technological capabilities like Electronic Data Interface (EDI). Each company now focuses on its core competencies and partners with other companies that have complementary capabilities for the design and delivery of products to market—and they are linked by computer to be able to share and transmit information instantly. Even so, every company in the chain must focus on improving its core competencies, to keep up with the fast pace of its markets and with technological change, as well as to satisfy its supply chain partners.

Retailers are no exception. To succeed in this competitive world, companies must learn to align their supply chains with the demands of the markets they serve. Supply chain performance is now a distinct competitive advantage for companies who excel in this area. The world's largest retailer, Wal-Mart, is a testament to the power of effective supply chain management. Much, if not most, of its success is directly related to its evolving capabilities to continually improve its supply chain.

DISCUSSION QUESTIONS

1. What is the difference between supply chain management and logistics?
2. What did you learn from the story of Alexander the Great that might be useful in a retail business? Do you see similarities between the business profiles in this chapter of Wal-Mart and Alexander the Great?
3. Find a supply chain service provider and write a report on the services it provides to retailers and how it fits into the retailers' total supply chain.
4. Why do you think the cost of information continues to drop, while costs associated with the other four supply chain drivers continue to rise?
5. Briefly describe the differences between the supply chains of Wal-Mart and Dell.

ENDNOTES

1. Lisa M. Ellram, Douglas M. Lambert, and James R. Stock, *Fundamentals of Logistics Management* (Boston: Irwin/McGraw-Hill, 1998).
2. Sunil Chopra and Peter Meindl, *Supply Chain Management: Strategy, Planning, and Operation* (Upper Saddle River, NJ: Prentice Hall, 2001).
3. Ram Ganeshan and Terry P. Harrison, *An Introduction to Supply Chain Management*, Department of Management Sciences and Information Systems (University Park, PA: Penn State University, 1995).

4. John T. Menzer, William DeWitt, et al., "Defining Supply Chain Management," *Journal of Business Logistics*, (Oak Brook, IL: Center for Supply Chain Research, Vol. 22, No. 2, 2001).

5. Henry Ford, *Today and Tomorrow* (Portland, OR; Productivity Press, Inc., originally published 1926; reissued 1988).

6. *Ibid.*

THE INCREDIBLE JOURNEY

Coauthor's Note: In doing the research for this book, I came across a fun and fascinating article—which is, to be honest, somewhat rare in the field of supply chain management! "The Incredible Journey" follows a single bottle of mouthwash on its trek through an actual supply chain. The publisher was kind enough to allow me to split the "journey" into multiple parts to use between chapters. The original article can be found in the August 15, 1998, issue of *CIO Enterprise* (now *CIO*) magazine. Many thanks to the original writer, Jennifer Bresnahan, and publisher Andrew Burrell of CXO Media, Inc. for permitting its use.

Please note that the speed at which supply chain technology moves automatically dates this article, at least somewhat. Wherever possible, I have updated the basic financial figures used in the original article. However, the 1998 copy mentioned several specific brands of SCM-related software, described various types of automated technology, and quoted individuals at some companies. Today, I cannot vouch for the continued use of those particular systems or brands by the supply chain partners in the article, or confirm that the people mentioned are still working in those positions at the same companies.

In this book, "The Incredible Journey" begins on page 43 and continues between each chapter and the next.

CHRIS THOMAS

2

THE RETAIL DISTRIBUTION CHANNEL

E arly in 2005, IBM Business Consulting Services released a survey that compiled in-depth interviews with more than 100 sales, marketing, and merchandising executives at over 20 consumer products and retail companies. Only 9 percent of the retailers felt their suppliers had "a good understanding" of their business objectives. The gist of the survey was that retailers felt the product manufacturers have focused their efforts on the end users of the products (the consumers), without giving as much priority to the needs of the other members of their distribution channels—namely, the retailers to whom they sell.[1]

In addition to a supply chain, manufacturers and retailers participate in another give-and-take relationship known as a **distribution channel** or *marketing channel*. A distribution channel is similar to, but different than, a supply chain. The distribution channel is where the "deals" are made to buy and sell products. Sales, negotiations, and ordering are done by these companies, or departments within companies. Then the supply chain kicks in, to do the "physical" work of manufacturing, transporting, and storing the goods; and facilitating the sales with services like consumer research, extending credit, and providing other services related to making the products attractive to customers and encouraging their ultimate sale.

In this chapter, you will learn about

- The members of a distribution channel and their functions
- How retailers fit into distribution channels
- How channel relationships are managed
- Strategic alliances

One of the catchphrases of the last decade or so is "B2B," short for "business-to-business." This is a type of distribution channel in which the end consumer is a business, not an individual.

The lines do blur between modern-day distribution channels and supply chains. But we will attempt to keep them separate as we describe the functions of each in relation to the other.

PARTICIPANTS IN THE DISTRIBUTION CHANNEL

There are several types of participants that make up a distribution channel, so let's begin by listing them, as in Chapter 1 with supply chain participants. You will notice some overlap because, as also previously mentioned, retailers belong to several (or many) different supply chains, each group focused on making and marketing different products.

Retailers

The characteristic that sets a retailer apart from other members of its distribution channel is that the retailer is the party who ultimately sells the product to its end user or consumer. As you know if you've ever shopped for anything, retailers come in many shapes and sizes, so to speak. Retailers may be grouped according to any of the following four categories:

- **Ownership.** Every brick-and-mortar retailer can be classified as a large, national chain store; a smaller, regional chain store; an independent retailer; or a franchisee.
- **Pricing philosophy.** Stores are generally either discounters or full-price retailers. Within the "discounter" category, there are several subcategories such as factory outlets, consignment stores, dollar stores, specialty discount stores, warehouse membership clubs, and so on.
- **Product assortment.** The breadth and depth of product lines carried by the store depends a lot on its ownership. An Ann Taylor store, for example, sells Ann Taylor branded clothing—not much breadth of product line there, but extensive depth in that line. A Kmart, on the other hand, carries thousands of brands, but perhaps does not have much depth (not many brands) in any given category of product.
- **Service level.** The more exclusive or specialized the store, the more types of services it will generally offer—from a name-branded credit card, to on-site alterations, to liberal return policies for its loyal customers. With the "big box" discounters, on the other hand, customers pay for convenience and bypass traditional service, by bagging their own groceries and the like.

These distinctions between various types of stores will be important as we discuss their participation in certain distribution channels.

Wholesalers

Wholesalers are intermediaries or middlemen who buy products from manufacturers and resell them to the retailers. They take the same types of financial risks as retailers, since they purchase the products (thereby taking legal responsibility for them), keep them in inventory until they are resold to retailers, and may arrange for shipment to those retailers. Wholesalers can gather product from around a country or region, or can buy foreign product lines by becoming importers.

The term "wholesale" is often used to describe discount retailers (as in "wholesale clubs"), but discounters are retailers, not technically wholesalers. And in B2B channels, wholesalers may be called distributors.

Agents and Brokers

Agents (sometimes called brokers) are also intermediaries who work between suppliers and retailers (or in B2B channels), but their agreements are different, in that they do not take ownership of the products they sell. They are independent sales representatives who typically work on commission based on sales volume, and they can sell to wholesalers as well as retailers. In B2B arrangements, this means they sell to distributors and end users.

Resident sales agents are good examples in retail. They reside in the country to which they sell products, but the products come from a variety of foreign manufacturers. The resident sales agent represents those manufacturers, who pay the agent on commission. A resident sales agent does not always have merchandise warehoused and ready to sell, but he or she does have product samples for which orders can be placed and is responsible for bringing the items through the importation process.

Retailers that don't have the money, time, or manpower to send someone overseas for manufacturers' site visits to check out the new product lines can depend on a resident sales agent to do the job.

Buying offices can also be considered a type of agent or broker, since they earn their money pairing up retailers with product lines from various manufacturers.

The Need for Distribution Channels

Why are all these layers needed in distribution? Why can't a producer simply sell to a retailer, who sells to a consumer? It's a fair question, and in some cases, that is exactly how it happens. But the fact is that many producers are either too small or too large to handle all the necessary functions themselves to get their products to market.

Consider the small, specialty manufacturer who is terrific at making fine leather handbags but may not have the expertise to market its products as well as it makes them, or they may not have the money to hire a team of full-time salespeople to court the customers and secure the orders. An intermediary who works for several small, noncompeting firms can easily handle those functions cost-effectively. An intermediary who specializes in importing and exporting can handle the intricacies of customs paperwork, overseas shipping, and foreign markets, too.

Conversely, large companies need intermediaries because they are also in the business of manufacturing, not marketing. Turning out tens of thousands of cases of soft drinks, for instance, do you think Pepsi has time to take and fill individual orders from households? Channel members like wholesalers and retailers are useful because they are best at specific aspects of sales in their markets, leaving the manufacturers to do what they do best—which is turn out the best possible product.

Having a distribution channel breaks the whole buying and selling process and all its related negotiations into manageable tasks, each performed by companies that specialize in certain skills. Using an import wholesaler, for example, can be handy because they know the laws and customs of the suppliers' nations; and they generally offer their own lines of credit so the retailer won't have to deal with currency exchange or negotiate payment terms with a bank in another country.

Another advantage of the distribution channel is its ability to even out the natural ebbs and flows of a supply chain. This comes from the ability of some channel members to store excess goods until they are needed, and to stockpile goods in anticipation of seasonal sales peaks. Depending on how close their relationships, channel members may also work together to purchase goods or services in greater quantity at discounts, passing the savings on to customers.

Even for consumers, the distribution chain is handy—*beyond* handy, in fact! It has become a necessity in our society. What if there were no supermarkets, for instance? Can you imagine how much more time and money you would spend having to buy every item at its source? How practical would it be to run out to the nearest farm to pick up a quart of milk and some salad ingredients on your way home from work?

TYPES OF CHANNELS

We'll set aside business-to-business channels for now and look at the four simple types of retail distribution channels for consumer products:

- **Direct channel.** This is when the same company that manufactures a product sells it directly to the consumer or end user. Dell, as mentioned in Chapter 1, is a direct channel marketer. Mail-order catalog sales companies, like Lands' End, are also direct channel sellers.
- **Retailer channel.** This is when the producer sells to the retailer, and the retailer sells to the consumer.
- **Wholesaler channel.** Intermediaries play a role here, as the manufacturer sells to a wholesaler . . . who sells to a retailer . . . who sells to the consumer.
- **Agent or broker channel.** The most complex arrangement involves several transactions, often because the merchandise is being imported. The producer sells to an agent . . . who sells to a wholesaler . . . who sells to a retailer . . . who finally sells to the consumer or end user.
- **Dual channel or multiple channel.** This term refers to the use of two or more channels to sell products to different types of customers. A lawnmower manufacturer, for example, might sell some product lines at retail and others to commercial lawn care companies, each requiring different intermediary services.

How Channels Are Chosen

Although retailers drive distribution channels, it is not usually the retailer who makes the decision to utilize one channel over the others. The producer of the product makes this decision. There are several characteristics of product lines that make them more or less appropriate for a particular type of channel. Briefly, these characteristics can be summarized as follows:

- **The products themselves.** If a product is perishable, like many grocery items, it requires the shortest, most direct distribution channel—which means the fewest possible intermediaries along the way. If a product is customized, like an expensive assembled-to-order computer system, it also benefits from a short distribution channel. There is no need for intermediaries when a customer orders a custom product directly from the company that makes it.

     Long distribution channels correspond to small purchases, either because the retailer doesn't carry much inventory or the consumer buys the item in small quantities.
- **The type of customer.** Who are the customers, what do they need and expect from their shopping experience, and where are they willing to go to buy this type of product? How much quantity do they buy at a time? A channel may be chosen because it best reflects the end users' buying habits. Business-to-business customers have completely different needs and buying habits than individual consumers.
- **Market size.** This factor encompasses two things: the population of an area and whether it is urban or rural. It is easier to sell direct to customers in a large city with lots of potential outlets for a product line. The more widely dispersed the stores, the more logical the dependence on agents and wholesalers—or on multiple retailers in different cities—to keep product sales strong and steady.
- **The producer's level of control.** Most top-dollar clothing designers and fragrance manufacturers do not want their products showing up anywhere and everywhere. They've worked hard to build an exclusive reputation, and they expect their distribution channel to work just as hard to protect and enhance their upscale image. These producers will choose a distribution channel that ensures no discount merchants have access to their lines, and they will count on the members of their channel to honor their wishes and not make bargain "deals."
- **The size of the producing company.** A producer is likely to sell direct when the company is large enough to handle the additional responsibilities that intermediaries would otherwise provide—credit to customers, warehouses for their own goods, the ability to hire and train their own sales representatives. Smaller producers require a larger distribution chain in order to fill these roles.
- **The size of the retailers.** A segment of the industry that is fragmented, with most of the stores operating as single units, requires the distribution channel to be longer. This was the case in the 1980s with video rental

stores, for example, until Blockbuster Video opened and began its climb to dominate the market.

Types of Distribution within Channels

The channel members may handle different portions of the transaction, but they must all agree on the end result—that the product(s) will be placed in the market in the manner desired by the producer or manufacturer, and that placement of the product(s) meets the contractual agreements of producer, retailer, and everyone in-between.

Once a channel is selected, the *distribution strategy* can take three different forms. They are listed as follows, from most restrictive to least restrictive—and remember, in retail, the term "restrictive" does not automatically have a negative connotation.

- *Exclusive distribution* is thought of most frequently for high-dollar products such as luxury cars or Rolex watches, but the fact is that even small-ticket items like toys are considered exclusive when they are in high demand.

  In an exclusive distribution agreement, one retail store or chain of stores has the legal right to market and sell the product line in a geographic area. Exclusive distribution is sometimes requested by the retailer, not the producer, to ensure that the retailer has something unique, that customers can't get anywhere else. This may also mean the retailer commits to *not* selling any products that are going to compete with the line. In exchange, the producer or manufacturer offers sales assistance, training, point-of-purchase materials, and other perks to the exclusive distributor.

  Such a distribution arrangement can work toward the "exclusive" image of the product (because it's harder to get), the retailer (for having "the only ones" available), and the manufacturer (by implying that the company is interested in marketing "quality, not quantity.")

  In B2B commerce, exclusive distribution works well for extremely specialized product lines, such as heavy equipment or high-tech products, ordered to the customer's specifications and budgeted for in advance of the purchase.

- *Selective distribution* means the retailers are carefully screened, and only a few are permitted to carry the product line. As with exclusive distribution, part of the goal here is to enhance the image of the product by making it harder (but certainly not impossible!) to obtain. This allows the retailer to charge full price. The ladies' clothing industry is full of selective distribution agreements between designer labels and so-called "finer" department stores. (The producers may have other, lower-priced merchandise lines to sell to discounters; but these are generally sold under separate, secondary brand names.)

SHARING INFORMATION: HOW FAR SHOULD COMPANIES GO?

Business realities do not always support the sharing of data among partners in distribution channels and/or supply chains. It makes sense that concerns about privacy and competitive advantage often lead channel partners to decisions *not* to share some data, such as sales and demand forecasts.

Jim Alexy is the CEO of Network Services Company, a multibillion-dollar distribution organization. Prior to coming to Network Services, he held senior management positions at several of the manufacturers whose products Network Services sells, so he speaks from the perspective of both manufacturer and wholesale distributor.

"In a perfect world, yes, [sharing data] is a great idea," Jim told us, "But if you do, it's only a matter of time before some company turns it against you. Each company has its own quarterly management incentive plans, and people will do what they need to do to meet their numbers."

Companies do share data about things such as product demand and inventory levels. The problem is that they often modify this data to their own advantage—inflating their demand numbers, for instance, in order to ensure that they will get the amount of product they think they will *really* need.

"Most manufacturers have some sort of productivity targets they need to hit," Jim explained. "When they look at the demand data they get from customers, it is so inaccurate that if they responded to all the fluctuations, their production costs would go up and they still wouldn't be producing the right items anyway."

So companies take the data that others share with them and run their own projections. "When I was CEO at Sweetheart Cups," Jim recalled, "there was a guy who worked for me who built great demand forecast models. He collected all the data and factored in historical trends and ran the model. Then, he looked at the results and tweaked them in places where he had a strong hunch or some special information. And then after all of that, his forecasts *still* weren't as accurate as they could be—because one of our major customers, like McDonald's, wouldn't tell us about a big promotion they were planning to run, and we'd be caught short in 12-ounce cups or something. They didn't always tell us, because they didn't want word to get out and then have a competitor take action to counter their promotion."

As a result of the tinkering that companies do, the data can get pretty distorted at times. Nonetheless, data sharing has enabled some major improvements.

"I think there has been a lot of inventory taken out of the system," said Jim. "Just-In-Time inventory has resulted in major savings for everyone."

Just-In-Time (JIT) inventory is often implemented through a technique called vendor-managed inventory (VMI). Using this technique, as Wal-Mart suppliers do, they can monitor inventory levels of their own products within the companies sell to. The retailers share inventory and sales numbers, so the supplier can keep the inventory stocked at the right levels.

Retailers continuously weigh the costs and benefits of sharing data and working together. Do they work with only a small group of trusted suppliers and allow them to manage their own inventory in-store? Can they risk the downsides of working with only a few suppliers, when things like labor strikes, sudden price hikes, or production problems might leave the stores in the lurch?

And there are more nagging questions: Can they risk confidential information being leaked to competitors? How open should they be with other channel members? It is very hard for companies to develop the level of credibility and trust needed to establish tight working relationships. In the meantime, they do realize the benefits of sharing tools and skills that allow them to analyze data and make decisions.

Like so many other aspects of business, information sharing is a trade-off.

- *Intensive distribution* is the closest thing to blanket coverage in retail, a "you can find it anywhere" theory of marketing. Snack items, like candy and soft drinks, are great examples of intensive distribution—their individual unit prices are so low that thousands must be sold to make a profit.

Ironically, this intensive product availability requires a large and complex distribution channel in order to cover all the sales outlets, from supermarkets and convenience stores to vending machines and restaurants. Manufacturers of these products depend heavily on their wholesalers to handle the sales functions—and will drop a wholesaler who is not performing well based on sales figures—which makes this type of wholesaling very competitive.

CHANNEL RELATIONSHIPS

The fact is that modern-day companies are often forced to participate in distribution channels for practical reasons—not really because they want to be "part of the team." They need the efficiency and the economy of scale, although in some ways, this kind of cooperation runs counter to the tough, competitive side of traditional retailing.

Channel cooperation would be ideal—a joint effort of all the members to create a supply chain that is flexible, gives each partner a competitive advantage, and ultimately provides the best product and related services to the customer. However, whether you're selling candy bars or luxury automobiles, conflict does occur when the members of a distribution channel choose different ways to operate within the system, have differing goals, or balk at sharing information. Areas of potential channel conflict are many. They can arise naturally from competition between multiple members of the same channel—retailers or wholesalers—who carry the same product line. They will also occur when retailers have service issues with the products and want to handle returns, repairs, or exchanges differently (say, more generously) than what the manufacturer is willing to do. A very common source of channel conflict is a producer's decision to either increase or decrease prices. The wholesalers take the flack about it from retailers—who, in turn, must listen to consumers' complaints, at least in the case of price hikes.

There is a hierarchy in all distribution channels, whether the participants like it or not. The company that has the most authority in the channel is referred to as the **channel leader** or **channel captain**. In this case, "authority" means the partner's ability to either influence or control the behavior of any of the other partners in the channel.

It's safe to say that no one in any distribution channel or supply chain wields as much authority in retail today as Wal-Mart. The world's largest retailer literally treats its suppliers like extensions of its own business—manufacturers and wholesalers have free access to real-time data about how their product lines are selling at any Wal-Mart store, any time. Sharing this information allows the suppliers to plan their production runs, make their importing decisions, and so on. Hundreds of manufacturers have offices in Bentonville, Arkansas, just to be conveniently located for Wal-Mart, and they consider it a small price to pay for increased access to their giant retail partner. In exchange, this Channel Captain Extraordinaire can require extraordinary things of its smaller partners, from price cuts to the acquisition and use of expensive new technology like radio frequency identification.

In business-to-business channels, Ford is known for its incredibly collaborative relationships with suppliers, who do more than provide materials and parts—they help design the vehicles Ford produces.[2] Similarly, any manufacturer that uses a Just-In-Time (JIT) system, with offices for supplier representatives on-site in its plants, has forged a unique type of channel relationship.

Like any kind of power, channel leadership can be wielded to the benefit or detriment of the other companies. Wal-Mart's situation aside, channel captains may take the lead in negotiating with a participating company that is not fulfilling its responsibilities—orders are late; the company hasn't updated its computer systems; it may be struggling financially; the CEO is uncommunicative or argumentative. Whatever the case, if the end result is that it's bogging down everyone else in the channel, then something must be done.

It is important to note that in a distribution channel, any of the participants can refuse to do business with any of the others—as long as someone amenable to the entire group is tapped to take over the role that the ousted business has played. This game of "musical chairs" is difficult at best, and disastrous at worst. It's better for everyone if the participants can figure out how to get along.

Strategic Alliances

A third and similar partnership arrangement between separate companies with products or skills to share is the **strategic alliance**, which allows them to share the use of already-established distribution channels in pursuit of business growth in new markets. Retailers have been forging strategic alliances since the 1950s, and the pace continues unabated today as stores continue to branch into international sales.

A strategic alliance is more than two companies holding shares of each others' stock, or ordering merchandise jointly for added buying power. In order to be truly strategic, the alliance must have all three of the following characteristics:

1. **It must be collaborative.** It should not involve the stronger channel member barking orders to the weaker one.
2. **It must be horizontal.** That is, it must be forged between companies of the same type, two retailers or two wholesalers.
3. **It must be beneficial to both.** This requires common objectives and the willingness to communicate and share knowledge.

A promising collaboration would be the alliance of two similar types of retailers in two different countries to share product lines, invest in technology together, and learn from each other. In so doing, they use each others' distribution channels in the new country.

Retailers commonly belong to several strategic alliances. They offer a way to share the risks of business expansion that, if undertaken separately, the individual companies may lack the time, money, or expertise to manage.

CHAPTER SUMMARY

Companies participate in distribution channels, which determine their supply chain relationships. Channel members negotiate with each other and offer complementary resources and services to move products "down the line" from manufacturers to consumers. Then, the supply chain partners provide the raw materials and logistics to meet the channel requirements.

Retail distribution channels consist of some combination of producers or manufacturers, agents or brokers, wholesalers or distributors, importers, and retailers. Each step along the channel has a specific purpose that is met by one or more member companies. Distribution channels are important because they allow for a continuous flow of product despite the natural peaks and slumps experienced in manufacturing and sales. They also provide efficiency, economies of scale, and cost savings to members of the channel. The types and numbers of channels a retailer participates in depend on many factors, all of which were listed and described in this chapter.

As with any type of business collaboration, pressure to perform can be intense among members of the channel, and numerous areas of potential conflict were discussed, including the dominance of channel leaders, for better or worse. However, most companies cannot avoid being channel members in this competitive and highly technological retail age.

The chapter ended with a brief definition of strategic alliances, partnerships that allow companies to use each other's existing distribution channels to grow business.

DISCUSSION QUESTIONS

1. If retailers "drive the distribution channel," as stated in this chapter, then why does the ultimate decision about which channel to choose rest with the manufacturers or producers of the products?
2. Think of a product that you buy in the supermarket regularly. Now, describe who the members of its distribution channel might be. From what you notice as a consumer, are they doing a good enough job? Why, or why not?
3. Do you think channel relationships can get too comfortable or cozy; that perhaps sharing information can work against the end users instead of to their benefit? Can you think of any steps or services in a supply chain that should *never* be entrusted to other members of a distribution channel—and if so, why not?
4. In the discussion of potential channel conflict and companies that aren't holding up their end of responsibilities, in each of the situations mentioned (orders are late, CEO is argumentative, etc.), write a paragraph describing what the other channel members might do to remedy the problem without dropping the business from the channel.
5. What would make a producer enter into a strategic alliance for international business? How is it different than what a retailer would consider?

ENDNOTES

1. *"Consumer Goods Industry Threatened, According to IBM Survey,"* © CRM Today, a publication of Contact Solutions, Ltd., Athens, Greece, February 18, 2005.
2. C. K. Prahalad and Venkatram Ramaswamy (University of Michigan), "Co-Opting Customer Competence," in *Working Knowledge*, newsletter of the Harvard Business School, Boston, Massachusetts, February 8, 2000.

THE INCREDIBLE JOURNEY

CONTINUES

By Jennifer Bresnahan

Swish it, spit it, feel the familiar burn. When you swig a mouthful of Listerine antiseptic mouthwash and watch it go down the bathroom drain, you're witnessing something much more significant than the disappearance of the fiery liquid that kills germs that cause bad breath, plaque, and gingivitis. You're seeing the last step in a complex value chain spanning several continents and requiring months of coordination by countless businesses and individuals. The resources involved in getting a single bottle of aqua Cool Mint Listerine into a customer's medicine cabinet boggle the mind. As it's transformed from raw material to finished product, the product wends its way around the globe and through the value chains and information technology (IT) systems of two "CIO-100" winners,* the $13 billion prescription drug and consumer products manufacturer Warner-Lambert Co. and the $30 billion drugstore chain CVS Corp. Most of the steps involved in manufacturing and distributing Listerine are ongoing, but we've assigned dates to each stage to illustrate the speed of a single bottle's trip through the value chain.

MAY 28—DOWN UNDER

Our journey begins in Australia where a farmer is harvesting his spring crop of eucalyptus for eucalyptol, the oil found in its leathery leaves. The farmer sells the crop to an Australian processing company, which spends about four weeks extracting the eucalyptol from the eucalyptus. Morris Plains, New Jersey–based Warner-Lambert (hereafter, WL) partners with a distributor in New Jersey to buy the oil from the Australian company and transport it to WL's Listerine manufacturing and distribution facility in Lititz, Pennsylvania. The load will arrive at Lititz about three months after the harvest, says Robert LeRoy, director of material procurement for WL.

JULY 13—BENEATH THE SAND

Half a world away, a Saudi Arabian government-owned operation is drilling deep under the desert for the natural gas that will yield the synthetic alcohol that gives Listerine its 43-proof punch. Union Carbide Corp. ships the gas via tanker to a refinery in Texas City, Texas, which purifies it and converts it to ethanol. The ethanol is loaded onto another tanker and transported from Texas City through the Gulf of Mexico to New Jersey, where it's transferred to storage tanks and transported via truck or rail to WL's plant. A single shipment of ethanol takes about six to eight weeks to get from Saudi Arabia to Lititz.

Note: *CIO* magazine names an annual "top 100" companies for supply chain excellence. The companies' profit figures were updated for 2005 for this article.

3

SUPPLY CHAIN OPERATIONS: PLANNING

The best retailers are expert jugglers, balancing the many challenges of planning for sales. They plan which product lines they will sell, and how to get these items from their original sources to the stores. They forecast sales figures by week and by month. They plan how to merchandise the items, often with a layout that shows exactly where they'll fit in the store, and how much shelf or rack space will be devoted to them. They plan special promotions and sales. And when things don't go according to plan, they revise their plans to remain on course!

After reading this chapter, you will understand the following concepts as they apply to planning functions in a supply chain:

- Forecasting product demand
- Pros and cons of various forecasting methods
- Importance of aggregate planning
- Cost structures and pricing plans
- Theories of inventory planning

There are also three short company profiles of paper industry distributors, in which their leaders discuss how they deal with their own planning and supply chain issues.

The retail industry has its own unique planning-related challenges. Chain stores must plan for different locations, often with different customer demographics. And today's merchant is likely to sell in multiple channels as well—traditional store locations, online, in catalogs—each requiring its own planning process. But there are common themes in the way supply chain members in any industry must plan, and retailers should become familiar with these processes. This knowledge will allow them to, among other things, be able to discern the well-organized manufacturers from the ones that are going to cause problems sooner or later by their lack of planning.

FIVE LINKS IN THE CHAIN

In the first chapter, you became acquainted with the five drivers of supply chain performance. These drivers can be thought of as the design parameters or policy decisions that define the shape and capabilities of any supply chain. Within the context created by these policy decisions, a supply chain goes about doing its job by performing regular, ongoing operations that are the "nuts-and-bolts" operations at the core of every supply chain.

To reach a higher-level understanding of these operations and how they relate to each other, we can use the Supply-Chain Operations Reference, or SCOR, model developed by the Supply-Chain Council of Pittsburgh, Pennsylvania (www.supply-chain.org). For years, the SCOR model identified four categories of operations, but it has been changed in recent years to include a fifth category. In the next few chapters, we'll examine each of these categories in terms of how supply chains are organized:

- Plan
- Source

- Make
- Deliver
- Return

Plan

This category refers to all the functions that are necessary to plan and organize the operations in the other four categories. We will investigate three functions in this category in some detail: demand forecasting, product pricing, and inventory management.

Source

Operations in this category include the activities necessary to acquire the raw materials or skills to create products or services. We will look at two operations here. The first is procurement, or the acquisition of materials and services. The second, credit and collections, is not traditionally seen as a sourcing activity, but it can be thought of literally, as the acquisition of cash. Both these operations have major impacts on the efficiency of a supply chain.

Make

This category includes the operations required to develop and build the products and services that a supply chain provides—product design, production management, and facilities management. The SCOR model does not specifically include the product design and development process, but it is included here because it is integral to the production process.

Deliver

These activities are part of receiving customer orders and delivering products to customers. The two main operations we will review are order entry/order fulfillment and product delivery. These two operations constitute the core connections between companies in a supply chain.

Return

This refers to the service-related functions that take place after the supply chain has achieved its primary mission—and, for retailers, these are critical functions that often make the difference in customer loyalty. They include credit policies and policies for things like returns, repairs, and exchanges of

SUPPLY CHAIN SKILLS—ADAPTABILITY

Paper Enterprises (www.paperenterprises.com) is a distributor of food service and paper disposables and janitorial supplies. Based in the Bronx, it serves the entire New York metropolitan area. Herb Sedler founded the company in 1961; his son Jordan has been working in the business for more than two decades.

Success in a market like New York City requires a combination of efficiency and high customer service levels. "You learn through trial and error but you learn," Jordan Sedler explains. "This is what adaptability is all about. For instance, in a lot of Manhattan buildings, you have to use a freight elevator manned by a guy who may not really care about your delivery schedule. You learn to bring him a doughnut and coffee!"

"In New York City, there are about 300 competitors for every market segment," adds Herb Sedler. "There are three or four big, overhead-laden corporations—and then 297 little guys running around with trucks, who buy cheap and sell cheap. Paper Enterprises straddles both worlds. On the one hand, we compete with the big corporations. On the other hand, we didn't want to compete with the little guys, so we decided to make them our customers. We became a re-distributor who could buy in bulk from manufacturers and resell to all the smaller operators."

Paper Enterprises encourages a mind-set of customer service in all employees, and then focuses on the day-to-day demands of delivering it.

"I have set the tone that the customer is king," says Herb. "You have to have a staff who loves the challenge of satisfying the customer. In today's ABC (activity-based costing) world this drive for customer satisfaction does not always look efficient. But it is the relentless dedication to satisfying the customer that ultimately pays off."

Logistics are a huge part of this, as well as the biggest challenge in the New York metropolitan area. Jordan says, "There's always a problem with delivery windows—70 percent of our customers have 2½-hour delivery windows that we have to meet. And the equipment you use has to fit the terrain—in lower Manhattan, you just can't use trucks over a certain size. Imagine trying to back an 18-wheeler into a loading dock across four lanes of traffic with pedestrians crossing back and forth."

In the years since the September 11 terrorist attacks, delivery hours have been restricted even further, as large trucks are not allowed into Manhattan overnight. Warehouse space is almost nonexistent, or far too pricey.

"Also in this city, there is an interesting situation that you have when it comes to people," Jordan observes. "We hire people from many different ethnic and cultural backgrounds, and there is a cliquish tendency in the employees from each of these cultures. It is a real trick to keep the cliques from distracting people and undermining the company and teamwork environment."

When they look at technology, the Sedlers take a very pragmatic approach. "We have two goals for using technology," says Jordan. "The first goal is to lower our cost of doing business in a measurable way. How can we use technology to lower costs in inventory control, warehouse management, and order fulfillment? The second goal is to lower our error rate. We don't want people to manually handle and re-handle data like purchase orders and invoices, because it just increases the error rate. Our motto is 'Get it right the first time.'"

"We also want to bring technology to our customer base," adds Herb. "The immigrants are the new entrepreneurs. They have no formal training in distribution and they are often one-man shows. I am a mentor in the Baruch College entrepreneurship program. As they succeed, Paper Enterprises will succeed. As we show them technology and practices that help them grow, we become a logistics organization and not just a paper distributor."

"I learn something every day. Running a business in New York is like working in a microcosm of the whole world. People from every country are here," said Jordan. "And it's funny, where you may think that there would be intense and cutthroat competition. Not so! A cooperative spirit has evolved, and that is an important part of how we do business."

"After 9/11," Herb recalls, "we called a meeting of distributors in the city and said we would make our trucks available to our competitors who needed to get into lower Manhattan if they would help us in New Jersey."

And that's adaptability.

goods. Remember, when something is wrong with a product that has been sold, it "returns" eventually to the supply chain to be dealt with by at least one member of the chain.

In this chapter, we begin with further detail in the planning category and an executive-level overview of three main operations that constitute the planning process. We'll follow in subsequent chapters with the other four major topics.

DEMAND FORECASTING

Supply chain management decisions are based on forecasts that define which products will be required, in what amounts, and when they will be needed. The demand forecast becomes the basis for companies to plan their internal operations and to cooperate among each other to meet market demand.

All forecasts deal with four major variables that combine to determine what the market conditions are likely to be:

1. Demand
2. Supply
3. Product characteristics
4. Competitive environment

Demand refers to the overall market's perceived need for a group of related products or services. Is the market growing or declining? If so, what is the yearly or quarterly rate of growth or decline, and how is this measured? Perhaps the market is relatively mature and demand is steady at a level that has been predictable for some period of years. Perhaps the product has a seasonal demand pattern—snow skis and heating oil are in greater demand as winter approaches; tennis rackets and sunscreen are more popular in the summer. Perhaps it is a developing market—meaning the products or services are new and there is not much historical data on demand, or the demand varies widely because new customers are just being introduced to the products. Markets where there is little historical data and lots of variability are the most challenging when it comes to demand forecasting.

Supply is determined by the number of producers of a product and by the lead times that are associated with a product. The more producers of a product and the shorter the lead times, the more predictable the supply. When there are only a few suppliers or when lead times are longer, there is more potential uncertainty in a market. Like variability in demand, uncertainty in supply makes forecasting more difficult. Also, longer lead times associated with a product require a longer time frame in which to forecast. Supply chain forecasts must cover a time period that includes the combined lead times of all the components that go into the creation of a final product.

Product characteristics are the features of a product that influence customer demand for it. Is it in a product category known for fast change and intense competition, like computers and home electronics? Or is the product mature and changing slowly or not at all, as is the case with many commodity products? Forecasts for mature products can cover longer time frames than forecasts for products that are developing quickly. It is also important to determine whether a product will steal demand away from another product—or even from other "members" of its own product line (a phenomenon perhaps unfortunately known as **cannibalizing**). Can it be substituted for another product? Or will the use of a product drive the complementary use of a related product? Demand for products that either compete with or complement each other should be forecast together.

Competitive environment refers to the actions of a company and its competitors. What is the market share of a company? Regardless of whether the total size of a market is growing or shrinking, what is the trend in the individual company's market share—growing or declining? How about the market shares of competitors? Market share trends can be influenced by product promotions and price wars, so forecasts should take into account such events that are planned for that time period, both by the company and its competitors.

Forecasting VARIABLES

1.	Demand	Overall market demand for product
2.	Supply	Amount of product available
3.	Product Characteristics	Product features that influence demand
4.	Competitive Environment	Actions of product suppliers in the market

Forecasting METHODS

1.	Qualitative	Relies on a person's intuition or opinions
2.	Causal	Assumes that demand is strongly related to certain factors
3.	Time Series	Based on historical demand patterns
4.	Simulation	Combines causal and time series methods

Figure 3-1. The four forecasting variables and the four forecasting methods.

Forecasting Methods

There are four basic methods to use when preparing forecasts, and most forecasts are done using various combinations of these methods. Chopra and Meindl define them as follows:

1. Qualitative
2. Causal
3. Time series
4. Simulation

Qualitative methods rely upon a person's intuition or subjective opinions about a market. These methods are most appropriate when there is not much historical data to work with. They are perhaps the most creative types of projections, which does not mean they are the least accurate! When a new line of products is introduced, people can make forecasts based on comparisons to other products or situations that they consider similar, or based on their best estimates about what will happen in the market.

Causal methods of forecasting assume that demand is strongly related to a particular cause, such as environmental or market factors. For instance, demand for commercial loans is often closely correlated to interest rates—so if interest rate cuts are expected in the next period of time, then loan forecasts can be made using a causal relationship with interest rates. Another strong causal relationship exists between price and demand. Generally, if prices are lowered, demand can be expected to increase, and conversely, if prices are raised, demand can be expected to fall.

A forecast that does not take causal factors into account is referred to as a **naïve model**, meaning that it appears to work "on paper" or in principle, but without real-world economic considerations factored in that may impact the true results.

Time series methods are the most common forms of forecasting. These naïve models are based on the assumption that historical patterns of demand are a good indicator of future demand, and that over a period of time, demand can be charted in three different ways: as an underlying trend (flat, up, or down), as a cycle (daily, weekly, seasonally, and so on), and as irregular fluctuations (peaks or valleys) over time.

A time series method is best when there is a reliable body of historical data and the markets being forecast are stable, with demand patterns that do not vary much from one year to the next.

Mathematical techniques, such as moving averages and data smoothing, are used to create forecasts based on performance over certain time periods. These techniques are built right into most computer software forecasting packages, but management students should know something about how they work. A **moving average** is a series of calculations in which a trend is measured and projected, then the numbers are "smoothed" (evened out just enough to measure a curve or cycle).

Simulation methods are combinations of causal and time series projections to imitate the behavior of consumers under different circumstances. A simulation may be used to answer questions such as, "What will happen to revenue if we put this entire line of clothing on sale next month?" "What will happen to our market share if our biggest competitor opens a store in this area?" and so on. Simulation models are useful because they are more efficient than, for example, doing actual tests that vary the output of a production facility "to see what will happen." Technology has made it relatively easy to input different projections into a computer program and let it do the calculating.

In retail settings, simulation is often used to determine what to do about **queuing problems**—that pesky waiting-in-line that annoys customers so much. In a simulation, a store can "try out" different numbers of cash wraps (counters where customers pay for merchandise), different lines for different types of sales (cash, credit card, express lanes), and so on, trying to come to a decent, average wait time without having to test all the various configurations on actual customers.

In most companies, retailers included, several of these methods are combined as a way of looking at a particular business situation from several different angles. This makes sense because different forecasting methods offer different types of insights. Studies have shown that creating forecasts using different methods and then combining the results into a final forecast usually produces greater accuracy than the output of any one method alone.

Regardless of the methods used, when creating and evaluating forecasts, you should keep several things in mind. First of all, short-term forecasts are inherently more accurate than long-term forecasts. The effect of business trends and conditions can be much more accurately calculated over short periods than over longer periods. When Wal-Mart began restocking its stores twice a week instead of twice a month, the store managers were able to significantly increase the accuracy of their forecasts because the time periods involved dropped from two or three weeks to three or four days. Most long-range, multiyear forecasts are highly speculative.

Aggregate forecasts are more accurate than forecasts for individual products or for small market segments. For example, annual forecasts for soft drink sales in a given metropolitan area are fairly accurate—but when these forecasts are broken down into sales by districts within the metropolitan area, they become less accurate. Aggregate forecasts are made using a broader base of data, which provides good forecasting accuracy. As a rule, the more narrowly focused or specific a forecast is, the less data is available and the more variability there is within the data, so its accuracy is diminished.

The final, and surely the most frustrating, thing about forecasts is that they are always wrong, to a greater or lesser degree. Quite simply, there is no such thing as a perfect forecast. No matter how scientifically it is prepared, it is still somebody's best guess, and retailers must therefore assign at least some degree of error to every forecast.

A forecast that is considered "accurate" has a typical degree of error of plus or minus 5 percent. A more speculative forecast may have an error range of plus or minus 20 percent! It is important to know the degree of error because the business must have contingency plans to cover those outcomes. What would a manufacturer do if raw material prices were 5 percent higher than expected? What would a retailer do if demand for the product was 20 percent higher than expected? How quickly could each business in the supply chain respond in these situations?

Aggregate Planning

Once demand forecasts have been created, the next step is to create a plan that maps out exactly how the company will meet the expected demand for what it makes or sells. This is called **aggregate planning** and its purpose is to satisfy

SUPPLY CHAIN SKILLS—MEETING CUSTOMERS' NEEDS

Service means different things to different customers, and their needs vary depending on their strengths and weaknesses and the business models that they use. Effective supply chain members learn to tailor their service offerings to match the individual customer's needs.

Service Paper Company (www.servicepaper.com) distributes retail food and food service products, industrial packaging, health-care disposables, and janitorial supplies. They have been in business since 1937, with locations in Seattle, Portland, and Spokane. Leonard Green is Service Paper's president. See if you can guess who the customer is as Green relates the story:

"We have customers in a number of different market segments and these customers are in different stages of their business growth," Leonard says. "We look at each customer and strive to provide a mix of products and services that will make us a valuable part of their operations. Let me illustrate this with an example of a customer that we have served for some time now and through several stages in their growth. Back in the '80s, we began doing business with a small company that operated a handful of coffee shops in Seattle.

"This small company insisted on using specially made products featuring their logo. Their original supplier was not willing to stock 'special print' inventory. At Service Paper, we viewed the request as a customer requirement rather than an inconvenience. We began taking large shipments of their logoed special-print items from various manufacturers and distributed these products to their coffee shops several times a week.

"They were growing rapidly and we were able to work with their staff to facilitate the procurement of their food service disposables. We knew the products and the manufacturers in the food service industry, so we were able to help in educating their purchasing people and in suggesting the products they needed. We also helped them with sourcing and even helped schedule production runs with manufacturers for products they needed.

"Early on, the company CEO was very hands-on in all of these areas. He knew what he wanted the company to be and was intent on finding the products they needed. We steered him to the maker of a new coffee cup lid called a 'Traveler Lid.' It allowed a person to sip hot coffee while they walked or drove, without getting too much in their mouth all at once. When he saw the lid, he liked it so much that he insisted the manufacturer give them an exclusive on the product. The manufacturer wasn't willing to do that and was ready to walk away from the business because of that demand.

"Since I knew both parties, I was able to act as a referee. I encouraged the CEO to see that he had a strong potential partner there and perhaps he could reconsider his position. I helped them start a business relationship that has been very beneficial to both companies ever since."

As the company expanded out of the Seattle area, Service Paper introduced them to a national cooperative of distribution companies, of which Service Paper is both a member and an owner. "We got Network Services involved when the company told us they were going to expand into Chicago.

I became their advocate within Network. We had lots of business in Seattle, but at first, there were only a few stores in Chicago. The Network member in Chicago was reluctant to stock the specially printed products and do the many small deliveries to the coffee shops. Then they expanded into San Francisco, and I had to work hard to explain to our member there why it was a good deal.

"We had to change our operating policies to meet the customer's needs. We had to carry a substantial inventory of proprietary items, and we had to accept orders that were often much smaller than our usual minimum orders. But, over time, they established credibility with us because they met their new store rollout plans and the promised volume did materialize."

Today, numerous Network members support the Starbucks locations nationwide—and no doubt, they're glad they took the risk! And it all started with one distributor's willingness to meet some unique customer demands.

demand in a way that maximizes profit for the company. The planning is done as an overview of the company's entire offerings (hence the term "aggregate") and not at the level of individual stock-keeping units (SKUs). It sets the optimum levels of production and inventory that will be followed over the next 3 to 18 months.

Depending on the type of company, its aggregate plan becomes the framework for its short-term decisions about production, inventory, and distribution:

- Production decisions include the rate of production (how fast or slow) and the amount of production capacity to use, the size of the workforce, and how much overtime to pay versus hiring subcontractors.
- Inventory decisions include how much demand will be met immediately by inventory on hand, and how much demand can be satisfied later with back orders.
- Distribution decisions define how and when product will be moved from the place of production to the place where it will be used or purchased by customers.

There are three basic approaches to take in creating the aggregate plan, and they involve trade-offs among three variables:

1. Amount of production capacity
2. Percentage or level of production capacity being used
3. Amount of inventory to carry

We will look briefly at each of these three approaches. Not all of them relate directly to retail management, so imagine instead the manufacturers that supply the product lines for retail stores, which will help you to envision the process. In practice, even the smallest manufacturing companies create aggregate plans that are combinations of the following three approaches:

1. **Use production capacity to match demand.** In this approach, the total amount of production capacity is matched to the level of demand. The objective here is to be working at 100 percent of capacity at all times. This is achieved by adding or eliminating plant capacity as needed, and hiring and laying off employees as needed. This approach results in low levels of inventory, but it can be very expensive to implement if the cost of modifying the plant capacity is high. It is also disruptive and demoralizing to the workforce if people are constantly being hired, then laid off as demand rises and falls. So this approach works best when the cost of carrying inventory is high and the cost of changing capacity—both of the plant and the workforce—is low.

2. **Use varying levels of total capacity to match demand.** This approach works well, but only if there is excess production capacity available. If existing plants are not used 24 hours a day, 7 days a week, then there is an opportunity to meet changing demand by increasing or decreasing the way the plants' capacity is used. The size of the workforce can be maintained at a steady rate, with overtime and flexible work scheduling used to match production rates. The result is low levels of inventory and also lower average levels of capacity utilization. The approach makes sense when the cost of carrying inventory is high and the cost of excess capacity is relatively low.

3. **Use inventory and backlogs to match demand.** This approach provides for stability in the plant capacity and workforce, and enables a constant rate of output. Production is not matched with demand—instead, inventory is either built up during periods of low demand (in anticipation of future demand) or inventory is allowed to run low and backlogs are built up in one period, to be filled in a following period. This approach results in higher capacity utilization and lower costs of changing capacity. However, it does generate large inventories and backlogs over time as demand fluctuates. It should be used when the cost of capacity and changing capacity is high, and the cost of carrying (storing) inventory and backlogs is relatively low.

PRODUCT PRICING

Companies and entire supply chains can influence demand by using price—and in a supply chain, we're not just talking about the retail prices of finished goods, but the prices of each and every ingredient or service that goes into manufacturing, storing, and transporting them before they arrive at the store.

Depending on how price is used, it will tend to maximize either revenue or gross profit. Typically, marketing and sales people want to make pricing decisions that will stimulate demand during peak seasons, with the obvious aim of maximizing total revenue. Financial or manufacturing people are more likely to favor pricing decisions that stimulate demand during slow periods, to even out the peaks and valleys. The latter goal is to maximize gross profit in peak demand periods, which then generates enough revenue to cover costs during periods of low demand for the product or service.

Relationship of Cost Structure to Pricing

So who's right? Is it better to do price promotion during peak periods to increase revenue—or during slow periods to cover costs? The answer depends on the company's cost structure. If a company has flexibility to vary the size of its

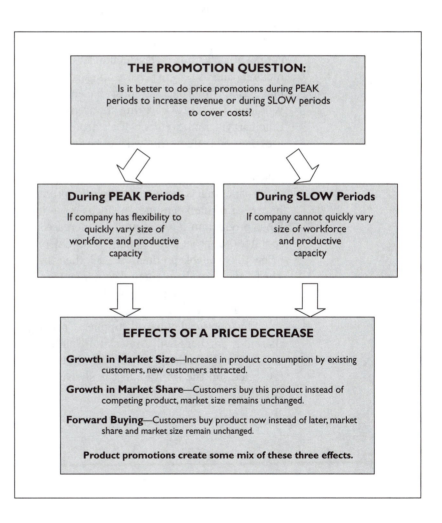

Figure 3-2. Product promotion and company cost structure.

workforce and productive capacity and the cost of carrying inventory is high, then it is best to create more demand in peak seasons. If there is less flexibility to vary workforce and capacity and if cost to carry inventory is low, it is best to create demand in low periods.

An example of a company that can quickly ramp up production would be an electronics components manufacturer. This type of company has typically invested in equipment and facilities that can be quickly reconfigured to produce different final products from an inventory of standard component parts. And this company doesn't want to carry a lot of product in inventory, because it soon becomes obsolete and must be written off.

Therefore, the electronic part supplier is generally motivated to run promotions in peak periods, to stimulate demand even further. Since it can quickly increase production levels, it can make up for a reduction in the profit margin with an increase in total sales—as long as it is able to sell all the product that is manufactured.

Conversely, a paper mill is an example of a type of manufacturing plant that cannot quickly ramp up production levels. The plant and equipment involved in making paper is very expensive and requires a long lead time to build. Once in place, a paper mill operates most efficiently if it is able to run at a steady rate, all year long. The cost of carrying an inventory of paper products is less expensive than carrying an inventory of electronic components because paper products are commodity items that will not become obsolete. These products also can be stored in less expensive warehouse facilities, and they are also less likely to be stolen.

A paper mill is motivated to do price promotions in periods of low demand. In periods of high demand, the focus is on maintaining a good profit margin. Since production levels cannot be increased anyway, there is no way to respond to—or profit from—an increase in demand. In periods where demand is below the available production level, then there is value in increased demand. The fixed cost of the plant and equipment is constant, so it is best to try to balance demand with available production capacity. This way, the plant can run steadily at full capacity.

Why do the details of suppliers' pricing policies matter to retailers? As senior partners Will Ander and Neil Stern of the prestigious retail consulting firm McMillan|Doolittle write in their book *Winning at Retail*: "Having low prices on the front end—the shelves—demands low costs on the back end."[1]

SUPPLY CHAIN SKILLS—BUILDING A BRAND

Waxie Sanitary Supply (www.waxie.com) is a distributor with locations throughout California, Nevada, Utah, Colorado, and Arizona. Over the last 20 years, they have been very successful in developing and promoting their own, Waxie brand-name products.

CEO Charles Wax recounts the company history: "It was founded in 1945 by my uncle Harry Wax, and then my father Morris joined him. The company started under the name of San Diego Janitorial Supply. We grew and in 1962 bought another company in southern California named Kleenline. We kept both names, because each had a loyal customer base. In the 1980s we expanded out of the southern California area and we felt the need for a new company name that would convey who we were as we entered new markets.

"Uncle Harry was a Seabee in the navy during World War II. That's where he got the nickname 'Waxie,' and the logo he chose when he started the company was a bee operating a floor-waxing machine. So it seemed natural for us to adopt the name Waxie and to use a bee as our logo.

"We wanted to develop our own brand name because a lot of companies buy product and then forget where they bought it," Wax explains. "If we put our name on the product, they would remember where they got it—and if they like the product, then they have to come to us to buy it. We redesigned and standardized our logo and the company slogan and put them on products, forms, trucks, brochures, everything."

The first step is to create a brand name; the next step is to sell its benefits to customers. "We sell a lot of value-added services," says Wax. "We educate the customer to use the best product for their specific needs. We show them how to use dilution control to optimize usage rates for chemicals. We show them how to use floor machines to cut labor costs. We train the customer's people in how to use our products.

"It is easy for a competitor of ours to say, 'We have the same item and at a lower price.' We respond to this by educating customers to the fact that 10 percent of their cost is product and the other 90 percent is labor. We can show them how to use our products to cut their labor costs, and that's where they'll see the big savings.

"We are always looking for ways to solve our customers' problems and customize our service offerings for them. For instance, we did a lot of work at the Winter Olympics in Salt Lake City. To meet their delivery schedules, we got security clearance for our drivers, and worked closely with people running the event to bring our trucks in at night, where and when they wanted them."

Waxie has also welcomed technology to help deliver services. Director of Information Technology Cliff Robbins says they've computerized the customer survey process, and field sales and service people carry laptops.

Continued

"They have the same access to information as they would if they were in the office—complete customer profiles, credit status, open issues, and sales history," Robbins explains. "There is a Web-based order entry system that lets customers view their own customized product catalogs and prices, and we've worked with the sales people to train our customers to use this system."

Wax adds, "There is great benefit to the customers. They can order 24/7, they can make up their own order guides, they can see product pictures, and they can see usage information. As customers start using the system, it cuts our cost to handle the orders and we are also seeing an increase in the average order size from these customers."

Delivering the value to the Waxie customers requires a coordinated effort from everyone in the company. The company tracks a few simple performance measures and has a bonus program for the non-sales employees, called "All Sell, All Grow."

"We post branch and overall company gross margin growth every month throughout the company, so all employees know how we are doing and how they stand on their yearly bonus," Wax explains.

"Having our own brand helps us manage our margins. It insulates us somewhat from the actions of the national brand-name manufacturers. We wanted to create a brand that stands for who we are—to remind us why we are here and to remind customers of our value."

INVENTORY MANAGEMENT

The demand forecasts and pricing policies discussed in this chapter should give each company in the supply chain the data it needs to decide how to manage its inventory. The term **inventory management** means using a set of techniques to manage the inventory levels within different companies in a supply chain. This task is an ongoing balancing act—making sure there is enough inventory to meet the demands while exploiting economies of scale to get the best prices for the products when they are sold; and reducing the costs associated with the inventory as much as possible while still maintaining the service levels that customers require.

Technology and computerization have had incredible impact in this part of the industry, allowing supply chain members to share data instantly. The term for increased efficiency in meeting the consumer's needs for a product is called efficient consumer response, or ECR. You'll learn more about the technology used to achieve ECR in Chapter 5.

As mentioned in Chapter 1, there are three kinds of inventory. Both *cycle inventory* and *seasonal inventory* are influenced by economy-of-scale considerations—that is, the cost structure of the companies in any supply chain will suggest certain levels of inventory based on how much it costs to produce and store the products. *Safety inventory* is influenced by product demand: The less predictable the demand for the product, the higher the level of safety inventory is required—more "backup" in storage, just in case of a demand swing.

The inventory management operation in a company (or an entire supply chain) is composed of a blend of activities related to managing the three different types of inventory. Each type of inventory has its own specific challenges, and the mix of these challenges will vary from one company to another and from one supply chain to another.

Cycle Inventory

Generally, in retail a **cycle** refers to the time period between orders of product—that is, enough goods must be ordered to keep the store stocked well enough during the cycle until the next order is placed. So cycle inventory is the inventory required to meet product demand between orders.

The whole reason cycle inventory exists is because economies of scale favor placing fewer, larger orders of just about any product, rather than continuous orders of small quantities. Of course, some perishable products and gourmet foods would be exceptions in the supermarket trade, but for the most part, supply chains "think" just like consumers—we can probably get a better deal buying in bulk.

The end user of the product may actually use or sell it in continuous small amounts throughout the year, but the distributor and manufacturer of the product often find it more cost-efficient to produce and sell it in large quantities that do not match the typical usage pattern. So cycle inventory might be described as the buildup of inventory in a supply chain, because production and stocking of inventory is done in quantities that are much larger than the ongoing demand for the product.

For example, a distributor may experience an ongoing demand for Item A of 100 units per week. However, the distributor finds that it is most cost-effective to order in batches of 650 units. Every six weeks or so, the distributor places a new order, which causes the cycle inventory to build up in the distributor's warehouse at the beginning of the order period.

Observing the rest of the supply chain, let's say the manufacturer of Item A sells to a number of distributors in different states and has found that production is most cost-effective when it manufactures in batches of 14,000 units at a time. This also results in the buildup of cycle inventory at the manufacturer's location.

Economic Order Quantity

For every company and every product, there is an order quantity that makes the most financial sense to purchase at a time. This "most cost-effective amount" for a single order is called the **economic order quantity (EOQ)**. The mathematical formula to calculate EOQ consists of very basic knowledge of square roots:

$$EOQ = \sqrt{2UO / hC}$$

where:

U = annual usage rate
O = ordering cost
C = cost per unit
h = holding cost per year as a percentage of unit cost

For instance, let's say that Item Z has an annual usage rate (U) of 240, a fixed cost per order (O) of $5, a unit cost (C) of $7, and an annual holding cost (h) of 30 percent per unit. Let's do the math:

$$EOQ = \sqrt{\frac{2 \times 240 \times 5.00}{.30 \times 7.00}}$$

$$EOQ = \sqrt{\frac{2400}{2.1}}$$

$$EOQ = \sqrt{1142.86}$$

$$EOQ = 33.81 \text{ (or rounded to the nearest whole unit, 34)}$$

If the annual usage rate for Item Z is 240, then the monthly usage rate is 20. An EOQ of 34 represents about 1 and 3/4 months supply. This may not be a convenient order size. Small changes in the EOQ don't have a major impact on total ordering and holding costs, so it is usually best to round off the EOQ quantity to the nearest standard ordering size. In the case of Item Z, there may be 30 units in a case, so it would make sense to adjust the EOQ for that item to 30.

The EOQ formula works to calculate an order quantity that results in the most efficient investment of money in inventory. Efficiency here is defined as the lowest total unit cost for each inventory item. If a certain inventory item has a high usage rate and it is expensive, the EOQ formula recommends a low order quantity—that is, more orders per year, but less money invested in each order.

If an inventory item has a low usage rate and is inexpensive, the EOQ formula recommends a high order quantity. This means fewer orders per year, but maximum efficiency when investing money to stock that item, since the unit cost is low.

Seasonal Inventory

Seasonal inventory happens when a company or a supply chain with a fixed amount of production capacity decides to stockpile products in anticipation of future demand. This is common when a manufacturing facility uses its slow periods to plan and get a head start on making fashions for an upcoming

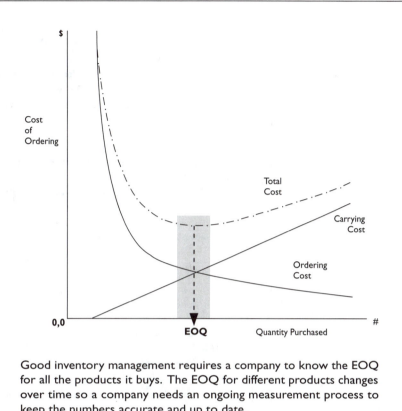

Good inventory management requires a company to know the EOQ for all the products it buys. The EOQ for different products changes over time so a company needs an ongoing measurement process to keep the numbers accurate and up to date.

Figure 3-3. Understanding the economic ordering quantity (EOQ).

high-demand season, rather than be swamped with work it would not have the production capacity to do when demand is high. For the manufacturer's employees, it also means steady work—instead of a seasonal rush and then a layoff when things slow down.

Decisions about seasonal inventory are driven by a desire to get the best economies of scale given the capacity and cost structure of each company in the supply chain. If it is expensive for a manufacturer to increase productive capacity, then its capacity can be considered as fixed. Once the annual demand for the manufacturer's products is determined, the most efficient schedule can be calculated to put that fixed capacity to its best use.

Managing seasonal inventory requires that the demand forecasts be as accurate as possible. Large amounts of inventory can be built up this way, with the risk that they will become obsolete—or at the least, expensive to store—if they don't sell as well as anticipated. Managing seasonal inventory also calls for manufacturers to offer price incentives to persuade distributors to purchase it and put it in their own warehouses, well before demand for it occurs.

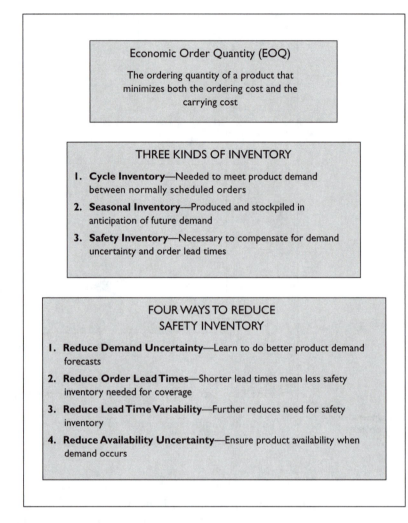

Figure 3-4. Key points to remember about inventory management.

Safety Inventory

Safety inventory is necessary to compensate for the uncertainty that exists in a supply chain. Retailers and distributors certainly don't want to run out of product if the demand is hot or their replenishment order is delayed, so they keep "safety stock" on hand. As a rule, the higher the level of uncertainty, the higher the level of safety stock required.

For any given item, its "safety inventory" can be defined as the amount of the item that is on hand at the time the next replenishment EOQ order arrives. Technically, this means that a store's safety stock is inventory that does not turn over. Inventory that is carried in this way—the backroom merchandise—becomes a fixed asset, in effect. It is always "around," and it must be stored and se-cured, which automatically adds to the store's overall cost of carrying inventory.

Retailers need to find a balance between their desire to carry a wide range of products and offer high availability on all of them, and their conflicting de-sire to keep these inventory costs as low as possible. That balance is reflected, quite literally, in the amount of safety stock that the company carries.

CHAPTER SUMMARY

The business operations that drive the supply chain can be grouped into five major categories: plan, source, make, deliver, and return. The functions that make up these categories are the day-to-day operations that determine how well the supply chain works, so companies must continually coordinate their plans and communicate their expectations in order to make improvements in these areas.

Planning refers to all the operations needed to organize the operations in the other four categories. Creating solid plans requires a combination of mathe-matics, competitive knowledge, and the ability to spot trends. It is also critical to know the strengths, weaknesses, and capacities of the other supply chain members—how flexible they are, how quickly they can work, and how much inventory they are willing to carry.

Planning begins with demand forecasting, and there are several reliable ways of looking at the past to determine possible future demands for products. Iron-ically, the more highly targeted and specific a forecast is, the less accurate it may be because the sample size is small. Aggregate plans are combinations of several types of forecasts, combined to get a clearer overall picture of a market or a business strategy.

A company's pricing policies for the goods they sell depend on how flexible the company is in terms of being able to hire or lay off people as needed, to pro-duce and store a lot or a little of an item, also as needed. Highly flexible com-panies can offer special sales promotions to create more demand in peak seasons; companies that cannot be especially flexible should try to create de-mand in low periods to maintain steady production (and a steady stream of revenue) year-round.

The chapter ended with an explanation of the three basic types of inventory, as well as what drives a company to carry each type of inventory and what factors must be considered in managing that type of inventory.

Increasingly, it is these planning operations—demand forecasting, product pricing policies, and inventory management—that determine the potential efficiency of the supply chain.

DISCUSSION QUESTIONS

1. This chapter asserts that, "The more producers of a product and the shorter the lead times, the more predictable the supply." But wouldn't supply be easier to predict if only a few companies produced the product instead of many? What do you think?
2. What makes data "historical"? With market conditions changing all the time, how far back should a retailer be able to look in order to make accurate forecasts about the future?
3. If you were a retailer in the process of selecting major suppliers, which type of aggregate planning would you expect to see from a large manufacturing company?
4. What types of planning would you assume each of the three paper products companies profiled in this chapter undertake? Briefly explain your answers.
5. Pick a store you admire that is not a "superstore" but might be a national or regional chain. How much safety inventory do you think they keep on hand, on-site? If something you want is not "in stock," how quickly can they get it? If they don't have it, where is it stored—that is, who maintains the costs associated with their safety inventory?

ENDNOTE

1. Willard N. Ander and Neil Z. Stern, *Winning at Retail* (New York: John Wiley & Sons, 2004).

THE
INCREDIBLE
JOURNEY

CONTINUES

AUGUST 25—SWEETENING THE DEAL

SPI Polyols, Inc., a manufacturer of ingredients for the confectionery, pharmaceutical, and oral-care industries, buys corn syrup from one of several corn-wet millers that purchases corn from farmers in the Midwest. SPI converts the corn syrup into sorbitol solution, which sweetens and adds bulk to the Cool Mint Listerine. The syrup is shipped to SPI's New Castle, Delaware facility for processing and then delivered on a tank wagon to Lititz. The whole process, from the time the corn is harvested to when it's converted to sorbitol, takes about a month.

How does WL determine the right quantity of raw materials to buy from its suppliers?

The sales and marketing group in Morris Plains forecasts demand with the help of Manugistics Inc.'s Demand Planning system. Used with other products in the Manugistic's Supply Chain Planning suite, the system analyzes manufacturing, distribution, and sales data against expected demand and business climate information to help WL decide how much product to make and distribute and how much of each raw ingredient is needed. For example, it can anticipate the impact of a seasonal promotion or of a production line being down. The sales and marketing group also meets monthly with folks in finance, procurement, and operations to project demand over the next several months. The procurement group enters the expected demand for mouthwash into a Marcom Corp. Prism Capacity Planning system, which schedules the production of Listerine in the amounts needed and generates electronic purchase orders for WL's suppliers.

4

SUPPLY CHAIN OPERATIONS: SOURCING MATERIALS AND MAKING PRODUCTS

I n this chapter, we examine the parts of retail supply chains that only senior managers and buyers are privy to—how the "production end" of a supply chain works to create the products eventually sold at retail. All too often, retail employees view this portion of the supply chain like preschoolers may view the supermarket meat counter when shopping with a parent—that is, they assume the meat comes "from the store," not from cows, pigs, or chickens, let alone the farms where these critters are raised to end up on a dinner table.

After reading this chapter, you will have a better understanding of what it takes to fill those store shelves. The topics include several cooperative functions between supply chain members:

- Procurement and consumption management
- Selecting and negotiating with suppliers
- Setting credit terms
- Collaborative product design
- Determining plant capacity and scheduling production

Many companies and supply chains in which they participate serve customers who are growing more sophisticated every year and demanding higher levels of service. Continuous improvements to the operations described in this chapter are needed to deliver the efficiency and responsiveness that evolving supply chains require.

PROCUREMENT

Purchasing the raw materials for making new products is serious business. In 2002, the 100 largest U.S. manufacturers spent 48 cents of every dollar in sales to buy materials—up from 43 cents in 1996.[1]

Traditionally, the aim of a good purchasing manager was to "beat up" potential suppliers on price—that is, threaten or induce enough guilt to get them to drop their prices—and then simply buy products from whomever turned out to be the lowest-cost supplier. Today, successful companies take a different approach that can best be described as embarking on partnerships. They rely on suppliers to improve quality, reduce costs, and assist with product design and development—and they learn to trust their suppliers. So other, related activities have become just as important as purchasing.

Because of this, the purchasing activity is now seen as part of a broader function called **procurement**. The procurement function can be broken into five main activities or categories:

1. Purchasing
2. Consumption management
3. Vendor selection

4. Contract negotiation
5. Contract management

Purchasing

Purchasing comprises the routine activities related to issuing purchase orders for needed products, and there are generally two types of products that a company buys:

- Direct materials are the supplies needed to produce whatever products the company sells to its customers. They may be known as raw materials or, in some companies, strategic materials.
- Indirect or **MRO** (maintenance, repair, and operations) products are things that a company consumes as part of its own daily operations.

The mechanics of purchasing both types of products are largely the same. Purchasing decisions are made, purchase orders are issued, vendors are contacted, and orders are placed. There is a lot of data communicated in this process between the buyer and the supplier—items and quantities ordered, prices, delivery dates, delivery addresses, billing addresses, and payment terms. Much of this activity is very predictable and follows well-defined routines, but the greatest challenge of the purchasing activity is to see to it that this data communication happens in a timely manner and without error.

The hottest trend in the business world today is **e-procurement**, the ability to handle purchasing functions online using software applications that are Internet-based. Vendors put their product catalogs, order forms, and other data on a Web site where others can access the site and place orders. In business-to-business applications, the transactions are secure, available only to selected buyers and suppliers, and can be tracked.

Consumption Management

Effective procurement begins with an understanding of how much of what categories of products are being bought across the entire company, as well as by each operating unit. Even in companies where different departments exercise a lot of autonomy, the procurement staff must keep track of who is buying what, and at what prices. This is necessary for several reasons, including theft prevention, waste management, and the ability to combine multiple, smaller purchases of the same goods to get better deals on them. Most major purchases made by a company are based on the terms of a sales contract, and companies discourage so-called **maverick spending**, or purchases made off-contract.

Expected levels of consumption for each product at the various locations of a company should be set and then compared against actual consumption on a regular basis. When consumption is significantly above or below expectations,

E-PROCUREMENT IS PAYING OFF

147 companies, most of them in North America, participated in a 2004 benchmark survey about e-procurement by Aberdeen Group, a market research firm in Boston, Massachusetts. Respondents said their e-procurement capabilities have allowed them to:

- Reduce off-contract "maverick spending" by 64 percent.

- Cut costs by 7.3 percent for spending that was brought back onto contract.

- Accelerate the cycle of requisition-to-order by 66 percent.

- Slash costs in requisition-to-order cycles by 58 percent.

The report also found that in 2001, companies did e-procurement business with an average of about 30 suppliers; by 2004, that number had increased to 250. The companies that have been successful with e-procurement have used some common tactics:

- They have the support of their senior management, which has made it easier to gain wide acceptance of the systems among users.

- They have made the use of e-procurement part of their strategic initiatives.

- They take time and effort to clearly define the costs, processes, and performance metrics. They measure things like adoption and usage rates, requisitions issued each money, and requests for off-catalog or off-contract items.

Like any relatively new technology, there are some downsides to e-procurement. So far, they seem to be as follows:

- Getting suppliers on the system can be challenging, especially if they are small and/or not technologically sophisticated.

- Most systems are being underutilized. Companies are using them to order goods, but not to make payments or reconcile invoices.

- The software developers have consolidated and/or gone out of business.

- Most companies still choose to spend their limited dollars updating other types of computer software with which they are more familiar.

Source: Adapted from Beth Stackpole, "E-procurement Systems Finally Paying Dividends," *Managing Automation* magazine (on-line), January 26, 2005. © Thomas Publishing Company, LLC, New York and reprinted with permission of Managing Automation.

it signals a possible problem that must be investigated. Consumption above expectations might be the result of pilfering, poor manufacturing practices, or outright wasting of materials, or it reflects inaccurate expectations that need to be reset. Consumption below expectations may point to an opportunity that should be exploited, but it also may simply reflect inaccurate planning or forecasting to begin with.

Vendor Selection

The first decision a manufacturing company makes about where to get any part or raw ingredient is "Do we need to find a supplier, or can we make (or do, or grow) this ourselves?" If an item is absolutely critical to the design of a product, or if the company wants complete control over the quality and production of a highly technical component, the result may be keeping it in-house. This is also true for specific supply chain functions (like customer service or deliveries of finished goods)—some companies outsource them; others do it themselves. When a company looks for outside vendors, it has three basic choices:

- **Multiple sourcing** means there is more than one supplier of the item or service, and the company chooses to use several. Multiple sourcing is important if the company absolutely never wants to run out of the product— multiple suppliers ensure there is always inventory on hand. Many companies refer to the suppliers that make the cut as their "preferred vendors." In theory, the competition among suppliers should result in a better deal for the company, in terms of price, payment terms, service, product quality, and so on, as each supplier works to impress the procurement team and gain a larger share of the business. In practice, though, multiple-sourcing relationships can be somewhat adversarial.
- **Single sourcing** means there are several sources of the item or service, but the company chooses to use only one. These "exclusive" arrangements typically involve long-term contracts and true partnerships. They put a lot of responsibility on the supplier to meet the demands of the client company, but the mutual loyalty allows both companies to lower their costs a bit.
- **Sole sourcing** is just what its name indicates—an item that is so specialized, it is available from only one company. It may be a complex or highly technical product, or one that is trademarked or patented to prevent competition. Companies also enter into partnerships with a sole source to develop a specific product, only for them.

The downsides of both sole and single sourcing are, of course, the problems that may arise from shortages caused by any number of factors—strikes, shipping delays, natural (or financial) disasters, or poorly planned production that results in too few items being produced. And then what? A company needs to ask questions like this before making contractually binding, single-source agreements.

In addition to the price of a vendor's product, the vendor's other capabilities must be considered. How important are they? The values of attributes like product quality, service levels, just-in-time delivery, and technical support can only be estimated in terms of what they mean to the company that is interested in doing business with them—its business plan, its operating model, the sizes and frequency of its potential orders, and its willingness to fine-tune a relationship with a new vendor.

As a general rule, a company seeks to narrow the number of suppliers it does business with. This way it can leverage its purchasing power with a few suppliers and get better prices in return for purchasing higher volumes of product.

Contract Negotiation

As particular business needs arise, contracts must be negotiated with individual vendors on the preferred-vendor list. This is where the specifics—items, prices, deadlines, and service levels—are worked out. The simplest contract negotiations are for the purchase of indirect products where suppliers are selected on the basis of lowest price. The most complex negotiations are for contracts to purchase direct materials that must meet exacting quality requirements, and where high service levels and technical support are needed.

Increasingly, though, even negotiations for the purchase of indirect items such as office supplies and janitorial products are becoming more complicated, because companies have learned to pay attention to these items in pursuit of their overall business plan. They want to use every opportunity to gain greater efficiencies in purchasing and inventory management.

Suppliers of both direct and indirect products need a common set of capabilities. Nowadays, maximizing purchasing efficiencies requires that suppliers have Electronic Data Interchange (EDI) capability—the systems and technical know-how to receive orders, send delivery notifications and invoices, receive payments, and so on—by computer. Better inventory management requires that inventory levels be reduced, which often means suppliers need to make smaller, more frequent deliveries and orders must be filled accurately and completely.

Anything that the "customer" company considers necessary is open to negotiation as part of the contract terms with the supplier. The negotiations often involve trade-offs between the unit price of a product and all the other value-added services that are desired. These other services might be paid for by a higher margin in the unit price, by separate payments, or by some combination of the two. Performance targets must be specified, and penalties and other fees must also be defined in the contract if performance targets are not met.

Contract Management

Once contracts are in place, vendor performance against these contracts must be measured and managed. Supplier performance is important, and suppliers should be willing to, and even enthusiastic about, participating in this process. A particular supplier may be the only source of a whole category of products that a company needs, and if it is not meeting its contractual obligations, the activities that depend on those products will suffer.

Therefore, a company must have the ability to track the performance of its suppliers and hold them accountable to meet the service levels they agreed to in their contract. Just as with consumption management, people in the company need to routinely collect data about suppliers' performance, both bad and good. Any supplier that consistently falls below requirements should be made aware of the shortcomings and asked to correct them, with a deadline stated in the request.

In many retail situations, the suppliers can be given responsibility for tracking their own performance, and should then be proactive about keeping their performance up to contracted levels. One example of this is the concept of vendor-managed inventory (VMI), which allows a vendor to monitor the inventory levels of its product within a customer's business. The vendor is responsible for watching usage rates and calculating economic order quantities (EOQs). The vendor proactively ships products to the customer locations that need them, and invoices the customer for those shipments under terms defined in the contract.

CREDIT AND COLLECTIONS

Procurement is the sourcing process a company uses to get the goods and services it needs. Credit and collections is the sourcing process that a company uses to get its money. The credit operation screens potential customers to make sure the company only does business with customers who will be able to pay their bills. The collections operation is what actually brings in the money that the company has earned.

Approving a sale is like making a loan for the sale amount, for a length of time defined by the payment terms. The goal of good credit management is to fulfill customer demand for products while also minimizing the amount of money tied up in receivables. This is analogous to the way good inventory management strives to meet customer demand and minimize the amount of money tied up in inventory.

The supply chains that a company participates in are often selected on the basis of credit decisions. Much of the trust and cooperation that is possible between companies who do business together is based upon good credit ratings and timely payments of invoices. Credit decisions affect who a company will sell to and also the terms of the sale. The credit and collections function can be broken into three main categories of activity:

1. Setting a credit policy
2. Implementing credit and collections practices
3. Managing credit risks

Setting Credit Policy

Credit policy is decided on by senior managers in a company—the controller, chief financial officer, treasurer, and chief executive officer. The first step in this process is to review the performance of the company's receivables. Every company has defined a set of measurements that is used to analyze receivables, such as:

- Days of sales outstanding (DSO)
- Percent of receivables that are past their customer payment terms
- The company's bad-debt write-off amount as a percentage of sales

Most of the number-crunching involves looking for trends and/or problems. Once management has an understanding of the company's receivables situation and the related trends, they can take the next step: to set or change risk acceptance criteria to respond to the receivables situation. These criteria should change over time, as economic and market conditions evolve, to define the kinds of credit risks that the company will take with different kinds of customers, and the payment terms that will be offered.

Implementing Credit and Collections Practices

These activities involve putting in place and operating the procedures to carry out and enforce the credit policies of the company. The first major activity in this category is to work with the company salespeople to approve sales to specific customers. As noted earlier, making a sale is like making a loan for the amount of the sale. Customers often buy from a company that extends them larger lines of credit and longer payment terms than its competitors. Credit analysis is necessary to ensure that this loan is only made to customers who will pay it off promptly, and according to the terms of the sale.

After a sale is made, people in the credit department work with customers to provide various kinds of service. They process product returns and issue credit memos for returned products. They resolve disputes and clear up questions by providing copies of contracts, purchase orders, and invoices.

The third major activity is collections, a process that begins with the ongoing maintenance of each customer's accounts payable status. Customers that have past-due accounts are contacted and payments are politely requested. Sometimes, new payment terms and schedules are negotiated.

The collections activity also includes the receiving and processing of customer payments, which can come in a variety of different forms. Some customers will pay by electronic funds transfer (EFT); others will use bank drafts, revolving lines of credit, or credit cards. If customers are in other countries, there are still other ways that payment can be made, such as international letters of credit from foreign banks.

Managing Credit Risk

The credit function works to help the company take intelligent risks that support its business plan. What may be a bad credit decision from one perspective may be a good business decision from another perspective. If a company wants to gain market share in a certain area, it may make credit decisions that help accomplish this. Credit department employees can work with other lenders to find innovative ways to lower the risk of selling to new kinds of customers. (Why do you think so many major retailers offer a "sponsored" Visa or Master-Card, sometimes in lieu of their own credit cards?)

Among members of a supply chain, offering and accepting credit is a business necessity. The inherent financial risk of offering credit can be managed by creating credit programs that are tailored to the needs of customers in certain market segments. Some credit grantors specialize in working with high-tech firms, start-up companies, construction contractors, or customers in foreign countries, devising payment terms that are attractive to customers in these market segments. Credit risks can be lowered by the use of credit insurance, liens on customer assets, and government loan guarantees for exports.

For important customers and particularly with large individual sales, people in the credit area work with others in the company to structure special deals just for a single customer. This increases the value that the company can provide to such a customer and can be a significant part of securing important new business.

PRODUCT DESIGN

We've found the suppliers, negotiated the contracts, and determined the credit-worthiness of the supply chain members. Now let's shift our focus to the next phase of the manufacturing process.

The design of a product—which determines the components needed to make or build it—is based on the technology available and the specific product performance requirements. Until recently, relatively little thought was given to how the design of a product and the selection of its components affect the supply chain; and yet these costs can account for 50 percent or more of the product's final cost. Smart company managers have learned to scrutinize them.

From a supply chain perspective, the goal of product design is fewer parts, fairly simple designs, and modular construction from generic subassemblies, so that the parts can be obtained from a small group of preferred suppliers. The fewer the parts, the less that can go wrong with the finished product. Inventory can be kept (in the form of the generic subassemblies) at appropriate locations in the supply chain. There will be no need to hold large inventories of finished goods, because customer demand can be met quickly. Some of the parts are already prepared and stored—they simply have to be fully assembled as customer orders arrive. This technique, called **variability pooling** or **postponement**, was pioneered by high-tech manufacturers like Hewlett-Packard because it allows them to keep large inventories of parts without the risk of holding finished inventory that might quickly become obsolete. The method requires the companies in the supply chain to collaborate on the design process, in order to shorten the time to market for the products that are assembled for sale.

The more flexible, responsive, and cost-efficient the supply chain, the more likely the product will succeed in its market. To illustrate this point, consider the following fictitious situation:

Fantastic Company designs a fantastic new home entertainment system with wide-screen TV, surround sound, the whole works! It performs to demanding specifications and delivers impressive results. But the electronics that power the entertainment center are built with components from 12 different suppliers.

Demand takes off and the company ramps up production, but soon finds that managing quality control and delivery schedules for 12 suppliers is a challenge. More procurement managers and staff are hired. Assembly of the components is complex, and delays in the delivery of components from any of the suppliers can slow down production rates. So buffer stocks of finished goods are kept to compensate for this.

Several new suppliers are required to provide the specified product components. One of them has quality control problems and has to be replaced. Another supplier decides after several months to cease production of the component it supplies to Fantastic Company. They bring out a new component with similar features, but it is not an exact replacement.

Fantastic Company has to suspend production of the home entertainment system while a team of engineers redesigns the part of the system that used the discontinued component so that it can use the new component. During this time, buffer stocks run out in some locations, and sales are lost when customers go elsewhere.

A competitor called Nimble Company is intrigued by the success of Fantastic Company and introduces a competing product. Its design is simpler, with fewer parts and components from only four suppliers. The cost of procurement is much lower, since only 4 suppliers must be coordinated instead of 12. There are no production delays due to lack of component parts, and product assembly is easier.

While Fantastic Company, who pioneered the market, struggles with a cumbersome supply chain, Nimble Company provides the market with a lower-cost and more reliable supply of the product. Nimble Company—with a more responsive and less costly supply chain—takes market share away from Fantastic Company.

What can be learned here? Product design defines the shape of the supply chain, and this has a great impact on the cost and availability of the product. If product design, procurement, and manufacturing people can work together in the initial design phase, there is tremendous opportunity to create products that will be successful and profitable.

The problem is that there is a natural tendency for design, procurement, and manufacturing people to have different agendas unless their actions are coordinated. Design people are concerned with meeting the customer requirements. Procurement people are interested in getting the best prices from a group of prescreened preferred suppliers. Folks in manufacturing are looking for simple fabrication and assembly methods and long production runs. You can't blame any of them for looking out for their own interests. They're all doing exactly what they are supposed to do.

Cross-functional product design teams with representatives from these three groups have the opportunity to blend the best insights from each group. At the same time they are designing the product, they should envision any accessories or services that can be bundled with it to add value, and discuss the relevant issues: Can the current suppliers provide the necessary components? How many new suppliers are needed? What opportunities are there to simplify the design and reduce the number of suppliers? What happens if a supplier stops producing a certain component? How can the assembly of the product be made easier?

At the same time they are reviewing product designs, a cross-functional team can evaluate existing preferred suppliers and manufacturing facilities. What components can existing suppliers provide? What are their service levels and technical support capabilities? How large a workforce and what kinds of skills are needed to make the product? How much capacity is needed, and which facilities should be used?

A product design that does a good job of coordinating the three perspectives—design, procurement, and manufacturing—will result in a product that can be supported by an efficient supply chain. This will give the product a faster time to market as well as a competitive cost.

SUPPLY CHAIN SKILLS—BUILDING STRONG PARTNERSHIPS

Two professors—Jeffrey K. Liker of the University of Michigan in Ann Arbor and Thomas Choi of Arizona State University's W.P. Carey School of Business in Tempe—have studied the American and Japanese automotive industry for more than 20 years. Between 1999 and 2002, their goal was to learn how Toyota and Honda managed to attain such solid relationships with their suppliers when American automakers seem unable to accomplish this. Their findings, published in the *Harvard Business Review* in December 2004, make for fascinating reading. Here are just a few of their conclusions and suggestions:

When we compared the elements of Toyota's partnering model with those of Honda's, we found that although the two companies used different tools, they had created strikingly similar scaffoldings. Experts usually emphasize the use of devices like target pricing, but we believe Toyota and Honda have built great supplier relationships by following six distinct steps:

First, they understand how their suppliers work.

- Learn about suppliers' businesses.
- Go see how suppliers work.
- Respect suppliers' capabilities.
- Commit to co-prosperity.

Second, they turn supplier rivalry into opportunity.

- Source each component from two or three vendors.
- Create compatible production philosophies and systems.
- Set up joint ventures with existing suppliers to transfer knowledge and maintain control.

Third, they supervise their vendors.

- Send monthly report cards to core suppliers.
- Provide immediate and constant feedback.
- Get senior managers involved in solving problems.

Fourth, they develop their suppliers' technical capabilities.

- Build suppliers' problem-solving skills.
- Develop a common lexicon.
- Hone core suppliers' innovation capabilities.

Fifth, they share information intensively but selectively.

- Set specific times, places, and agendas for meetings.
- Use rigid formats and have a structure for sharing information.
- Insist on accurate data collection.

Sixth, they conduct joint improvement activities.

- Exchange best practices with suppliers.
- Initiate kaizen projects at suppliers' facilities.
- Set up supplier study groups.

Toyota and Honda have succeeded not because they use one or two of these elements, but because they use all six together as a system.

Most vendors believe that Toyota and Honda are their best—and toughest—customers. The two companies set high standards and expect their partners to meet them. However, the carmakers help suppliers fulfill their expectations. Clearly, Toyota and Honda want to maximize profits, but not at the expense of their suppliers.

Source: Thomas Y. Choi and Jeffrey K. Liker, "Building Deep Supplier Relationships," *Harvard Business Review*, Boston, Massachusetts, December 2004.

PRODUCTION SCHEDULING

Production scheduling assigns the available capacity to the work that needs to be done. First, of course, the capacity has to be determined. American companies are known for a preoccupation with numbers—that is, they think in terms of how many garments they can manufacture in a day on a production line, or how many customers they can serve in an hour at a fast-food counter. This type of measurement may be accurate, but it is only a small part of a far more complex concept that involves what have been nicknamed "The Four M's of Manufacturing"—machinery, manpower, materials, and money.[2] (For the most part, these apply to businesses other than manufacturers as well.) Seen in these terms, capacity says as much about what a company *cannot* do as what it can do. It is a measurement of the limits, or "Here's the maximum of what we are capable of."

So the goal is to use available capacity in the most efficient and profitable manner. The production scheduling operation is a process of finding the right balance between several competing objectives:

- **High utilization rates.** This often means long production runs and centralized manufacturing and distribution centers. The idea is to generate (and benefit from) economies of scale.
- **Low inventory levels.** This usually means short production runs and just-in-time delivery of raw materials. The idea is to minimize the assets and cash tied up in inventory.
- **High levels of customer service.** This often requires high levels of inventory or many short production runs. The aim is to provide the

customer with quick delivery of products and not to run out of stock in any product.

There are also three different types of scheduling:

- **Aggregate scheduling.** The long-term view of what a plant is going to be doing and making over a time period of a year or more, this schedule is created as part of the aggregate planning process.
- **Master scheduling.** This is what is typically thought of as "the schedule," the assignments of work to meet specific deadlines over one month, three months, six months, and so forth.
- **Dispatching.** This involves day-to-day tweaks in the schedule at the point of production to match up supply and demand.[3]

Most of today's manufacturing for the retail market is known as **mass customization**—yes, it does sound like a contradiction in terms—or **build-to-order**. Manufacturers can no longer afford to produce thousands of items, warehouse them, and hope that they will remain in style or in demand over a long time period, so they wait until orders are placed and make enough to fill those orders—perhaps with a little overage just to be safe, but not much. Plants are designed for flexibility so they can adapt to retailers' needs, which depend in turn on consumers' changing tastes.

When a single product is to be made in a dedicated facility, scheduling means organizing the operations as efficiently as possible and running the facility at the level required to meet demand for the product. When several different products are to be made in a single facility or on a single assembly line, this becomes instantly more complex. Each product will need to be produced for some period of time, and then more time will be needed to switch over to production of the next product.

The first step in scheduling a multiproduct production facility is to determine the economic lot size (ELS) for the production runs of each product. This is a calculation much like the EOQ calculation used in the inventory control process. The calculation of economic lot size involves balancing the production setup costs for a product with the cost of carrying that product in inventory. If setups are done frequently and production runs are done in small batches, the result will be low levels of inventory but the production costs will be higher due to increased setup activity. If production costs are minimized by doing long production runs, then inventory levels will be higher and product inventory carrying costs will be higher.

Once production quantities have been determined, the second step is to set the right sequence of production runs for each product. The basic rule is that if inventory for a certain product is low relative to its expected demand, then production of this product should be scheduled ahead of other products that have higher levels of inventory relative to their expected demand. A common technique is to schedule production runs based on the concept of a product's

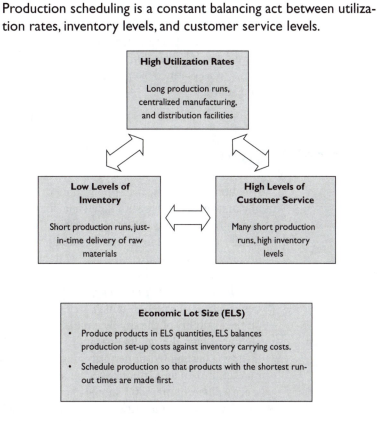

Production scheduling is a constant balancing act between utiliza-tion rates, inventory levels, and customer service levels.

High Utilization Rates

Long production runs, centralized manufacturing, and distribution facilities

Low Levels of Inventory

Short production runs, just-in-time delivery of raw materials

High Levels of Customer Service

Many short production runs, high inventory levels

Economic Lot Size (ELS)

- Produce products in ELS quantities, ELS balances production set-up costs against inventory carrying costs.

- Schedule production so that products with the shortest run-out times are made first.

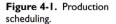

Figure 4-1. Production scheduling.

run-out time. The run-out time is the number of days or weeks it would take to deplete the product inventory on hand given its expected demand. The run-out time calculation for a product is expressed as:

$$R = P \div D$$

where:

R = run-out time
P = number of units of product on hand
D = product demand (in units) for a day or week

The master scheduling process is a repetitive process that begins by calcu-lating all the run-out times for all of the products—their "R values." The first production run is then scheduled for the product with the lowest R value. The production scheduler assumes that the economic lot size for that product has been produced, and then recalculates all product R values. Again, the one with the lowest R value is selected, and its production is next on the schedule . . . and so forth. This scheduling process can be repeated as often as necessary to create a production schedule going as far into the future as needed.

After scheduling is done, the resulting inventory should be continuously checked against actual demand. Is inventory building up too fast? Should the demand number be changed in the calculation of run-out time? Reality rarely happens as planned, so production schedules are constantly being monitored and adjusted.

FACILITY MANAGEMENT

Location is one of the five supply chain drivers discussed in Chapter 1. It is usually quite expensive to shut down a facility or to build a new one, so companies live with the consequences of decisions they make about where to locate their facilities. Ongoing facility management takes location as a given and focuses on how best to use the capacity available. This involves making decisions in three areas:

The role each facility will play involves decisions that determine what activities will be performed in which facilities. These decisions have a huge impact on the flexibility of the supply chain. They largely define the ways that the supply chain can change its operations to meet changing market demand. If a facility is designated to perform only a single function or serve only a single market, it usually cannot easily be shifted to perform a different function or serve a different market if supply chain needs change.

How capacity is allocated in each facility is dictated by the role that the facility plays. Capacity allocation decisions determine how much labor and what types of equipment are part of the facility. It is easier to change capacity allocation decisions than it is to change locations—but still it is not cost-effective to make frequent changes in allocation. So, once decided, capacity allocation strongly influences supply chain performance and profitability. As with so many other supply chain considerations, it is a balancing act for manufacturers with multiple locations. Allocating too little capacity to a facility creates inability to meet demand and loss of sales. Saddling a facility with having to carry too much capacity results in low utilization rates and higher supply chain costs.

The allocation of suppliers and markets to each facility is influenced by the first two decisions. Depending on the role that a facility plays and the capacity allocated to it, the facility will require certain kinds of suppliers, and the products and volumes that it can handle mean that it can support certain types of markets. Decisions about the suppliers and markets a facility will serve affect transportation costs, both for getting supplies to the facility and transporting the

SUPPLY CHAIN SKILLS—WORKING WITH GLOBAL PARTNERS

Faced with shrinking margins and intense competitive pressure, officials at Hunt Corp. (in Philadelphia, Pennsylvania) knew something had to change. So, in 2002, the privately owned maker of office and graphics supplies decided to outsource manufacturing of its high-volume products to contractors in China and to use other lower-cost offshore suppliers.

The good news: Hunt, a supplier of office supplies used worldwide by businesses, consumers, educational institutions, and professional photographers and framers, got the lower manufacturing costs it was after. The bad news: The switch to offshore sourcing and manufacturing put new strains on the company's supply chain. Lead times—the time it took for Hunt orders to arrive at its shipping dock—grew from days or weeks when manufacturing was done in-house to an average of 95 days, for example. Inventory costs and overnight shipping charges also rose.

As a result, says Bill Bracey, Hunt's materials manager, the company has been forced to "undergo a model change." This means Hunt had to switch from being a company that could respond quickly to customer requests for supplies such as paper clips, pens, and X-ACTO brand items by depending on its manufacturing prowess to one that has to rely on its partners.

"Our role in the market is changing from [one centered on] our strength as a manufacturer to [one in which] our strength [is] our distribution and supply chain prowess," adds Bracey.

To get the most out of this changing business model, Hunt began designing and implementing new supply chain processes intended to improve communication and collaboration with suppliers. So far it's working. Hunt has been able to reduce its lead times from 95 to 65 days, cut airfreight charges and reduce inventory levels on imported items by 10 percent.

Hunt isn't the only company that, having outsourced some manufacturing offshore, will be forced to revamp its supply chain. With many companies turning to overseas suppliers to lower unit prices, Bracey says, manufacturers that focus only on lowering manufacturing costs will eventually lag behind.

"Companies can afford to acquire a lot of inventory while the cost of money is low, but that won't always be the case," he says. "As companies begin to pay the same amount for goods, that cost benefit also goes away. The only way to create sustainable advantage is through a well-run supply chain."

As Hunt has learned, there are challenges to doing business overseas. Outsourcing production can significantly reduce the cost of goods. But it also typically means working around long lead times and accepting large lot sizes. Long lead times lead to less accurate forecasts and make it difficult to manage unplanned spikes in demand, while large lot sizes can mean carrying excess inventory. It soon became clear to Hunt officials that a 95-day lead-time was "unacceptably long," according to Tony Stafford, Hunt's purchasing manager. The long lead time was not only driving up inventories, it

Continued

was also making it difficult for Hunt to service customers quickly and to efficiently manage returns, a significant issue as retailers increasingly move to a consignment model where they return any unsold inventory to Hunt.

In order to cut lead times, Hunt officials realized they had to work much more efficiently with suppliers. "We had to schedule capacity and get [suppliers] to operate as an extension of our organization," says Bracey.

Hunt set its sights on developing supply chain processes that would provide "a more continuous flow of product so when price is less of a factor, we still have competitive advantage in being able to service our customers without carrying excess inventory," Bracey explains. That means continuing to improve communication and collaboration with its suppliers to shorten the order-to-delivery cycle.

To help suppliers plan capacity, Hunt first modified its forecasting process. Rather than giving suppliers just one level of commitment—a discrete order—Hunt established what Bracey calls "firm, slushy, and free time zones in our forecasts." In the firm zone, the company is committed to buying the finished goods in the amount specified. In the slushy zone, the company is committed to purchasing the raw materials and standard components so the supplier can plan its purchases and production. In the free zone, Hunt has no commitment to buy.

"The free zone is typically three to five months out and is strictly for reference information to help them manage capacity," says Bracey.

At the same time, Hunt worked to give suppliers better visibility into its forecasts and inventory levels. Hunt uses the full suite of QAD Inc. (based in Carpinteria, California) MFG/PRO enterprise resource planning (ERP) applications to run its internal business, so it was natural for the company to use QAD's hosted Supply Visualization application. The application, hosted by QAD on its MFGx.net site, is designed to provide suppliers with visibility into a manufacturer's forecasts and inventory levels. Using a hosted version of the application, says Bracey, helped Hunt get a quick return on its investment.

Supply Visualization helped Hunt communicate effectively with suppliers and, ultimately, drive lead times down to 60 days. The Supply Visualization application is integrated with the company's MFG/PRO software applications. Inventory and forecast data from MFG/PRO are published to partners over standard Internet browsers, which means suppliers can access inventory and forecast information as soon as it's updated rather than waiting for a fax or e-mail from Hunt when the data is rolled up monthly or quarterly. So now, even if suppliers can only meet part of Hunt's demand, they can more quickly and easily communicate that, and Hunt can make contingency plans.

Hunt updates its forecasts monthly and can update a forecast on individual products or by group as needed. To develop its forecasts, Hunt uses the Demand Solutions forecast applications from Demand Management Inc. (based in St. Louis, Missouri) and imports/exports that data into its

MFG/PRO ERP system. In the new process, Hunt meets with suppliers once a month (or more frequently if necessary) via conference call to discuss the forecast and plans and how they compare to Hunt's actual needs.

"In the past, we didn't have a tool that would force us to get together and work out the details," says Bracey. Sharing forecast data and improving communication with suppliers also means all members always have the same data from which to work. Stafford says Hunt's partners look at the Web site for changes or new information "daily, if not more often." One advantage of the browser-based system is that supplier browsers can be set up in Chinese so the information appears in their native language. That way Hunt doesn't have to depend on just a few people who are fluent in English.

Shorter lead times have delivered several benefits to Hunt. For one thing, they've made for more accurate forecasts because, with 35 fewer days between order and delivery, there is less data to try to analyze and less time for surprises to hit the process. "The further out you look, the less accurate your forecasts are and the more you have to hedge on that forecast. Having a 50 percent longer lead time more than doubles the work with far less certain results," says Stafford.

Shorter lead times also let Hunt cut off product pipelines more efficiently when it sees the end of an item's selling period. That's important as product life cycles shorten. Shorter lead times also reduce the need for safety inventory. That's important to Hunt because "if that inventory goes obsolete, it's a real struggle to get rid of it without contaminating your market," says Stafford.

Hunt also found that by moving its manufacturing processes to suppliers, it moved its work-in-progress (WIP) and raw materials inventory to those suppliers. It's then the suppliers that have to improve the way they manage that inventory. To do that, suppliers need more accurate and timely demand and forecast data from Hunt.

Besides cutting lead times and inventory levels, Hunt has been able to reduce its airfreight costs for items it couldn't wait 35 travel days to receive. Under the previous process, when it needed product in less than 95 days, the company would have to airfreight product from China to its distribution center. The new process let the company cut $200,000 in airfreight charges in the first half of 2003.

But Bracey says Hunt isn't stopping there. The next step in improving its supply chain is for the company to use the Supply Visualization tool to move away from creating a discrete purchase order for each item and toward generating a firm release of the forecast so suppliers can simply package product and send it to Hunt efficiently.

"Letting our schedule float could shorten lead times to 45 days," says Bracey. "With a floating schedule, when our customer orders change, we don't have purchase orders clouding the picture of what we really need. At the latest possible moment, our suppliers could take the latest requirements, load the container, and let us know what's coming."

Continued

To make the supply chain even more efficient, Bracey is also beginning to discuss with Hunt's product-engineering group the standardization of parts. That would mean, rather than carrying a finished goods inventory, Hunt's suppliers could carry a parts/materials inventory. That could allow the company to carry less total inventory and possibly reduce the company's risk and need for safety stock.

Already, though, Hunt has increased its level of service and reduced cost by improving its supply chain. "If you don't have the right processes in place when the cost of money rises and the price of goods levels out for everyone, you won't be competitive," Bracey says. "We assume that day will come, and we're developing processes that will put us ahead of the curve."

Source: This article originally appeared as "Syncing the Supply Chain" by David Kodama, *Managing Automation* magazine, March 2004. © Thomas Publishing Company, LLC, New York and reprinted with permission of *Managing Automation*.

finished goods to the customers. In turn, these decisions also affect the overall supply chain's ability to meet market demands.

More companies are facing the reality that at least some of their supply chain partners—notably suppliers, manufacturers, and customer service functions—are located in foreign countries. The information in this book about procurement, inventory levels, credit terms, manufacturing schedules, and so on applies just as surely to them as to any United States-based company. The article about Hunt Corp. (*see sidebar*) has been included in this chapter as an introduction to the shifts in supply chain operation that become necessary when its member companies span the globe.

CHAPTER SUMMARY

Manufacturing is a critical part of the supply chain. Without it, there would be little for retailers to sell.

This chapter began with a look at the *sourcing* or *procurement* process—terms for how companies purchase everything they need to do business, from paper clips to fleet vehicles to the products that they resell to their own customers. They make decisions about whether to use multiple or single sources of each product, and the chapter included information about what to look for in a reliable supplier. Once trusted suppliers are in place, routine procurement is often done nowadays on secure Internet Web sites, which saves time and money.

Credit and collections are considered part of sourcing, since they are the ways companies "procure" the money for what they have sold to customers.

Sourcing of supplies and the actual manufacturing of products go hand in hand—and the design or development process should include input from cross-functional teams to ensure real-world considerations: Can we get the parts we need to do this? Is the design more complex (and therefore, more expensive) than it needs to be? Can we design services to bundle with the product for added value?

When the design is complete and the raw materials have been procured, the manufacturing process cannot begin without scheduling the production of the item. Plant capacity must be determined and a certain portion of that capacity must be allocated to each product the plant produces. The processes of scheduling and facility management sound simple and logical, but they are a constant juggling act in order to balance the workloads of people and machinery with desired inventory levels and customers' orders.

The chapter ended with a look at how one U.S.-based supplier, Hunt Corp., has modified its business operations in order to work with supply chain partners in China.

DISCUSSION QUESTIONS

1. Find out more about e-procurement and compare the benefits and sales claims of three different e-procurement software systems based on their Web sites. As a purchasing manager for a multiplant manufacturer, which would you choose and why?
2. As a retailer, what would *you* expect from a good supplier, in terms of added services and perks?
3. As a retail executive, you are at the mercy of the credit policies of your suppliers. How generous do you think they should be if your store is having financial difficulties and has fallen behind on some payments?
4. Why should designers of a product have to be constrained by the limitations of a supply chain? Explain the theory here. If you were designing the product, how would you try to work around ineffective or unresponsive supply chain partners?
5. How are the "Four M's of Manufacturing" impacted by mass customization? How are they impacted by the use of foreign suppliers?

ENDNOTES

1. Thomas Y. Choi and Jeffrey K. Liker, "Building Deep Supplier Relationships," *Harvard Business Review*, December 2004.
2. Eliza G.C. Collins and Mary Anne Devanna, *The Portable MBA* (New York: John Wiley & Sons, 1990).
3. *Ibid.*

THE
INCREDIBLE
JOURNEY

CONTINUES

AUGUST 31—WARNER-LAMBERT MIXES IT UP

By now the ethanol, eucalyptol, and sorbitol solutions have all arrived at WL's plant in Lititz, where employees test them—along with the menthol, citric acid, and other ingredients that make up Listerine—for quality assurance before authorizing storage in tanks. To mix the ingredients, flow meters turn on valves at each tank and measure out the right proportion, according to the Cool Mint formula developed by WL R&D (Research & Development) in 1990. (The original amber mouthwash was developed in 1879.) This blending process is constant; as ingredients are added to the several-thousand-gallon vat, the properly blended liquid is continuously transferred to a separate holding tank. Next the Listerine flows through a pipe to fillers along the packaging line. The fillers dispense the product into bottles delivered continuously from a nearby plastics company for just-in-time manufacturing.

The bottles are capped, labeled, and fitted with tamper-resistant safety bands, then placed in corrugated shipping boxes (known as "shippers") that each hold a dozen 500-milliliter bottles. During this process, machines automatically check for skewed labels, missing safety bands, and other problems. The entire production cycle, from the delivery via pipe of the Listerine liquid to the point where the bottles are boxed and ready to go, takes a matter of minutes. The line can produce about 300 bottles per minute—a far cry from the 80 to 100 bottles that the line produced per minute prior to 1994. In that year, WL switched from glass bottles to sturdy plastic bottles, modernized its production line with high-speed equipment, and went from mixing batches of mouthwash one tank at a time to the continuous mixing process.

Each shipper travels on a conveyor belt to the palletizer, which organizes and shrink-wraps shippers into 100-case pallets. Stickers with identifying bar codes are affixed to the pallets. Drivers forklift the pallets to the distribution center located in the same Lititz facility and store them in a designated spot where they will sit for two to four weeks.

What sets Warner-Lambert's supply chain apart?

WL's supply chain excellence stems from its innovative Collaborative Planning, Forecasting and Replenishment (CPFR) program, says Hau L. Lee, CIO-100 judge and Stanford University professor. WL launched CPFR a few years ago when it started sharing strategic plans, performance data, and market insight with Wal-Mart Stores Inc. over the Internet. The company realized that it could benefit from Wal-Mart's market knowledge, just as Wal-Mart could benefit from its product knowledge.

During the CPFR pilot, WL increased its products' shelf-fill rate—the extent to which a store's shelves are fully stocked—from 87 percent to 98 percent, earning the company about $8 million in additional sales, or the equivalent of a new product launch, says Jay Nearnberg, director of global demand management for WL. Every major supply chain vendor now offers CPFR software. Eventually, WL hopes to use the Internet to expand the CPFR program to all its suppliers and retail partners, says Nearnberg.

5

SUPPLY CHAIN OPERATIONS: DELIVERIES AND RETURNS

I t's probably not surprising that the service sector is the fastest-growing segment of the economy. Most of us are crunched for time, and we're willing to pay to have people take care of some of the necessary chores that people of past generations did for themselves—lawn care, housekeeping, cooking, child care, pet sitting, errand running, and more.

Corporations in supply chains are no exception. They are busy, and they realize they can't specialize in everything—or do it all perfectly—so they entrust some of the details to other companies. In manufacturing and retail businesses, this means tasks like transportation and warehousing of goods. Unlike consumers—who spend more money to have others do work for them—corporations outsource work in order to get it done more cheaply than they could do it themselves. This also impacts their supply chain, however, by adding complexity and increasing the risk of failure.

The final step in the SCOR model introduced in Chapter 3 is "Returns." This means the process of accepting returned or defective goods and sending them "back through" the system to the appropriate supply chain partners, sometimes known as **reverse logistics**.

So this chapter focuses on service-oriented functions and the decisions required to make them effective within a supply chain, including the following topics:

- Managing the ordering process
- Scheduling deliveries
- The impact of returned goods on the supply chain
- Outsourcing supply chain functions

According to research by Procter & Gamble, Number 28 on the Fortune 500 list and the nation's largest manufacturer of household products, blame can be placed equally on three supply chain partners for product out-of-stocks (OOS) at stores: One-third are manufacturers that shipped the wrong order; one-third are problems in a distribution center; and one-third are problems in the store, where the product may have arrived but is not on the correct shelf.[1] This chapter examines the supply chain functions that, when not working well, are the causes of some of these retail headaches.

ORDER MANAGEMENT

Order management is the process of passing order information from customers back through the supply chain from retailers to distributors to service providers and producers. This process also includes passing information about order delivery dates, product substitutions, and back orders forward through the supply chain to customers.

You may ask, "How difficult would it be to get an order right?" After all, there's not that much to it—or is there? Stephen David, former chief information and business-to-business officer at Procter & Gamble, estimated that at least $250 million of product in the United States is refused by retailers and returned to manufacturers—largely because of "bad data in the system."[2] The wrong product arrived, or it arrived at the wrong store. Somebody, somewhere, botched the order, and the mistake may have been as simple as a single transposed digit on an order form.

For decades, the order process relied on the use of the telephone and a flurry of paper documents: purchase orders, sales orders, change orders, pick tickets, packing lists, and invoices. (A **pick ticket** is the document that signals to a warehouse which items in which amounts must be "picked out" from inventory to be transported to a store as part of an order.)

A company generates a purchase order and calls a supplier to fill the order. The supplier who gets the call either fills the order from its own inventory or sources the required products from other suppliers. If the supplier fills the order from its inventory, it turns the customer purchase order into a pick ticket, a packing list, and an invoice. If products are sourced from other suppliers, the original customer purchase order is turned into a purchase order from the first supplier to the next supplier. That supplier in turn will either fill the order from its inventory or source products from other suppliers. The purchase order it receives is again turned into documents such as pick tickets, packing lists, and invoices. This process is repeated through the length of the supply chain.

In the last 20 years or so, supply chains have become noticeably more complex than in previous generations. Companies now deal with multiple tiers of suppliers, outsourced service providers, and distribution channel partners. This complexity has evolved in response to changes in the way products are sold, increased customer service expectations, and the need to respond quickly to new market demands.

The traditional order management process has longer lead and lag times built into it due to the slow movement of data back and forth in the supply chain. This slow movement of data works well enough in some simple supply chains. However, in complex supply chains, faster and more accurate movement of data is necessary to achieve the responsiveness and efficiency that is needed. Modern order management focuses on techniques to enable faster and more accurate movement of order-related data.

In addition, the order management process must be capable of handling exceptions and providing people with ways to quickly spot problems and give them the information they need to take corrective action. This means the processing of routine orders should be automated and orders that require special handling because of issues such as insufficient inventory, missed delivery dates, or customer change requests need to be brought to the attention of people who can handle these issues. Because of these requirements, order management has overlapped or merged with a function called *customer relationship management* (CRM), that is often thought of as a marketing and sales function.

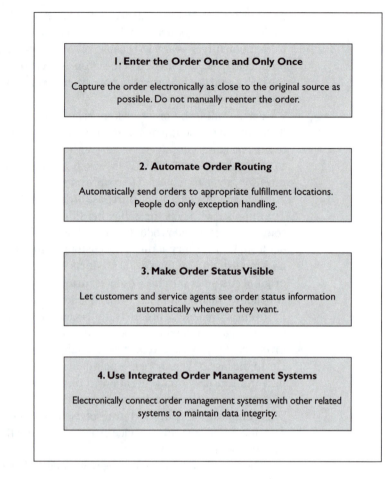

I. Enter the Order Once and Only Once

Capture the order electronically as close to the original source as possible. Do not manually reenter the order.

2. Automate Order Routing

Automatically send orders to appropriate fulfillment locations. People do only exception handling.

3. Make Order Status Visible

Let customers and service agents see order status information automatically whenever they want.

4. Use Integrated Order Management Systems

Electronically connect order management systems with other related systems to maintain data integrity.

Figure 5-1. Four rules for efficient order management.

No matter how sophisticated the system, order management requires a handful of basic principles for any company:

- **Enter the order data once and only once.** Capture the data electronically as close to its original source as possible, and do not manually reenter the data as it moves through the supply chain. It is usually best if the customers themselves enter their orders into an order entry system. This system should then transfer the relevant order data to other systems and supply chain participants as needed for creation of purchase orders, pick tickets, invoices, and so on.
- **Automate the order handling.** Manual intervention should be minimized for the routing and filling of routine orders. Computer systems should send needed data to the appropriate locations to fulfill routine orders. Exception handling should identify orders with problems that require people to get involved to fix them.

- **Make order status visible to customers and service agents.** Let customers track their orders through all the stages from entry of the order to delivery of the products. Customers should be able to see order status on demand, without having to enlist the assistance of other people. When an order runs into problems, bring the order to the attention of service agents who can resolve them.

- **Integrate order management systems with other related systems to maintain data integrity.** Order entry systems need product descriptive data and product prices to guide customers in making their choices. The systems that maintain this product data should be able to communicate with order management systems, because the order data is needed by other systems to do things like update inventory status, calculate delivery schedules, and generate invoices. (Interestingly, the Procter & Gamble research cited earlier in this chapter found that from 25 to 70 percent of some key trading partners' master data was inaccurate.) Order data should automatically flow into these systems in an accurate and timely manner.

DELIVERY SCHEDULING

Retailers in the United States spent more than $118 billion on logistics in 2003—that is, getting products from the proverbial Point A to Point B.[3] And yet, despite all the technology that's been deployed to avoid it, estimates of OOS incidents in retail range from 8 to 10 percent of the items in a store. The customer looks for a product that's just not there, which often signals a delivery problem.[4]

The delivery scheduling operation is, of course, strongly affected by the decisions made about the modes of transportation that will be used—so the way deliveries are scheduled must fit the constraints of the transportation decisions. For most modes of transportation, there are two types of delivery methods: direct deliveries and so-called **milk run deliveries**.

Direct Deliveries

Direct deliveries are made from one originating location to one receiving location. With this method of delivery, the routing is simply a matter of selecting the shortest path between the two locations. Scheduling this type of delivery involves decisions about the quantity to deliver and the frequency of deliveries to each location. The advantages of this delivery method are found in the simplicity of operations and delivery coordination. Since products are being moved directly from the location where they are made or stored in inventory to a location where the products will be used, it eliminates any intermediate operations that combine different, smaller shipments into a single, combined larger shipment.

Direct deliveries are efficient if the receiving location generates economic order quantities (EOQs) that are the same size as the shipment quantities needed to make best use of the transportation mode being used. For instance, if a receiving location gets deliveries by truck and its EOQ is the same size as a truck load (TL), then the direct delivery method makes sense. If the EOQ does not equal TL quantities, then this delivery method becomes less efficient. Receiving expenses incurred at the receiving location are high, because this location must handle separate deliveries from the different suppliers of all the products it needs.

Milk Run Deliveries

This term refers to the old-fashioned milkman, the dairy delivery driver who stopped at every house to deliver fresh milk in glass bottles. (Probably not in our lifetimes, however.) Today, milk runs are

- Deliveries routed to bring products from a single originating location to multiple receiving locations, or . . .
- Deliveries that bring products from multiple originating locations to a single receiving location.

Scheduling milk run deliveries is a much more complex task than scheduling direct deliveries. Decisions must be made about delivery quantities of different products, about the frequency of deliveries, and most importantly, about the routing and sequencing of pickups and deliveries.

The advantages of this method of delivery are that more efficient use can be made of whatever mode of transportation is used, and that the cost of receiving deliveries is lower because the receiving locations get fewer and larger deliveries. If the EOQs of different products needed by a receiving location are less-than-truckload (LTL) amounts, milk run deliveries allow orders for different products to be combined until the resulting quantity equals a truckload amount. If there are many receiving locations that each require smaller amounts of products, they can all be served by a single truck that starts its delivery route with a full truckload of products.

There are two main techniques for routing milk run deliveries. Each routing technique has its strengths and weaknesses, and each technique is more or less effective depending on the situation in which it is used and the accuracy of the available data. Both of these techniques are supported by software packages that, of course, are only as reliable as the accuracy of the data being input.

The **savings matrix** technique is the simpler of the two techniques. It can be used to assign customers to vehicles, and to design routes where there are delivery time windows at receiving locations and other constraints. The technique can be modified to take many different constraints into account. It provides a reasonably good routing solution that can be put to practical use. Its weakness lies in the fact that it is often possible to find more cost-effective solutions using the generalized assignment technique. This technique is best used when there are many different constraints that need to be satisfied by the delivery schedule.

The **generalized assignment** technique is more sophisticated and usually gives a better solution than the savings matrix technique—that is, when there are no constraints on the delivery schedule other than the carrying capacity of the delivery vehicle. The disadvantage of this technique is that it has a harder time generating good delivery schedules as more and more constraints are included. This technique is best used when the delivery constraints are simple: total vehicle capacity or total travel time.

SUPPLY CHAIN SKILLS—RELOCATING TO INCREASE EFFICIENCY

Getting up at the crack of dawn each day to make fresh donuts, pastries, and coffee is a way of life for the thousands of tireless Dunkin' Donuts franchisees around the country. But that is not all they have to do. These small-business owners are responsible for purchasing, transportation, logistics, and warehouse operations at the five distribution centers that provide all baking materials, supplies, and much of the equipment for the Dunkin' Donuts stores throughout the United States.

The United Kingdom-based parent company, Allied Domecq, is essentially a marketing company. The franchisees are responsible for just about everything else. In each region of the country, the franchisees own separate distribution companies that are managed by professional logistics managers. For example, the Dunkin' Donuts Mid-Atlantic Distribution Center (MADC) is a franchisee-owned, stand-alone nonprofit corporation that services 1,400 restaurants in eight states and the District of Columbia.

These hard-working small-business owners know the value of efficiency and productivity, as well as the importance of the right location. By 2004, the current DC location in the southernmost part of New Jersey had become a problem. MADC had been operating out of the cramped 125,000-square-foot DC for six years, and the growing base of Dunkin' Donuts restaurants in the mid-Atlantic region cried out for expansion. But because of the marginal nature of the current location and resistance to expansion from the local municipality in Swedesboro, New Jersey, the company looked elsewhere.

"We liked New Jersey, but we needed to be farther north, closer to New York City where the business climate is better for distribution operations," says Warren Engard, director of distribution operations for MADC. "Just as important, we needed a facility better suited to our operations with more space, more doors, and cross-docking capabilities."

Continued

Before deciding on a new location, the company looked at its changing restaurant network. While the New York City area remained the largest single market, more store expansion was planned in Pennsylvania, Baltimore, and Washington. "We had to stay in the middle of these growing markets, so we only moved about 36 miles north to Burlington, New Jersey," says Engard. "If we went much farther north, the costs would have become much higher, and we would have had a problem retaining employees."

The company selected a site in a small industrial park in Burlington, New Jersey, that it shares with a trucking terminal. The site is immediately adjacent to two major highways (the New Jersey Turnpike and Interstate 295) with easy access to several bridges going into Pennsylvania.

The new Burlington facility is a vast improvement over the previous DC in Swedesboro, according to Engard. The old DC was a mere 125,000 square feet with 22 doors. It was so cramped that the pickers and receivers overlapped in time and space. Receiving was done over 16 to 18 hours, while picking was done for 21 hours a day.

"My pickers hated the receivers, the receivers hated the pickers," says Engard. "Everyone was in the aisles at the same time."

The Burlington DC is 300,000 square feet, with 134 doors and a cross-dock layout. The facility is not just larger, but dedicated pick and put-away aisles eliminate congestion. While this arrangement takes up more space, it allows simultaneous picking and receiving 24 hours a day, if need be. Because of the more efficient layout and operations, there is rarely a need for extended hours of picking and receiving.

"We are more capable in eight hours than we were in 21 hours at the old facility," says Engard, adding that all picking is usually done in one 8-hour shift. Receiving from outside carriers starts at 4 A.M. for frozen goods and dry goods receiving begins at 7 A.M. After 1 P.M., only goods carried on the private fleet are received. Since the vast majority of inbound goods come in as backhauls on the private fleet, the volume of afternoon receiving is significant. Workers and aisle space must be available, and the new facility provides all the space needed.

The DC building has the ability to be expanded another 100,000 square feet, but Engard doesn't anticipate the need for such an expansion anytime soon, even with the likely addition of other Allied Domecq restaurants. (MADC is being asked to service Baskin-Robbins and the Togo sandwich chains, since many of the franchisees have combination shops.)

"Because of our much greater throughput and ability to handle all orders in one shift, we will have all the space we need for years to come," says Engard.

Another way that MADC tightly manages its DC operations is with intense use of its private fleet that it leases from Ryder Transportation. The fleet consists of 62 road trucks and 110 trailers in its road division. In the route division that serves stores directly, there are 95 tractors, 108 trailers, and 12 straight trucks. Most of the 300 employees at the DC are drivers and driver helpers. In fact, only

40 employees are receivers and pickers, so the trucking operation is a critical part of the MADC operations.

"The straight truck fleet is increasing because of growing restrictions on tractor-trailers in New York and other cities," says MADC's transportation manager, Tim Kennedy.

MADC is Ryder's largest U.S. customer in one facility, and the truck lessor even operates a three-bay full maintenance and repair facility on MADC's property. Ryder also helps MADC manage its longer-haul trucking routes, half of which used to require one or even two overnight layovers. With the help of Ryder, MADC now uses drivers domiciled in the more remote areas. Its home-based drivers shuttle trailers to Ryder facilities in the outlying regions where they are staged for pickup by the domiciled drivers who will do local delivery and backhaul pickups. These local drivers, in turn, drop off backhaul trailers loaded with supplier materials at the Ryder facilities for the home-based drivers to bring back to Burlington.

"Right now, 85 percent of our supplier material is backhaul freight for our trailers," says Kennedy. "The goal is to build this up to 100 percent."

The MADC private fleet also has 48-state for-hire trucking authority that it uses to fill excess back-haul capacity with freight from selected partners, including GE appliances, Pepsi, and Juicy Juice. "Our own logistics staff carefully coordinates the movement of these trailers and the available capacity with our Appian Logistics transportation management system, so the trucks are available when we need them," says Kennedy.

MADC also coordinates front and backhaul moves with its sister DCs operated by other Dunkin' Donuts regions. For example, MADC ships bagels up to the New England DC and brings back dairy products and shortening.

"Although we are separate companies, the DCs work closely together," says Engard, adding that three of the DCs are using the same warehouse management and enterprise resource planning (ERP) systems from Integrated Distribution Systems (IDC). "The Midwest and Southeast center will be running off our system, and one of them will have a redundant site to deal with any computer crashes or down time."

Source: Thomas A. Foster, "Dunkin' Donuts' Short Relocation Brings Big Change," *Global Logistics & Supply Chain Strategies,* © Keller International Publishing, New York, March 2005.

Delivery Sources

Deliveries can be made to customers from two sources. *Single product locations* are facilities such as factories or warehouses, where a single product or a narrow range of related items are available for shipment. These facilities are

MODERN CONSIDERATIONS FOR DC LOCATIONS

There are huge cost differences in operating distribution warehouses in the 50 top markets around the United States. In a study by The Boyd Company, a site location consulting firm in Princeton, New Jersey, operating a DC in any of the top ten highest-cost U.S. locations would cost a company more than $14 million annually to operate; while the lowest-cost (ranked #41–50) are less than $10 million annually. Some of the major concerns of companies shopping for a new DC site are:

- **Land values.** It costs 50 percent more to lease a DC site in New York City (#1) than it does in Mobile, Alabama (#50), for example.

- **Labor cost and quality.** Paying unskilled warehouse workers an hourly wage is no longer sufficient, and the issue also is not necessarily union-versus-nonunion labor. Many DC facilities are automated and highly computerized, which requires more training and skills that command higher wages.

- **Traffic.** Congestion of nearby ports and highways can significantly delay shipments.

- **Security.** Some companies avoid large population centers simply because of the increased risk of supply disruptions from terrorism threats—not against the company, but in the overall area, shutting down airports, freeways, and the like.

Source: "The Best DC Locations in the U.S.," *Global Logistics & Supply Chain Strategies,* © Keller International Publishing, New York, March 2005.

appropriate when there is a predictable and high level of demand for the products they offer, and where shipments will be made only to customer locations that can receive the products in large, bulk amounts. They offer great economies of scale when used effectively.

Distribution centers are facilities where bulk shipments of products arrive from single product locations. When suppliers are located a long distance away from customers, the use of a DC provides for economies of scale in long-distance transportation to bring large amounts of products to a location close to the final customers.

The distribution center is usually a huge, regional warehouse that stores inventory for future shipment, or it may be used primarily for cross-docking.

Cross-docking is a technique pioneered by Wal-Mart, in which truckload shipments of single products arrive at a DC and are unloaded. As these trucks are being unloaded, their bulk shipments are being broken down into smaller lots, combined with small lots of other products, and loaded immediately onto other trucks. These trucks then deliver the products to their final locations.

Distribution centers that use cross-docking provide several benefits. The

SUPPLY CHAIN STRATEGIES—DELIVERY SCHEDULING AS A CORE COMPETENCY

Eastern Bag & Paper Company (www.easternbag.com) is a distributor of paper products, industrial packaging, food service, and janitorial and sanitary maintenance products. It operates out of two distribution centers, one in Connecticut and one in Massachusetts, and has a fleet of 44 straight trucks and 4 tractor trailers. More than 4 million cases are shipped, and 200,000 deliveries are made each year.

Eastern Bag & Paper has developed a very efficient delivery scheduling operation, and it continues to innovate and refine the processes that support this operation. Meredith Reuben is the company's CEO.

The process begins at 4:00 P.M. every business day. All orders received up to that time are downloaded from the enterprise resource planning computer system to an automatic delivery routing system called RoadShow. Don Burton, director of operations, explains, "We have built in customized parameters—things like tight delivery windows for certain customers, and route preferences, so the system creates routes and schedules that are very efficient."

It takes the RoadShow system and router about two hours to calculate the routes and schedules for all the trucks. At 6:00 P.M. the routes and schedules are uploaded back into the ERP system and the picking labels are printed in each of the distribution centers. By 6:30 P.M., each location has a complete set of pick labels, which correspond to the way each warehouse is laid out. The pick labels tell the employee (called a "picker") where to go for each item and what quantity to retrieve. Along with the labels that are attached to each case, a pick list is generated to accommodate a quality control audit.

"We have a QA process that randomly selects orders to audit," Don says. "We use the pick list and check it against the set of labels on each case. We probably audit about 10 percent of orders. We track errors such as 'right label on wrong case' or 'short, case not on truck,' or 'short, can't find case.' " Errors are traced back to the individual pickers.

Loading the trucks takes 8 to 10 hours, starting by 7:00 P.M. and finishing by 4:00 A.M. The trucks are on the road soon after. All trucks are equipped with a global positioning satellite (GPS) system. It can pinpoint the location of each truck during the day, creating an activity log that records the truck's movements.

"RoadShow creates a delivery schedule, and the GPS allows us to compare the actual route versus the planned route," Don says. "The drivers are always saying RoadShow doesn't accurately reflect conditions. So we can now create very realistic schedules using corrective information that we get from GPS. Drivers are able to achieve 95 percent on-time performance against the schedules that we create."

Continued

The company continuously measures its performance and makes adjustments as needed to maintain high levels of customer service. There is a zero-defect program in place that follows a customer order from entry to delivery, with the goal of "perfect orders"—right place, right time, with the invoice completely correct. When Eastern started tracking orders, it was at only 53 percent "perfect." Now, the percentage is approaching 90!

The system results in individual responsibility for errors and corrections.

"Our performance measurements allow us to track individual productivity and error rates by worker," says Don. "We have developed standard productivity rates for different jobs that we can use to compare against the actual productivity of each person. Our error reports allow us to identify the person and the department where an error originated. This is the information we need to continuously make adjustments to our operations so as to keep up high service levels and also keep our costs as low as possible."

It is the continuous measuring and adjusting that makes the activities of delivery scheduling and order fulfillment into a core competency. No matter what the size of the distributorship of the types of products it distributes, these two activities must be core competencies if the company is to be successful.

"Bottom line, distribution is a 2 percent to 4 percent net business—there is no room for errors and low productivity," observes Eastern CEO Meredith Reuben. "Measuring people and processes to look for improvements is something that goes on all the time. Process reengineering and investments in new technology to decrease errors and increase productivity is something that we do every year."

first is that product flows faster in the supply chain, since very little inventory is held in storage. The second is less handling expense, because the goods don't have to be put away and then retrieved later from storage. The benefits of cross-docking can be realized when there are large, predictable product volumes, and when economies of scale impact both the inbound and outbound transportation. However, cross-docking is a demanding technique; it requires a considerable degree of coordination between inbound and outbound shipments.

One of the future trends for distribution centers is the idea of putting other functions into the DC location, like customer call centers, order processing, and accounting. With office space scarce and expensive in many cities, the cost per square foot of warehouse-style space is far more economical, so companies may choose to locate services that used to be at their headquarters at DC locations instead.

Another financial reality—with today's fuel prices, transporting and delivering goods is expensive and not getting any cheaper. Capabilities in this area are closely aligned with the actual needs of the market that the supply chain serves. For instance, highly responsive supply chains usually have high transport and delivery costs, because their customers expect quick delivery, and this means many small shipments of product. Less responsive supply chains can combine orders over a period of time and make fewer, larger shipments, which results in more economies of scale and lower transport costs.

THE REALITY OF RETURNS

Returned goods, packaging, parts, and waste materials flow through the supply chain in a stream or system commonly known as **reverse logistics**. To a certain extent, improving the accuracy of sales forecasting, order management, and delivery systems will minimize returns, but not entirely. How well retailers and their suppliers manage these items will either add to or detract from the overall efficiency of the supply chain, as well as each company's costs of doing business.

Too often, reverse logistics has been a rather informal process in retail, with no particular plan or budget. In fact, a survey of more than 300 logistics managers in various industries by the nonprofit Reverse Logistics Executive Council found that 40 percent considered the issue "relatively unimportant." That is not the case, however, for companies on the lookout for cost-saving methods.

While liberal returns policies are certainly convenient and have been used as marketing tools by retailers since the 1980s, customers have become so accustomed to this courtesy that the resulting "fallout" for supply chains has become a real challenge to manage. For example, Americans return

- 4 to 5 percent of consumer electronics items
- Up to 15 percent of mass merchandise items
- Up to 30 percent of books

For online sales, since customers can't "try before they buy," return rates can be well above 50 percent! These statistics really add up. Reverse logistics is estimated to consume $40 billion, or about 4 percent, of the overall logistics costs in the United States. It can also drain as much as one-third of an individual company's profits.[5]

The reality of returning these products is more complex than satisfying the end user or consumer with the resolution of a problem or complaint. Reversing the supply chain is not as tidy, you might say, as keeping it in forward motion. Items come in without packaging, as singles instead of cases or lots or pallets. Their "delivery" is certainly not scheduled! Unless the returned item is going to sit unnoticed in a store's backroom or warehouse forever, even something as

TYPES OF RETURNS AND REVERSE LOGISTICS CHALLENGES

	BUSINESS TO BUSINESS	*BUSINESS TO CUSTOMER*
Reasons for return	• Product defects • Damage • Warranty • Discontinued product • Return allowances • Stock adjustments (such as raw-material surplus)	• Product defects • Damage • Warranty and service • Recall • End of use • Did not like, no trouble found
Supply chain challenges	• Nonuniform product quality and packaging (sold in pallets, returned singly), which also affects transportation utilization and expense • Outdated and possibly obsolete returned items	• Unpredictable demand with little or no advance notice of the return quantity or quality • High number of transactions necessitating efficient disposition, evaluation, and customer credit processes
Opportunities	• Opportunities include refurbishing, repair, and remanufacturing to reduce the need to purchase new parts and incentives that would motivate customers to be more efficient in ordering • A customer-focused strategy requires streamlined, no-hassle policies and fast crediting to the customer's account • Detailed data can be gathered to perform root-cause analysis for product innovation	• Opportunities include refurbishing, repair, and remanufacturing the product while delivering customer service that will result in return business. • A customer-focused strategy would shift responsibility for handling returns from customer to supplier • Seamless integration of supply chain partner systems helps rapidly and accurately dispose of returned product

simple as an exchange or repair will require at least *some* further supply chain involvement. For example, the store inventory must be updated to reflect the status of the returned item. Then, someone must be responsible for deciding what to do with the item—return it to inventory? Return it to the distributor, importer, or manufacturer? Get it repaired? By whom? Where is it stored in the meantime? Who pays for the repair? Who pays for the return shipping? Who replaces a defective item in the retailer's inventory, or refunds the money originally paid for it? If a new order must be placed, what kind of priority does it receive and who notifies the customer when it arrives? Each of these seemingly routine decisions involves a policy and procedure that must be agreed on by the affected supply chain partners, or problems will surely arise.

One of the reasons it is critical to track returns and have procedures in place to handle them is that they can point to bigger-picture issues, such as product defects or safety concerns. In the case of some products that contain hazardous materials (batteries, electronics equipment, and so on), there are safe disposal requirements that must be adhered to and reported. A tracking system can also point to communication problems tied to customer expectations about the product—for instance, if many customers return an item saying it "doesn't work as well as I thought it would," this may require ads, marketing materials, or product instructions to be modified to prevent future buyers' disappointment.

Today's consumers take liberal returns policies for granted, and this adds some competitive pressure to the system. Customer service has become as important in the returns process as it was in the initial purchase of the item. People don't want to have to wait "too long," in line or on the phone—and if they do have to wait, they want to know approximately how long the wait will be, and perhaps even the reason for the delay. If they are asking for a replacement item, they want it and they want it now! A key component of the retailer's returns plan must be to have sufficient capacity (staff, policies, inventory, and so on) to make the transaction or complaint process as quick and hassle-free as possible—for the customer, that is.

Even other members of the supply chain that don't deal directly with consumers must plan for returns. They may be in the form of overstocks, end-of-season items, unsold or damaged goods, products that have been recalled, and mountains of packaging materials. An attempt should be made to recover at least some of the items' original value, if possible. They may be repaired or reconditioned, resold to discounters, used for spare parts, and so on. One consideration that is not directly related to customer satisfaction but important in terms of public perception is the recycling of packaging materials and reusable parts. The general expectation is that companies will be good corporate citizens, which means having an environmental strategy to minimize waste.

OUTSOURCING SUPPLY CHAIN OPERATIONS

In a survey of more than 300 retailers in the United States, 21 percent listed "outsourcing" as a major priority for 2005.[6] Outsourcing logistics functions (like deliveries) is sometimes known as **third-party logistics (3PL)**. When considering outsourcing service functions to other companies, any member of any supply chain must ask itself the following questions:

- Which of these operations can we handle ourselves?
- At which do we truly excel? (These are known, in "corporate-speak," as **core competencies**.)
- How many of these operations bring money into the company?
- How many of these operations consume money?

The relentless pressure on profit margins that free markets create is a driving force behind the growth of outsourcing. What may be considered as overhead for Company A may be a service that Company B can offer and make a profit doing so. Company B may be able to offer this service for a price lower than it costs Company A to do it in-house. Company A is going to consider outsourcing.

The traditional participants in supply chains are producers, logistics providers, distributors, and retailers. How many of the supply chain operations can be called core competencies of any of these organizations? There are some operations—like credit and collections, product design, and order management—that may not be core competencies of any of the traditional participants. This creates opportunities for new service providers to take on these operations and offer them to the other supply chain participants. Every one of the operations in this book needs to be performed for the supply chain as a whole, but they do not all need to be done by any single company. Indeed, they cannot all be done well by any single company.

Speed and efficiency are the reasons most companies decide to outsource their customer service functions. Third-party providers already have the people, processes, and infrastructure in place to handle the customer calls—and it doesn't really matter if there are 10, 100, or 1,000 calls a day, a system must be in place and operational in order to manage the call activity, answer questions, and satisfy customers. Smaller retailers find that hiring a third-party call center improves their image, by giving their customers the same service level they would receive from a larger business. Manufacturers also use third-party service providers, often when they first introduce a product and call volume is highest. Later, they may take over the customer service function themselves as the volume tapers off.[7]

The other force that drives outsourcing is the growing sophistication of the markets that supply chains serve. Gone are the days when Ford Motor Company could run a vertically integrated company that did everything from mine iron ore to produce steel, to design and build automobiles. That structure was only possible because the markets it served were content to buy mass quantities of standard products.

A third reason companies outsource is that they are small and/or growing. They have (or make) the product and people want to buy it, but they don't have the money to build their own infrastructure for added services like delivering it themselves, hosting a 24/7 customer call center, and so on. Instead, they hire outside specialists to handle these functions.

Mass customization is different than past generations' mass production. Markets today demand and pay for all sorts of innovations, customized features, and services. This creates complexity in the supply chain, and participants who specialize in certain areas bring the expertise and efficiencies that are required to manage this complexity.

CHAPTER SUMMARY

The ordering, delivery, and returns processes are core connections between members of a supply chain, and the first two are critical functions to prevent retail out-of-stocks. This makes accuracy and timeliness paramount in these systems. This chapter introduced four basic rules for ensuring correct orders.

Orders are fulfilled either directly from the manufacturer, or through an intermediary facility such as a warehouse or distribution center. The types of transportation used and the frequency of orders will determine the delivery schedule and ultimately impact the cost of getting the goods to market. Much of the logistics function is now organized with computer software, but it is only as good as the data being input.

Because consumers expect liberal return policies, customer service has become as important in the returns process as it is in the initial purchase of the item. Returns create a backflow of merchandise, packaging, and unsold items—not just for the retailers, but for everyone in the supply chain who has handled the goods at some point. These must be repaired, resold, recycled, and so on, in an attempt to recover as much of their original value as possible while minimizing waste.

Companies today are very likely to consider outsourcing ordering, delivery, and at least part of the returns process, but they should do so only if it is more economical to outsource and if it prompts their own people to focus on the company's core competencies.

DISCUSSION QUESTIONS

1. Why would a company's own product descriptive data be inaccurate? Whose job should it be to update it, and how often should this be done?
2. What kind of retailers would be best suited to direct deliveries from manufacturers? What kind of retailers would be better served by milk run deliveries?

3. Using the topics in the sidebar "Modern Considerations for DC Locations," pick a city and find out the pros and cons of locating a distribution center there. What is the economy like? Where are other, similar facilities located? Does the city, county, or state offer some economic incentives?
4. How would an Internet-based retailer handle transportation needs? Would its overhead be less than a brick-and-mortar store in terms of moving, storing, picking, and shipping?
5. If you were a retailer, are there any business functions that you would not even consider outsourcing to a third-party service provider? If not, why not?

ENDNOTES

1. Marc Millstein, "P&G Transforms Supply Side Dynamics," *Women's Wear Daily*, New York, February 15, 2005.
2. *Ibid.*
3. David Hannon, "Retailers Push the Logistics Learning Curve," *Purchasing* magazine, © Reed Business Information, Inc., New York, September 2, 2004.
4. Ram Reddy, "Tried and True," *Information Supply Chain*, a newsletter of Intelligent Enterprise, CMP Media, LLC, San Francisco, California, September 4, 2004.
5. Charles Harthan, Sean Monahan, and Patrick Van den Bossche, "Shifting Your Supply Chain Into Reverse," *Executive Insights*, © A.T. Kearney, an EDS Company, Chicago, Illinois, 2004. All rights reserved. Quoted with permission.
6. Study results, "Retail Horizons: Benchmarks for 2004," conducted by BearingPoint, Inc. (McLean, Virginia) for the National Retail Federation Foundation (Washington, DC), January 18, 2005.
7. "Outsourcing Your Supply Chain Management Function," © DecisionOne Corporation, Frazer, Pennsylvania, July 2001.

THE
INCREDIBLE
JOURNEY

CONTINUES

SEPTEMBER 14—ORDER OF THE DAY

WL receives an EDI order from CVS for 20 pallets of 500-milliliter bottles of Cool Mint Listerine to be delivered by September 16 to CVS's Woonsocket (Rhode Island) warehouse, which serves all New England CVS stores. The order is automatically screened to make sure the numbers requested are reasonable and the source for the order is legitimate before it is passed on to WL's SAP system, an enterprise resource planning tool from SAP AG. SAP prices the order and determines how much of it is already in stock and how much needs to be manufactured. Generally, the order is in stock, since the E3 Merchandise Transaction System would have predicted store demand.

That same day, SAP transfers the order to WL's Strategic Transportation Planner made by Manugistics. The Manugistics' system determines how best to consolidate order delivery and which shipping companies to use to minimize costs and meet the required delivery time specified by CVS. An action plan specifying those details is drawn up. WL then sends an electronic alert to the chosen shipping companies via EDI.

Meanwhile, the Manugistics action plan is automatically downloaded to SAP, which sends it back to WL's McHugh Software International Inc. warehouse system around 1 A.M. for use by the people on the WL warehouse floor. The McHugh system specifies how the warehouse employees should pick and ship the day's orders.

How does CVS determine prices?

The oral hygiene category manager at CVS headquarters in Woonsocket, Rhode Island, is responsible for deciding what products to stock and how to price them—as well as how to develop promotions with manufacturers to boost sales. To do this, she relies on Category Map, a decision support tool that's connected to the company's massive data warehouse. Category Map draws on data on the past performance of all products as well as market research fed into the system from research firms such as ACNielsen Corp. Using the tool, she can figure out how well Listerine sells compared with other mouthwash brands and how much money CVS makes on the product, given price and sales rates. Category Map also lets her adjust for special promotions. To set the standard sales price for Listerine, she uses a pricing tool with historical performance data, intelligence gathered on competitors' prices, and market data. The tool updates CVS's data warehouse with the official price and also downloads the pricing data to the individual CVS stores, where computers print out shelf tags as prices change. The category manager's recommendations automatically feed into another system, the Merchandise Transaction system made by E3 Corp. The E3 system takes Category Map data and combines it with point-of-sale (POS) data from the CVS stores as well as inventory information to calculate the exact quantities of Listerine CVS should purchase to meet forecasted store demand. On the same day that E3 figures out how much Listerine to order, it generates a purchase order and sends it via electronic data interchange (EDI) to WL; the information is also sent to CVS's warehouse management system made by EXE Technologies Inc., so that CVS warehouse employees and computer systems know when to expect the order. The E3 system has taken three days out of CVS's order cycle process, says Leo Hartnett, vice president of efficient consumer response.

6

TECHNOLOGY AND SUPPLY CHAIN COORDINATION

Some people insist that the "human touch" will always be necessary in retail—that most customers are more comfortable dealing with a person than a computer screen or an automated telephone line. Still, technology has its benefits, notably speed and consistency. A computer system may get a virus now and then, but it never plays favorites, talks on its cell phone while it's supposed to be working, or is intentionally rude to a customer.

Technology has meant good things for supply chains as well. The spread of high-speed data communications networks and computer technology has made it possible to manage a supply chain with a level of precision that was not feasible 20 years ago. The organizations that learn to use the latest techniques and technologies can create customer service throughout their supply chains—from their suppliers to the consumers—that give them a competitive advantage in their markets.

After reading this chapter, you will be able to

- Explain the bullwhip effect on retailers and supply chains.
- Explain the benefits of collaborative planning, forecasting, and replenishment (CPFR).
- Describe the types and uses of information systems in a supply chain.
- Assess the technology that supports and enables effective supply chain coordination.

The widespread availability and use of the Internet offers companies opportunities that did not exist before. These opportunities are made possible because it is now so easy and relatively inexpensive for companies to connect to the Internet. Once connected, companies can send data to and receive data from other companies with which they do business, regardless of the computers or software that each company uses to run its internal operations. Data sharing allows companies to work together to achieve tremendous supply chain efficiencies and significant increases in customer service and responsiveness. The term for this type of coordination is known as **supply chain integration**. It allows companies to react much more quickly to changes in market demand, and business competition based on supply chain efficiency is becoming a central fact in many markets.

To develop this capability, individual companies and entire supply chains need to first learn new behaviors and then enable these new behaviors with the use of appropriate technology. Before you learn about the technology, however, let's examine one of the reasons coordination of these efforts is so important.

THE "BULLWHIP EFFECT"

One of the most common dynamics in supply chains is a phenomena known as the **bullwhip effect**. Small changes in product demand by the consumer at the "front end" of the supply chain translate into wider and wider swings in demand as they are experienced by companies "further back" in the supply chain. As a result, companies at different stages in the supply chain come to have very different pictures of market demand, and there is a breakdown in supply chain coordination. Companies behave in ways that at first create product shortages and then lead to an excess supply of products. It's a ripple effect, except that for every member of the supply chain, the economic reality is more like the lash of a real bullwhip!

This dynamic plays out on a larger scale in certain industries in what is called a **boom-to-bust business cycle**. In particular, this affects industries that serve developing and growth markets—cell phone equipment, computer components, and the like—where demand can spike suddenly. The cycle begins with the "boom," when a hot new product sells out, creating shortages in the market. Distributors and manufacturers steadily increase their inventories and production rates in response to the demand. But at some point, either the demand changes or the supply of product exceeds the demand level. Distributors and manufacturers seem to be the last to realize this—they're going all-out, continuing to build the supply.

Finally, the glut of product is so large that everyone realizes there is too much. Manufacturers shut down plants and lay off workers. Distributors are stuck with inventories that decrease in value and can take years to work down. The cycle ends with a "bust."

This dynamic can be modeled in a simple supply chain that contains a retailer, a distributor, and a manufacturer. In the 1960s, a simulation game was developed by the Massachusetts Institute of Technology's Sloan School of Management that illustrates how the bullwhip effect develops. The "Beer Game" shows what happens in a hypothetical supply chain that supports a group of retail stores that sell beer, snacks, and other convenience items. The results of this simulation teach a lot about how to coordinate the actions of different companies in a supply chain—how the bullwhip gains its momentum, and how to avoid its dangerous boom-and-bust consequences.

The Beer Game starts with retailers experiencing a sudden but small increase in customer demand for a certain brand of beer, called "Lover's Beer." Orders are batched up by retailers and passed on to the distributors who deliver the beer. Initially, these orders exceed the inventory that distributors have on hand, so they ration out their supplies of Lover's Beer to the retailers and place even larger orders for the beer with the brewery that makes Lover's Beer. The brewery cannot instantly increase production of the beer, so it rations out the beer it can produce to the distributors and begins building additional production capacity.

At first, the scarcity of the beer prompts panic buying and hoarding behavior. Then as the brewery ramps up its production rate and begins shipping the product in large quantities, the orders that had been steadily increasing due to panic buying suddenly decline. The glut of product fills up the distributors' warehouses, fills all the retailers' unfilled back orders, and exceeds the actual consumer demand. The brewery is left with excess production capacity, the distributors are stuck with excess inventory, and the retailers either cancel their beer orders or run discount promotions to move the product. Everybody

Inventory levels in a supply chain over time illustrating the wild swings that develop as product demand distortion moves from customer to retailer to distributor to manufacturer. Swings in product demand appear more pronounced to companies further up the supply chain. This distortion makes effective supply chain management very difficult.

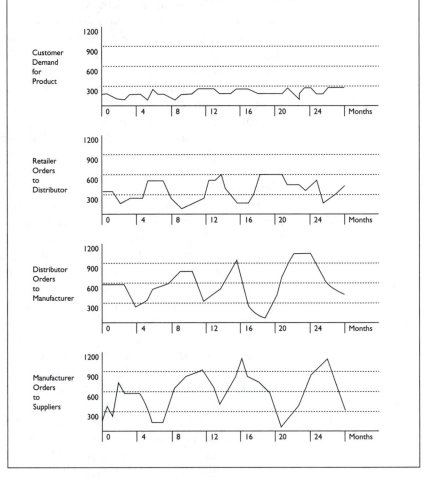

Figure 6-1. Product demand distortion swings: the bullwhip effect.

loses money. Figure 6-1 illustrates how each company sees the product demand and the distortion that causes the problems.

Anything that disrupts a steady and orderly supply of product can create a bullwhip effect: a retailer who stops ordering in an attempt to reduce inventory, for example, or delays in material or information that cause backlogs in some parts of the supply chain. A study by Georgia Technical University estimated supply chain problems cost companies between 9 and 20 percent of their overall value in a six-month period.[1] The costs of the bullwhip effect are felt by all members of the supply chain:

- Manufacturers add extra production capacity to satisfy an order stream that is much more volatile than actual demand, and/or production schedules are thrown off as the plant scrambles to supply the inflated demand numbers.
- Distributors carry extra inventory to cover the variability in order levels, which ties up additional funds.
- Transportation costs increase because excess transportation capacity has to be added to cover the periods of high demand.
- Labor costs also go up in order to respond to the high demand periods.
- Retailers experience problems with product availability and extended replenishment lead times, which results in poor customer service and out-of-stocks.
- During periods of high demand, there are times when the available capacity and inventory in the supply chain cannot cover the orders being placed. This results in product rationing, longer order replenishment cycles, and lost sales due to lack of inventory.

COORDINATING THE SUPPLY CHAIN

Research has identified five major factors that cause the bullwhip effect. These factors interact with each other in different combinations in different supply chains, but they are all the result of inadequate or incorrect information, and the net effect is that they generate the wild demand swings that make it almost impossible to run an efficient supply chain.

These factors must be understood and addressed in order to successfully coordinate the actions of any supply chain, and we'll examine them one at a time. They are as follows:

1. Demand forecasting
2. Order batching
3. Product rationing
4. Product pricing
5. Performance incentives

Demand Forecasting

Demand forecasting based on orders received instead of end user demand data will inherently become more and more inaccurate as it moves "up" through the supply chain. Remember, the companies that are removed from direct contact with the end user can lose touch with actual market demand if they view their role as simply filling the orders placed with them by their immediate customers.

If a supply chain participant sees only the data from the business either directly "above" or "below" them in the chain, they see only part of the picture. If the fluctuations in the orders that come to them are being caused by the bullwhip effect, then when they use this order data to do their own demand forecasting, they end up adding further distortion to the demand picture, passing it along in the form of orders they place with their suppliers.

SUPPLY CHAIN SKILLS—TAMING THE BULLWHIP EFFECT

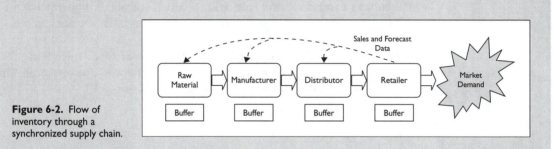

Figure 6-2. Flow of inventory through a synchronized supply chain.

A very effective response to the bullwhip effect is to manage the entire supply chain as a single entity and synchronize it to the timing of actual market demand. This requires the supply chain participants closest to the end use customers (generally, the retailers) to share their sales numbers and forecasts with the other companies in the supply chain. Each company can then manage its actions based on the most accurate data about market demand.

Buffers in the supply chain are determined by the degree of uncertainty about future market demand and the service levels required by the market. The lower the levels of uncertainty about demand, the smaller the buffers can be and still maintain high service levels. Companies can manage their buffers by using either productive capacity or inventory, whichever is most cost-effective for them.

Synchronized supply chains avoid the volatile waves of demand generated by the bullwhip effect, and increased predictability makes the productivity of each company easier to manage. The whole supply chain becomes more efficient and profitable.

This model is called "drum-buffer-rope." Market demand is the constraint on the system, and it sets the "drum beat" or pace of the supply chain. Individual companies manage uncertainty in their stage of the supply chain by using their "buffer"—either inventory or productive capacity. Buffers are kept low because uncertainty is minimized by sharing data. This data is the "rope" that ties the participants together and allows them to synchronize their actions.

Clearly, one way to counteract this distortion is for all companies in a supply chain to share a common set of demand data from which to do their forecasting. The most accurate source of this demand data is the supply chain member closest to the end use customer, if not the customers themselves. Sharing point-of-sale data among all the companies in a supply chain goes a long way toward taming the bullwhip effect, because it lets everyone respond to actual market demand instead of supply chain distortions.

Order Batching

Order batching occurs because companies place orders periodically for amounts of product that will minimize their order processing and transportation costs. As discussed in the "Inventory Management" section in Chapter 3, companies tend to order in lot sizes determined by the EOQ (economic order quantity) of the product. Because of order batching, these orders vary from the level of actual demand, and this variance is magnified as it moves up the supply chain.

The way to address this type of demand distortion is to find ways to reduce the cost of order processing and transportation. This will mean smaller EOQ lot sizes and more frequent ordering, but the result will be a smoother flow of orders that distributors and manufacturers will be able to handle more efficiently. Ordering costs can be reduced by computerization of the order process, something most companies already do. Transportation costs can be reduced by using third-party logistics suppliers (3PLs) to cost-effectively pick up many small shipments from suppliers and deliver small orders to many customers.

Product Rationing

Product rationing is the response that manufacturers take when they are faced with more demand than they can meet. One common rationing approach is for a manufacturer to allocate the available supply of product based on the number of orders received. Thus, if the available supply equals 70 percent of the orders received, the manufacturer will fill 70 percent of the amount of each order and back-order the rest. This leads distributors and retailers in the supply chain to raise their order quantities artificially, in order to get the amount they think they deserve as "good customers." This type of behavior, known as **shortage gaming**, can be disastrous to the supply chain because it greatly overstates product demand. Indeed, it becomes quite a game with some merchants.

There are several ways to respond to this. Manufacturers can base their rationing decisions on the historical ordering patterns of a given distributor or retailer, rather than on their present order sizes. This eliminates much of the motivation for the shortage gaming that otherwise occurs. Manufacturers and distributors can also alert their customers in advance if they see demand outstripping supply. This way product shortages will not take buyers by surprise and there will be less panic buying.

Product Pricing

When prices of products fluctuate, distortions in demand can result. If special sales are offered and product prices are lowered, it will induce customers to buy more or buy sooner than they otherwise would (so-called forward buying). Then prices return to normal levels and demand falls off. Instead of a smooth flow of products through the supply chain, price fluctuations can create waves of demand and surges of product flow that are hard to handle efficiently. Even very liberal (or "free") return policies can skew demand figures one way or the other and end up cracking the bullwhip.

With a nod to Wal-Mart, answers to this problem generally revolve around the concept of "everyday low prices." If the end customers believe that they're getting a pretty good price whenever they purchase the product, they will make their purchases based on real need and not other considerations. This, in turn, makes demand easier to forecast, and companies in the supply chain can respond more efficiently.

This does not mean retailers can't have sales without the approval of all other members of their supply chains! It just means the sale events should be structured to move product already in stock at the store, such as end-of-season or slow-moving merchandise, or product that the other partners can supply without an artificial ramp-up of production or distribution.

Performance Incentives

Performance incentives are often different for different companies and individuals in a supply chain. Each company views itself as managing its role or position in isolation from the rest of the supply chain. Within companies, individuals can also see their jobs in isolation from the rest of the company. It is common for companies to structure incentives that reward its sales force on sales made each month or each quarter.

Therefore, as the end of a month or a quarter approaches, the sales force offers discounts and takes other measures to move the product in order to meet the quotas. This results in product—for which there is no real demand—being pushed into the supply chain. It is also common for managers within a company to be motivated by incentives that conflict with other company objectives. For instance, a transportation manager may take actions that minimize transportation costs at the expense of customer service or inventory carrying costs.

Alignment of performance incentives with supply chain efficiencies is a real challenge. It begins with the use of accurate activity-based costing (ABC) data that can highlight the associated costs. Companies must be able to quantify the expenses incurred by forward buying due to month-end or end-of-quarter sales incentives. Companies also need to identify the effect of conflicting internal performance incentives. The next step is to experiment with new incentive plans that support efficient supply chain operation. This is a process that each company needs to work through in its own way.

COLLABORATIVE PLANNING, FORECASTING, AND REPLENISHMENT

To facilitate the coordination that is needed in supply chains, an industry group known as the Voluntary Interindustry Commerce Standards (VICS) Association keeps up-to-date on the technique known as collaborative planning, forecasting, and replenishment (CPFR) and its related issues. This committee documents best practices for CPFR and creates guidelines to follow for CPFR.

The CPFR process is divided into the three activities of planning, forecasting, and replenishment. Within each activity there are several steps.

Collaborative Planning

- Negotiate a front-end agreement that defines the responsibilities of the companies that will collaborate with each other.
- Build a joint business plan that shows how the companies will work together to meet demand.

Collaborative Forecasting

- Create sales forecasts for all the collaborating companies.
- Identify any exceptions or differences between companies.
- Resolve the exceptions to provide a common sales forecast.

Collaborative Replenishment

- Create order forecasts for all the collaborating companies.
- Identify exceptions between companies.
- Resolve the exceptions to provide an efficient production and delivery schedule.
- Generate actual orders to meet customer demand.

CPFR in Action

For an example of how CPFR can work, let's return to the example of Nimble Company. In the discussion of product design in Chapter 3, you learned how Nimble Company developed a home entertainment system that was much simpler to manufacture than a competitor's system. The simpler design is supported by a less complex supply chain that reduces production costs and increases responsiveness to market demands. All of this is central to the competitive success that Nimble Co. is enjoying.

Nimble Co. has collaboration agreements in place with its supply chain partners and has an ongoing planning, forecasting, and replenishment process in place with these partners. Nimble Co. receives POS data, showing the actual sales of its systems in retail stores. From these same retailers, Nimble Co. receives regular updates of their sales forecasts and their inventory levels of Nimble Co. home entertainment systems. Nimble Co. uses this data to plan its production schedule. It also shares this data with the component manufacturers who provide parts for its home entertainment system, so the component manufacturers can plan their own production schedules.

In looking at the sales data and forecasts, Nimble Co. sees that demand for its product is growing faster than anticipated in the company's yearly plan and makes the decision to increase production. Nimble Co. revises its production schedule for the year and takes the new plan to its key component suppliers to negotiate additional purchases of their components.

It turns out that one component supplier cannot quickly ramp up production—but a second supplier has a component that could fill the need with just a slight design modification. Because all affected parties know what is going on and have enough lead time, the design changes are made and production schedules are increased to meet the rise in product demand without any retailers running out of inventory.

The benefits illustrated here clearly show supply chain collaboration in action:

- First, the bullwhip effect is diminished because all companies in the supply chain can see real-time sales data and share sales forecasts. This allows everyone to optimize their production schedules, inventory levels, and delivery schedules.
- Next, there are the benefits associated with Nimble Co. being able to quickly see a real rise in customer demand and coordinate with its suppliers to increase production schedules over previously planned levels.
- Third, even though one component supplier was not able to accommodate Nimble Co.'s increased production schedule, another supplier had a workable substitute. Changes were made to the product design, production was increased, and no retailer lost sales revenue due to running out of inventory.

Companies that can integrate their supply chains will have a significant competitive advantage, but this type of collaboration is not easy to implement, and it will take time to become more common in business. However, prominent companies are already beginning to lead the way. Wal-Mart, Dell, and Procter & Gamble share point-of-sale data with all the other companies in their respective supply chains, including inventory data. Sharing this kind of information provides a basis for each company to make decisions about its own activities that will yield better efficiencies and profits—for itself and for the supply chain as a whole.

STARTING SUPPLY CHAIN COLLABORATION

The best place to start in an effort to promote collaboration is to measure the bullwhip effect within a company. Over a period of time—perhaps a quarter or a year—compare the volume and frequency of orders received from customers with the volume and frequency of orders the company places with suppliers. Plot them out on a graph so everyone can see the difference between the company's incoming customer orders and its outgoing supplier orders. What is the extent of this divergence? Where is the company located in the supply chain? Retailers are, of course, at the "front" of the chain (close to the end customer), but the same calculations work for companies at the "back" of the chain (manufacturers or their suppliers). Remember, the distortion caused by divergence of incoming orders with outgoing orders increases as it moves back through the supply chain.

Many companies are not aware of the supply chain costs that are associated with the bullwhip effect. Traditionally, demand variability caused by the bullwhip effect was taken as a given, and companies worked on their own to develop better ways to respond to the fluctuations in demand. But increasingly, the experts have decided it is far more efficient for companies to work together to combat the bullwhip effect, by collaborating with other supply chain partner companies to reduce the fluctuations together.

Once the magnitude of the bullwhip effect has been established in a particular company, it is up to the people in that company to estimate the cost consequences in different departments. Production costs, production scheduling, transportation costs, and shipping and receiving costs all are impacted to a certain extent by bullwhip conditions. What inventory levels are needed to maintain service levels in such a volatile situation, versus what they would normally be without these fluctuations? What is the effect on product availability and order lead times—are sales lost because of lack of inventory? These are the kinds of factors that will show a company how much it actually costs to deal with the constant hypervigilance that is required by having to adapt to these unnecessary demand fluctuations. This is the basis upon which to discuss what it might be worth to fix the bullwhip effect.

INFORMATION SYSTEMS

One of the requirements for successful CPFR is known as **global data synchronization**. The name means just what it says—every company should be able to synchronize its data with partner companies' data so they can work together to plan, forecast, produce, and deliver the right amounts of goods. This requires information technology (IT) that can support a company's internal operations and also enable collaboration among companies in a supply chain. Using high-speed data networks and databases, companies can share data to better manage the supply chain as a whole, as well as their individual positions within the supply chain. Today, the effective use of this technology is key to a retailer's success.

You would think in this highly wired Internet age that this would be fairly easy—just start e-mailing data! But the business world runs on a mishmash of different types of computers and software. Many companies don't have compatible systems and either cannot or will not upgrade them. Even if they did, they collect different types of data that may or may not be useful to their partner companies. In this environment, "collaboration" and data synchronization become increasingly complex feats.

All information systems are composed of technology designed to perform three main functions: data capture and communication, data storage and retrieval, and data manipulation and reporting. Different systems have different combinations of capabilities, and the specific combination necessary for the retailer (or other supply chain partner) depends on the demands of the job.

Data Capture and Data Communications

The first functional area is composed of systems and technology that create high-speed data capture and communications networks. This is the technology that can overcome the lag times and lack of big-picture information that gives rise to the bullwhip effect. We will look at the following:

- The Internet
- Broadband
- EDI (electronic data interchange)
- XML (eXtensible Markup Language)

The Internet

The Internet is the global data communications network that uses what is known as Internet Protocol (IP) standards to move data from one point to another. The Internet is the universal communications network that can connect with all computers and communication devices. Once a device is hooked to the

Internet, it can communicate with any other device that is also connected to the Internet, regardless of the different internal data formats that they may use.

Before the Internet, companies had to put in expensive, dedicated networks to connect themselves to other companies and move data among their different computer systems. Now, with the Internet already in place, companies have a way to quickly and inexpensively "connect" their computer systems. If needed, extra data protection and privacy can be provided by using technology to create virtual private networks (VPNs) that utilize the Internet to create very secure communication networks.

Broadband

Basically, this means any communications technology that offers high-speed (faster than a 56K dial-up modem) access to the Internet with a connection that is always on. This includes technologies such as coaxial cable, digital subscriber line (DSL), metro Ethernet, fixed wireless, and satellite. Broadband technology is spreading, and as it does, it becomes possible for companies in a supply chain to easily and inexpensively exchange large volumes of data in real time.

Most companies have connected themselves internally using local area network (LAN) technology (such as Ethernet) that gives them plenty of internal communications capability. Many companies have connected some or all of their different geographical locations using wide area network (WAN) technology (such as T1, T3, or frame relay). What is then required are additional high-speed, relatively low-cost connections between separate companies, and that is the role that broadband will play.

Electronic Data Interchange

Electronic data interchange (EDI) is a technology that was developed to transmit common types of data between companies that do business with each other. It was first deployed in the 1980s by large companies in the manufacturing, automobile, and transportation industries. It was built to automate back-office transactions such as the sending and receiving of purchase orders (known as "850" transactions), invoices (810), advance shipment notices (856), and back-order status (855), to name just a few. It originally was built to run on big, mainframe computers using value-added networks (VANs) to connect with other trading partners. That technology was expensive.

EDI allows retailers and suppliers to improve their supply chain performance with a technique called **vendor-managed inventory** (VMI). The vendor (supplier) is responsible for (and now technologically capable of) checking the product quantities in stores themselves and filling as needed to prevent out-of-stocks. Salespeople aren't crazy about VMI, and neither are distributors—it takes some of their control away, including the ability to use sales promotions and discounts as incentives to move product. But, in effect, VMI shortens the retail supply chain and can reduce both overstocking and out-of-stock problems.

Many companies have large existing investments in EDI systems and find that it is very cost-effective to continue to use these systems to communicate with other businesses. Standard EDI data sets have been defined for a large number of business transactions. Companies can decide which data sets (and/or which parts of each data set) they will use. EDI systems can now run on any type of computer, from mainframe to PC, and they use the Internet for data communications as well as VANs. Costs for EDI technology have come down considerably.

XML

An abbreviation for **eXtensible Markup Language**, XML is a technology that has been developed to transmit data in flexible formats among computers, and between computers and humans. Where EDI uses rigid, predefined data sets to send data back and forth, XML is extensible—that is, it can be extended or expanded. It can be used to store any type of structured information and to encapsulate information to pass between computers that would otherwise be unable to communicate.

A little background in "computerspeak" here will help in understanding the importance of XML. Most Internet users by now are familiar with HTML (HyperText Markup Language), which is used to create Web pages. HTML is part of a larger language, a "mother tongue" for computers called SGML (Standard Generalized Markup Language). SGML is so huge that using it would bog down most applications, which do not require that much complexity anyway. So XML is a handier, scaled-down version of SGML that is easy for programmers to use and understand. And XML is a public format—the technology is not owned by any particular company. Anyone can use or view documents written in XML if he or she has a browser that works with XML, and most modern browsers either can read it outright or have the capability to process it by default.[2] (The clearest and most in-depth information we've been able to find about XML and related technological developments is from the University of Cork in Ireland, a "Frequently Asked Questions" page that is updated regularly, at www.ucc.ie/xml/.)

Once certain standards have been agreed upon, XML can be used to communicate a wide range of different kinds of data and related processing instructions among different computer systems. XML can also be used to communicate between computers and humans, because it can drive user interfaces (like Web browsers) and respond to human input. Unlike EDI, the exact data transactions and processing sequences do not have to be previously defined when using XML.

There are many evolving XML standards in different industries, but as yet, none of these standards has been widely adopted. The industry that has made the most progress in adopting XML standards is the electronics industry. They have implemented the RosettaNet XML standards (www.rosettanet.org).

In the near term, XML and EDI are merging into hybrid systems, evolving to meet the needs of companies in different supply chains. At this point, it is not cost-effective for companies with existing EDI systems that are working well enough to replace them with newer XML systems all at once. Instead, XML extensions are being grafted onto EDI systems. Software is available to quickly translate EDI data to XML and then back to EDI. Service providers are now offering Internet-based EDI to smaller suppliers who do business with large EDI-using customers.

In the longer term, EDI will be wholly consumed by XML as XML standards are agreed upon. As these standards become more widely accepted, they will enable very flexible communications among companies in a supply chain. XML will allow communications that are more spontaneous and free-form, like any human language. This kind of communication will drive a network of computers and people interacting with other computers and other people. The purpose of this network will be to coordinate supply operations on a daily basis.

And who said computer programming was boring?

Data Storage and Retrieval

The second functional area of an information system is the technology to store and retrieve data, known as database technology. A database is an organized grouping of data that is stored in an electronic format. The most common type of database uses what is called **relational database technology**. As the name suggests, a relational database stores related groups of data in individual tables and allows for retrieval of the data with the use of a standard language called structured query language (SQL).

A database is a model of the business processes for which it collects and stores data. The model is defined by the level of detail in the data it collects. The design of every database has to strike a balance between highly aggregate data at one extreme and highly detailed data at the other extreme. This balance is arrived at by weighing the needs and budget of a business against the increasing cost associated with more and more detailed data. The balance is reflected in what is called the data model of the database.

As events occur in a business process, there are database transactions. The data model of the database determines which transactions can be recorded, since the database cannot record transactions that are either more detailed or more aggregated than provided for in the data model. These transactions can be recorded as soon as they happen, called "real-time" updating, or they may be captured and recorded in batches that happen on a periodic basis, called "batch" updating.

A database also provides for the different data retrieval needs of the people who use it. People doing different jobs will need different combinations of data from the same database. These different combinations are called "views." Views can be created and made available to people who need them to do their jobs. For instance, a database may contain the sales history for a range of different products to a range of different customers. A view of this data designed for a customer might show the customer the different products and quantities they purchased over a period of time and show detail of the purchases at each customer location. A manufacturer's view might show all the customers who bought their group of products over a period of time and show details of each of the products that each customer bought.

Data Manipulation and Reporting

Different supply chain systems are created by combining processing logic to manipulate and display data with the technology required to capture, communicate, store, and retrieve data. The way that a system manipulates and displays the data that flows through it is determined by the specific business operations the system is designed to support. Information systems contain the processing logic needed by the business operations they support. Chopra and Meindl define several kinds of systems that support supply chain operations:

- *Enterprise resource planning (ERP)* systems gather data from across multiple functions in a company. ERP systems monitor orders, production schedules, raw material purchases, and finished goods inventory. They support a process-oriented view of business that cuts across different functional departments. For instance, an ERP system can view the entire order fulfillment process and track an order from the procurement of material to filling the order to delivery of the finished product to the customer.

  ERP systems come in modules that can be installed on their own or in combination with other modules. There are usually modules for finance, procurement, manufacturing, order fulfillment, human resources, and logistics. The focus of these modules is on carrying out and monitoring daily transactions; the downside of most ERP systems is that they lack the analytical capabilities needed to optimize the efficiency of these transactions.

- *Procurement systems* track the procurement activities that take place between a company and its suppliers, with the purpose of streamlining the procurement process and making it more efficient. Such systems typically replace supplier catalogs with an online product database that contains all the needed information about products the company buys. They also keep track of part numbers, prices, purchasing histories, and supplier performance.

Procurement systems allow people to compare the price and performance capabilities of different suppliers. This way the best suppliers are identified so that relationships can be established with these suppliers and prices negotiated. The routine transactions that occur in the purchasing process can then, for the most part, be automated.

- *Advanced planning and scheduling (APS)* systems are highly analytical applications. Their purpose is to assess plant capacity, material availability, and customer demand. These systems then produce schedules for what to make in which plant and at what time. APS systems base their calculations on the input of transaction-level data that is extracted from ERP or legacy transaction processing systems. They then use linear programming techniques and other sophisticated algorithms to create the recommended schedules.

- *Transportation planning* systems calculate what quantities of materials should be brought to what locations at what times. The systems enable people to compare different modes of transportation, routes, and carriers, and use the comparisons to create transport plans for goods. The software for these systems is sold by system vendors. Other providers (known as "content vendors") provide the data required for these systems—mileage, fuel costs, shipping tariffs, and so on.

- *Demand planning* systems use special techniques and algorithms to help a company forecast demand. These systems take historical sales data and information about planned promotions and other events that can affect customer demand, such as seasonality and market trends, and use this data to create models that help predict future sales.

  Another feature often associated with demand planning systems is *revenue management,* which lets a company experiment with different price mixes for its various products in light of the predicted demand. The idea is to find a mix of products and prices that maximizes total revenue to the company. Companies in the travel industry (airlines, rental car agencies, hotels) are major users of revenue management techniques. Other industries are just catching on to the value of this feature.

- *Customer relationship management (CRM)* systems automate many of the tasks related to servicing existing customers and finding new ones. They track buying patterns and histories of customers, and they consolidate it in a place where it is quickly accessible to customer service and salespeople. This enables them to better respond to customer requests.

- *Sales force automation (SFA)* systems allow a company to better coordinate and monitor the activities of its sales force. These systems automate many sales-related tasks—scheduling sales calls and follow-up visits, preparing quotes and proposals for customers and prospects, and so on.

Any of the preceding types of systems can be combined to form a supply chain management (SCM) system—a suite of different supply chain applications, tightly integrated with each other. An SCM system could be an integrated suite that contains advanced planning and scheduling, transportation planning, demand planning, and inventory planning applications. SCM systems rely on ERP or relevant legacy systems to provide them with the data to support the analysis and planning they do. These systems have the analytical capabilities to support strategic-level decision making.

INVENTORY MANAGEMENT SYSTEMS

Retailers and most of the companies that service them also require computerized inventory management systems for the types of activities described in Chapter 3—tracking historical demand patterns for products, monitoring inventory levels of different products, calculating economic order quantities, and determining the levels of safety inventory that should be held for each product. These systems are used to find the right balance for a company between the cost of carrying inventory and the cost of running out of inventory, which also includes the resulting loss of sales revenue.

The latter consequence can be significant. Research has shown that when a product is out of stock, 31 percent of customers buy it at another store, 26 percent substitute another brand, 19 percent substitute another item of the same brand, 15 percent delay the purchase, and 9 percent end up not purchasing anything in that category.[3] Add the first and last categories on the list, and the store has only a 60 percent chance of making a sale in an OOS situation. Some of these consequences are bad for the retailer; others are bad for the manufacturer.

The same study indicates that so far, neither SCM nor POS technology has been able to impact the overall global out-of-stock numbers, which hover at between 8 and 10 percent in most stores. However, software manufacturers continue to try.

Along the way, before the finished merchandise arrives at a store, there are several types of inventory control systems at various points on the supply chain. These include the following:

- A *manufacturing execution system (MES)* focuses on carrying out the production activities in a factory. This kind of system is less analytical than an APS. It produces short-term production schedules and allocates raw materials and production resources within a single manufacturing plant. MES is similar in its operation to an ERP system; frequently, MES software is produced by ERP software vendors.
- *Transportation scheduling systems (TSS)* are similar to ERP and MES applications in that they are less analytical and more focused on daily operational

SUPPLY CHAIN SKILLS—THE THEORY OF CONSTRAINTS

We mentioned the book *The Goal* in Chapter 1, Eliyahu Goldratt's tale of a fictitious factory manager's quest to save the business from being closed for lack of profitability. What the manager and his staff members learn is how to apply the principles of what Goldratt calls the "Theory of Constraints."

This theory can apply to an entire supply chain as readily as it applies to a single business. In another book, *Basics of Supply Chain Management* (Boca Raton, FL: St. Lucie Press, 2001), Lawrence Fredendall and Ed Hill explain how to apply the Theory of Constraints in this manner.

It is based on the idea that all systems have at least one constraint, and that it is better to manage constraints than to try to eliminate them—because when one part of a system ceases to be a constraint, a different constraint will crop up in another part of the system. Constraints are inevitable because the capacities of each part of a system are not all the same. So, instead of forever reacting to new constraints or bottlenecks as they appear, why not choose a small group of constraints and manage them, deliberately and efficiently?

To apply this model, the first step is to define the goal and decide how to measure progress toward it. Goldratt's goal for a manufacturing company also works for a supply chain: "Increase throughput while simultaneously reducing both inventory and operating expense." (Remember, throughput is the rate at which sales to end customers occur.)

Once a goal has been defined and there is agreement on how to measure progress toward it, five steps can be taken to focus and clarify the situation, which should lead to the decisions necessary to reach the goal. The five steps are as follows:

- **Identify the system's bottlenecks or constraints.** Trace out the workflows and the paths that materials travel in a factory or a supply chain. Find out where slowdowns and backups occur.

- **Decide how to exploit these bottlenecks.** Figure out how to maximize the bottleneck activities. The rate of throughput for the entire system is set by the rate of throughput achieved by the bottlenecks. Ensure the bottlenecks operate at maximum capacity by providing them with enough inventory so they can continue to operate even if there are occasional slowdowns elsewhere in the system.

- **Do not try to maximize the operation of a non-bottleneck operation.** Additional productivity achieved by non-bottleneck operations that exceeds the capacity of the bottlenecks to process will be neutralized anyway by the slowdowns and backups caused at the bottlenecks. Synchronize all system operations to the rates that can be efficiently processed by the bottleneck operations.

- **Elevate the system's bottlenecks.** Add additional processing capacity to the bottleneck activities. Since the rate of throughput of the entire system is set by the throughput of the

Continued

bottlenecks, improvements in the bottlenecks will increase the efficiency of the entire system and provide the best return on investment.

- **If in a previous step a bottleneck has been broken, go back to Step 1.** As the capacity of one system bottleneck is elevated, it may cease to be a bottleneck. The bottleneck may transfer to another operation that could keep up before but now cannot keep up with the new increase in capacity. Watch the entire system to see where slowdowns and backups occur; they may shift from one area to another. If this occurs, start again at Step 1.

issues. A transportation scheduling system produces short-term transportation and delivery schedules that are used by a company.

- *Warehouse management systems (WMS)* support daily warehouse operations. They provide capabilities to efficiently run a warehouse. These systems keep track of inventory levels and stocking locations within a warehouse, as well as the actions needed to pick, pack, and ship product to fill customer orders.

ASSESSING TECHNOLOGY AND SYSTEM NEEDS

When evaluating different systems that can be used to support a supply chain, it is important to keep in mind the goal—that is, the ultimate reason for using any of these systems. Customers want good service and good prices, and that's generally what guides them when they select companies with which to do business. Technology is a means for a company to be of service to its customers. Companies that keep this in mind do well.

In business, technology is only important insofar as it enables a company (or a supply chain) to deliver valuable products and services to its own customers profitably. Do not let the complexity or the details of any technology or system distract from this basic truth. Technology can be impressive, but it is not an end in itself.

Success in supply chain management comes from delivering the highest levels of service at the lowest cost. Technology is expensive and can quickly add a lot of cost to a business. It is a far better thing to use simple technology well than to use sophisticated technology without the skill to handle it.

E-Business and Supply Chain Integration

E-business absolutely requires the principles and practices of supply chain integration. In the words of Professors Hau Lee and Seungjin Whang of Stanford

University, e-business specifically refers to "planning and execution of the front-end and back-end operations in a supply chain using the Internet."

In a November 2001 research paper entitled "E-Business and Supply Chain Integration" (and still available on Stanford University's Global Supply Chain Management Forum Web site, www.stanford.edu/group/scforum/), professors Lee and Whang introduce four key technological dimensions that create a sequence of greater integration and coordination among supply chain participants—culminating in entirely new ways to conduct business. The four dimensions are as follows:

1. *Information integration* is the ability to share relevant data among companies in a supply chain—sales history and demand forecasts, inventory status, production schedules, production capacities, sales promotions, and transportation schedules. This data should be available to the people who need it in a real-time, online format—over the Internet or a private network.
2. *Planning synchronization* is the joint participation of companies in the demand forecasting and the scheduling or inventory replenishment. It also includes collaborative design, development, and bringing new products to market.
3. *Workflow coordination* is the streamlining and automation of ongoing business activities across companies in the supply chain, like purchasing and product design.
4. *New business models* can emerge as a result of supply chain integration made possible by the Internet. Roles and responsibilities of companies in a supply chain can be redesigned to allow each company to truly concentrate on its core competencies, outsourcing the non-core activities to other companies. New capabilities and efficiencies will become possible.

The role of technology in global supply chains is discussed further in Chapter 10.

CHAPTER SUMMARY

One of the most common dynamics in supply chains is the bullwhip effect. Small changes in product demand by the consumer at the front of the supply chain translate into wider and wider swings in demand as experienced by companies further back in the supply chain—the tail wagging the dog, so to speak. Without a well-coordinated supply chain that includes global data synchronization, companies at different stages in the supply chain come to have very different pictures of market demand. The chain fails to communicate accurate data, and each member suffers financial and logistical problems as a result.

Companies have learned that the bullwhip effect is no longer a business necessity—that it is more efficient for them to work together to reduce demand fluctuations by sharing data and coordinating their efforts.

The use of supporting technology is necessary for effective supply chain operations. This chapter explained the three major functions of information technology (IT) systems, as well as listed and defined all the types of software systems a company might use to forecast, schedule, manufacture, deliver, and/or track sales of goods and customer data. Together, various combinations of them are also sold as supply chain management (SCM) packages.

Clearly, technology has transformed the retail industry, allowing collaboration as never before. But the same problems are evident in the most sophisticated system as they were in the old-fashioned paper-in-triplicate invoice: The data must be accurate.

DISCUSSION QUESTIONS

1. Aren't there some advantages to having a product that is in short enough supply to be considered "exclusive"? How would the bullwhip effect impact that type of product and its supply chain?
2. What kinds of extra or unnecessary costs would the bullwhip effect add to a retail supply chain?
3. What would a retail supply chain management system need in the way of types of data manipulation and reporting capabilities? Briefly list and explain your choices.
4. What is the difference between an APS, a CRM, and an ERP system, and which of the three would be the most beneficial to a retailer who could not afford to have them all?
5. How does the Theory of Constraints apply to retail stores? Are there "bottlenecks" in retail as there are in traditional manufacturing, shipping, and so on? Describe a couple of potential situations in which Goldratt's five points might be used to improve a store's operations.

ENDNOTES

1. "The Bullwhip Effect," newsletter of Factory Logic, Inc., Austin, Texas, 2001.
2. Peter Flynn, ed., "The XML FAQ v. 4.0," (online at www.ucc.ie/xml), University of Cork, Ireland, January 1, 2005.
3. Daniel S. Corsten, Thomas W. Gruen, and Bharadwaj Sundar, "Retail Out of Stocks: A Worldwide Examination of Extent, Causes, and Consumer Responses," Goizueta Business School, Emory University (Atlanta, Georgia), in *IntelligentCRM*, a newsletter of Intelligent Enterprise, CMP Media, LLC, San Francisco, California, March 27, 2001.

THE
INCREDIBLE
JOURNEY

CONTINUES

SEPTEMBER 15—SHIPPING OUT

Because CVS usually orders products in volume, the pick quantities tend to be full pallets, so forklifts are used to transport the order instead of WL's network of automatic conveyor belts used for smaller orders. Every morning WL forklift operators use computers attached to their forklifts as well as handheld scanners with instructions screens linked to the McHugh system to learn what they need to pick up, where it's located, and where to transport it. When the lift operators get to the appropriate pallet, they scan the bar code with the handheld device so that the software can confirm it's the correct product. They next bring the pallet to the designated shipping door and use the onboard computer system and handheld to inform the McHugh system that the job is finished. Workers at the shipping door then load waiting trucks with the Listerine and other Warner-Lambert products ordered by CVS, says Mark Kuester, WL's director of logistics and customer support systems.

SEPTEMBER 16—THE HANDOFF TO CVS

The load appears at the CVS warehouse in Woonsocket. The trucking company sends WL confirmation of the delivery and who signed for it via EDI. As soon as the truck is unloaded, the CVS warehouse team generates an electronic receiving invoice telling the CVS accounts payable department that it received the goods from WL. The team also downloads the document to the company's data warehouse for future forecasting purposes and to the warehouse management system, which routes the pallets to the appropriate storage site in the warehouse. There they'll sit for as long as three weeks until they are shipped to fill orders placed by CVS stores.

What's noteworthy about CVS's supply chain?

CVS has 9 main warehouse facilities and 15 satellite facilities.* The company's claim to supply chain fame comes from its ability to spread fixed costs across many stores by consolidating orders and coordinating demand and delivery between stores, says Gregory J. Owens, CIO-100 judge and worldwide managing partner for Andersen Consulting's supply chain management practice in Atlanta. If a truck has to deliver to one store, it might as well deliver to three others on the way. This saves money for CVS, which passes on the savings to its customers, says Owens.

Note: This figure has not been updated for 2005.

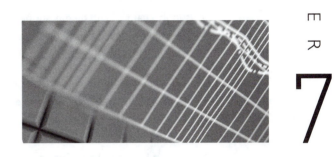

7

MEASURING PERFORMANCE: SUPPLY CHAIN METRICS

S upply chains are fluid, as they continuously adjust to changes in supply and demand for the products they handle. This kind of flexibility is absolutely necessary, but it also requires that the performance of the companies in the chain be monitored and controlled for the good of the group, and to make course corrections along the way if necessary.

Nowadays, even with advances in technology, this type of control is difficult at best. Especially in supply chains that stretch across the globe, with suppliers on different continents than retailers, each new subcontractor adds a layer of complexity that, in effect, lengthens the chain. Some refer to it as a pipeline rather than a chain, which is an apt description—when the pipeline is too long, it is dark and hard to see what's going on in various parts of it, let alone measure progress.

This chapter introduces four performance categories that each participant in a supply chain should be measuring regularly, along with the performance metrics for each of these categories. We also discuss the collection and storage of data. After reading this chapter, you will understand

- The four basic market conditions in which companies operate
- Four categories that gauge a company or supply chain's performance, how and why to measure each of these categories
- The importance of data collection and retrieval/reporting of data
- How companies use performance data to spotlight problems and opportunities.
- How supply chain confidence is measured

FOUR TYPES OF MARKETS

A supply chain exists to support the market that it serves, so we cannot decide on the type of performance it must deliver unless we first understand the market being served. In support of this analysis, we'll use a simple model that allows us to categorize a market and identify various requirements and opportunities that it presents to its supply chain. Reality is, of course, a lot more subtle and complex than any model can represent—but this should at least provide the basics.

We'll start by defining a market using its two most basic components—supply and demand. Any market is characterized by its combination of supply and demand. This model defines four basic kinds of markets, or market quadrants, as seen in Figure 7-1:

- The first quadrant is a market where both supply and demand for its products are low and unpredictable. Let's call this a *developing market*. These are usually new markets that are just emerging, created by new technology just hitting the market, or by social and economic trends that cause a group of

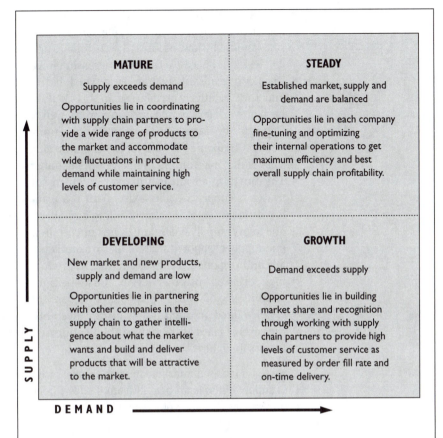

MATURE

Supply exceeds demand

Opportunities lie in coordinating with supply chain partners to provide a wide range of products to the market and accommodate wide fluctuations in product demand while maintaining high levels of customer service.

STEADY

Established market, supply and demand are balanced

Opportunities lie in each company fine-tuning and optimizing their internal operations to get maximum efficiency and best overall supply chain profitability.

DEVELOPING

New market and new products, supply and demand are low

Opportunities lie in partnering with other companies in the supply chain to gather intelligence about what the market wants and build and deliver products that will be attractive to the market.

GROWTH

Demand exceeds supply

Opportunities lie in building market share and recognition through working with supply chain partners to provide high levels of customer service as measured by order fill rate and on-time delivery.

SUPPLY

DEMAND

What are the markets your company serves? What quadrants are they in? How can your company respond to the opportunities in these markets?

Figure 7-1. Each market quadrant presents different opportunities.

customers to perceive some new set of needs—say, long-term care insurance for baby boomers, for example. Opportunities in a developing market are in the areas of partnering with other players in the supply chain to gather intelligence about what the market wants. Cost of sales is high in this market, and inventories are low because the product is still new and not all potential sellers have jumped on the bandwagon.

- The second quadrant is a market where supply is low and demand is high. This is a *growth market*. Since the demand is higher than supply, the supply is often uncertain. If a developing market solidifies and builds up momentum, it can suddenly take off, and for a time, there is a surge in demand that suppliers have difficulty keeping up with. Opportunities in a growth market involve providing a high level of customer service as measured by order fill rates and on-time deliveries. Customers in a market like this value a reliable source of supply and will generally pay premium prices for reliability. Cost of sales should be low, because the customers are easy to find, and inventories can be higher because they are increasing in value.

- The third quadrant is a market in which both supply and demand are high and, thus, relatively predictable. In this *steady market*, the market forces have been at work for a while and have pretty well balanced supply and demand. Opportunities here lie in fine-tuning or "optimizing" internal company operations. Companies should focus on minimizing their inventory and cost of sales while maintaining high levels of customer service.

- The fourth quadrant is a market in which supply has overtaken demand, so excess supply capacity exists. This is a *mature market*, in which demand is reasonably stable or slowly falling but—because of the fierce competition due to oversupply—demand seems uncertain from the point of view of any one supplier. Opportunities in mature markets hinge on the ability to be flexible and respond quickly to changes in product demand while maintaining high levels of customer service. Customers in a market like this value the convenience of "one-stop shopping," where they can purchase a wide variety of related products at low prices. Inventories should be minimized, and the costs of sales are somewhat higher due to the expense of attracting customers in an already crowded market.

As you can see, markets in each quadrant have their own characteristics that supply chains can benefit from if they understand the opportunities and can work together to exploit them.

MARKET PERFORMANCE CATEGORIES

In Chapter 1 we introduced two characteristics that describe the best supply chain performance—responsiveness and efficiency. We intuitively know what these two characteristics imply, but we need to define them in more precise terms in order to measure them objectively. This requires four measurement categories:

- *Customer service* measures the ability of the supply chain to meet the expectations of its customers—and, depending on the type of market being served, the customers have different expectations of service. Some customers both expect, and will pay for, high levels of product availability and quick delivery of small purchase quantities. Customers in other markets will accept longer waits for products and will purchase in large quantities. Whatever the market being served, the supply chain must meet the customer service expectations of the people in that market.

- *Internal efficiency* refers to the ability of a company (or an entire supply chain) to operate in ways that generate an appropriate level of profitability. As with customer service, market conditions vary and that "appropriate level" of profit varies. In a risky, developing market, the profit margins must be higher in order to justify the investment of time and money. In a mature market with little uncertainty or risk, profit margins can be somewhat lower and still satisfy the business partners, because high volume of sales can make up in gross profit what is given up in gross margin.
- *Demand flexibility* is the ability to respond to uncertainty in levels of product demand—notably, how much of an increase over current levels of demand could be handled if necessary by a company or its supply chain. It also includes the ability to respond to uncertainty in the range of products that may be demanded—that is, the ability (in a mature market, for example) to shift production to a better-selling new item suddenly if necessary.
- *Product development* encompasses a company and a supply chain's ability to continue to evolve along with the markets it serves, developing and delivering new products in a timely manner. This ability is key when serving developing markets.

There are other demands that real-world markets place on their supply chains; however, by using these four performance categories, we can create a useful framework. This framework describes the mix of performance required from companies and supply chains that serve the four market quadrants.

When a company identifies the markets it serves, it can then define the performance mix required by those markets in order to best respond to the opportunities they provide. Figure 7-2 lists the performance categories that have the most impact on each quadrant. The most profitable companies and supply chains are those that deliver the performance skills that "match" their markets.

But even when they believe they're "delivering like crazy," how can they be sure? Some **metrics**, or ways to measure the performance, are necessary so that they can be tracked and compared over time to the goals and standards of the company and/or supply chain. And here's where things can get sticky. Companies are often reluctant to share data that may be used against them by their competitors, or that point out weaknesses to their customers or suppliers. There are issues of trust and confidence building to work out before these metrics can readily be collected for an entire supply chain, which will be discussed in greater detail later in this chapter. And yet, you can't hit a target that you can't see. Measurement is the only way to determine how close to the target the supply chain partners are coming, individually or collectively.

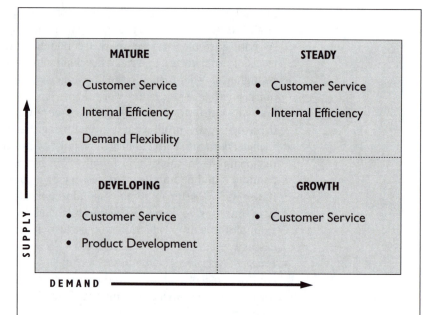

Does your company excel in the performance categories that relate to the markets you serve? Profit opportunities lie in being a leader in the mix of performance categories that your markets call for.

Figure 7-2. Market quadrants require a different mix of performance.

CUSTOMER SERVICE METRICS

In the words of Stanford University professor Warren Hausman: "Service relates to the ability to anticipate, capture and fulfill customer demand with personalized products and on-time delivery."[1] The reason that any company exists is to be of service to its customers. The reason that any supply chain exists is to serve its market. Customer service metrics indicate how well a company serves its customers and how well a supply chain supports its market.

There are two sets of customer service metrics depending on whether the company or supply chain is in a **build-to-stock (BTS)** or **build-to-order (BTO)** situation. Retail buyers routinely encounter both BTS and BTO situations when placing orders.

Build-to-Stock

BTS is how common, commodity-type products are supplied to a large market or customer base—products such as office supplies, cleaning supplies, building supplies, and so on. These items are made in advance, with the idea that they may sit in inventory for a while before being purchased; however, customers fully expect to get them right away, anytime they need them. Supply chains for these products must make and stock them accordingly.

Because the customer wants their complete order to be filled immediately, there is added expense to some supply chain partners. It is costly for them to carry enough stock to fill orders that may contain a wide range and number of items. So they usually have backup plans—rush delivery of items not in stock or substitution of upgraded items.

Typical metrics for a build-to-stock situation are as follows:

- Complete order fill rate and order line-item fill rate
- On-time delivery rate
- Value of total back-orders and number of back orders
- Frequency and duration of back orders
- Line-item return rate

The order fill rate measures the percentage of total orders where all items on the order are filled immediately from stock. The line-item fill rate is the percentage of total line items on all orders that are filled immediately from stock. Used together, these two measures track customer service from two important perspectives. Can you figure out whose perspectives they are?

Build-to-Order

A BTO product is customized to meet a specific customer order, configured to meet the requirements defined by the customer. Examples of this are the way Boeing builds airplanes for specific customers, or the way Dell Computer assembles PCs to fit individual customer orders and specifications. Some BTO products are made up of premade components that are simply assembled to order; others are literally made from scratch.

Following are popular metrics for a build-to-order situation:

- Quoted customer response time and on-time completion rate
- On-time delivery rate
- Value of late orders and number of late orders
- Frequency and duration of late orders
- Number of warranty returns and repairs

In a BTO environment, it is important to track both the quoted customer response time and the on-time completion rate, because it is easier for a company to achieve a high on-time completion rate if it quotes longer customer response times. The question becomes whether the customer really wants a short response time or will accept a longer response time. The quoted response time needs to be aligned with the company's competitive strategy.

INTERNAL EFFICIENCY METRICS

Internal efficiency refers to the ability of a company or a supply chain to use its assets as profitably as possible. Assets include anything of tangible value: plant, equipment, inventory, and cash. Some popular measures of internal efficiency are as follows:

- *Inventory value* should be measured both at a point in time and also as an average over time. The major asset of any supply chain is the inventory contained throughout the length of the chain, because the individual assets to make the inventory are owned by the individual companies. Supply chain members are always looking for ways to reduce inventory while still delivering high levels of customer service. This means trying to match inventory availability (supply) with sales (demand) and not have excess inventory left over. The only time a company would want to let inventory exceed sales is in a growth market, where the value of the inventory will increase. However, markets can be fickle, and as a rule, it is best to avoid excess inventory.

- *Inventory turns* are a measurement of the profitability of inventory by tracking the speed with which it is sold or turned over during the course of a year. This measure is often referred to as **T&E**, short for "turn and earn." It is calculated by the equation:

$$\text{Turns} = \frac{\text{Annual Cost of Sales}}{\text{Annual Average Inventory Value}}$$

Generally, the higher the turn rate the better, although some lower-turning inventory must be available in order to meet customer service and demand flexibility.

- *Return on sales* is a broad measure of how well an operation is being run. It measures how well fixed and variable costs are being managed, and also takes into account the gross profit generated on sales:

$$\text{Return on Sales} = \frac{\text{Earnings before Interest and Tax}}{\text{Sales}}$$

Again, as a rule, the higher the return on sales, the better. However, there are times when a company may deliberately reduce this number in order to gain or defend market share, or to incur expenses that are necessary to achieve some other business objective.

- *Cash-to-cash cycle time* is the time it takes from when a company pays its suppliers for materials to when it gets paid by its customers. This time can be estimated with the following formula:

$$\text{Cash-to-Cash Cycle Time} = \text{Inventory Days of Supply} +$$
$$\text{Days Sales Outstanding} -$$
$$\text{Average Payment Period on Purchases}$$

The shorter this cycle time, the better. A company can often make more improvements in its accounts payable and receivable areas than can be made in its inventory levels. Accounts receivable may be large as a result of late payments caused by billing errors or selling to customers who are bad credit risks. These are things a company should be able to manage just as well as inventory.

DEMAND FLEXIBILITY METRICS

Demand flexibility describes a company's ability to be responsive to new demands in the quantity and range of products and to act quickly—which is absolutely necessary in today's marketplace in order to cope with fast-changing trends and the related uncertainty. There are three chief measurements of flexibility:

- *Activity cycle time* is a very simple concept—the amount of time it takes to perform a supply chain activity such as order fulfillment, product design, product assembly, and so on. This cycle time can be measured within an individual company or across the whole supply chain. In retail, order fulfillment is a critical measure of efficiency. But within a supply chain, what's important is the cycle time for the *total* order fulfillment—from the time the first item was made to its sale to the ultimate end user, the customer.
- *Upside flexibility* is the ability of a company or supply chain to respond quickly to additional order volume for the products they carry. Normal order volume may be 100 units per week for a product—but can an order be filled that is 25 percent greater one week, or will the extra product demand wind up as a back order? Upside flexibility can be measured as the percentage of increase *over the expected demand* that the supply chain can accommodate.
- *Outside flexibility* is the ability to quickly provide the customer with additional products outside the bundle of products normally provided. As markets mature and technologies blend, products that were once considered outside the range of a company's offerings can become a logical extension of them. There is danger in trying to provide customers with a new and unrelated set of products that has little in common with the existing product bundle. However, there is opportunity to acquire new customers, and sell more to existing customers, when outside flexibility is managed skillfully.

PRODUCT DEVELOPMENT METRICS

Product development metrics are measurements of a company or supply chain's ability to design, build, and deliver new products to serve its markets as those markets evolve over time. Technical innovations, social change, and economic developments all cause or contribute to market changes, and as important as they are, this is the category that is most often overlooked in terms of trying to measure performance.

A supply chain simply must keep pace with the market it serves, or sooner or later, it will be replaced. The ability to keep pace with an evolving market can be measured by metrics such as:

- Percentage of total products sold that were introduced in the last year
- Percentage of total sales from products introduced in the last year
- Cycle time to develop and deliver a new product

Metrics by Operation

Sometimes what to measure can be determined by just taking a closer look at the operation itself. The Supply-Chain Council's SCOR Model, introduced in Chapter 3, divides any supply chain into five functions. Here are a few metrics that would be useful in each function. Can you think of others?

1. **Plan.** Costs of planning activities; inventory financing costs; inventory days of supply on hand; forecast accuracy
2. **Source.** Material acquisition costs; cycle times for receiving and using goods; raw materials' days of supply on hand
3. **Make.** Production cycle times; numbers of product defects; other quality issues
4. **Deliver.** Fill rates; order management costs; order lead times; transportation costs
5. **Return.** Numbers of complaints; speed of customer service calls; customer follow-up measures

And those are just a few examples. The efficiency with which these activities are carried out will ultimately determine how well a company performs.

COLLECTING AND USING PERFORMANCE DATA

Historically, companies based their management decisions on periodic, standard reports that showed what happened during some period in the past. In stable and slow-moving business environments, this worked well enough—but there are not many companies that work in stable and slow-moving environments anymore! Working from traditional, periodic, accounting-oriented reports in a fast-paced retail business is somewhat like trying to drive a car by looking only in the rearview mirror.

Today's shorter product life cycles, mass markets dissolving into smaller niche markets, and new technology and distribution channels are constantly opening up new opportunities. To keep pace, a company requires a reporting system that presents data at three levels of detail:

- **Strategic.** To help the senior management team decide what to do
- **Tactical.** To help middle management decide how to do it
- **Operational.** To help employees in general actually do it

In a supply chain management context, *strategic data* consists of current or "actual," as well as plan and historical numbers, that show the company's standing in the four performance categories: customer service, internal efficiency, demand flexibility, and product development. In the Supply-Chain Council SCOR model, data of this type is referred to as "Level 1" data. This data is the overview or top-level data, summarized by major business unit and for the company as a whole. Strategic data also consists of data from outside the company—things like market sizes and growth rates, demographics, and economic indicators such as inflation rates and interest rates. There should also be benchmark data from industry trade associations and studies that show the operating standards and financial performance levels of the best companies in the markets being served.

In the planning operation, for example, measures of complexity would be the number and percentage of order changes, number of stock-keeping units (SKUs) carried, production volumes, and inventory carrying costs. Configuration measures track things such as product volume by channel, number of channels, and number of supply chain locations. Measures of management practices in the plan operation are such things as planning cycle time, forecast accuracy, and obsolete inventory on hand.

Tactical data consists of actual, plan, and historical numbers in the four performance categories displayed at the "branch office" level of detail—in retail, the individual store level. This data also includes the performance metrics labeled "Level 2" in the SCOR model. SCOR breaks them into 30 core process categories that make up any supply chain. Companies use Level 2 measurements to uncover process inefficiencies and try out possibilities—what if we did things this way? What if we changed just this part of the process?

Operational data consists of the measures labeled "Level 3" in the SCOR model. These measurements help people who are charged with getting a job done to understand what is happening, fine-tune, and find ways to make improvements to meet the performance targets that have been set. The SCOR model refers to these measurements as diagnostic metrics. Companies use Level 3 metrics to analyze information flow and workflow, among other things.

There are also "Level 4" metrics in the SCOR model, but these are company-specific and therefore highly customized. The higher the level of metrics, the more detailed they are, but all are used to analyze some aspect of the complexity and configuration of the supply chain, and to study the effectiveness of specific management practices.

The important thing to note here is that most of us are awash in data, so if it is not presented in ways that are useful and meaningful, we are more likely than ever to discard it. By organizing data into distinct levels, people can quickly access only what they need to do their jobs:

- Upper management uses strategic level data to assess market conditions and set business performance objectives. They can drill down to the tactical level or even the operational levels when necessary.
- Store managers use tactical data to do planning and resource allocation to achieve the performance objectives set by upper management.
- Department managers and their staffs use operational data to solve problems and get things done.

The Data Warehouse

A central repository or **data warehouse** is necessary so that data may be drawn from a variety of operating systems and accounting systems within a company and sent to a single source—secure, but easily accessible to those who need it. Technology makes data collection easy to accomplish directly from its sources, as part of daily operations.

The data warehouse includes a database software package and the automated connections to other systems needed to collect the relevant data on a regular and timely schedule. Working in conjunction with the database software is other software that allows for the creation of standard, predefined reports and graphic displays that people can use to monitor operations. In addition to predefined reports and displays, the software must also allow people to make queries in the data warehouse when they need to find things or do more detailed investigations.

A company's IT (information technology) department and/or an outside contractor handles the design and updating of the data warehouse, but it is smart for anyone who uses it to have a basic idea of how it operates. Smaller retailers can get by with a simple, smaller-scale software package, but large or multistore retailers require larger and more complex data warehouses.

Remember, the most important component in any data warehouse system is not the technology, or even the data, but the people who use the system and their ability to use it effectively. Chapter 8 goes into further detail about the design and building of these kinds of systems.

In addition to helping the people inside a company to become more efficient in their own jobs, a data warehouse is the foundation for collaboration with other companies in the supply chain. Information is shared electronically, either automatically (reports sent at certain intervals to certain people in other firms) or retrieval-on-demand capability (certain external people are given proprietary "password" access to the data warehouse over the Internet and can download what they need). Figure 7-3 gives an overview of the information flow.

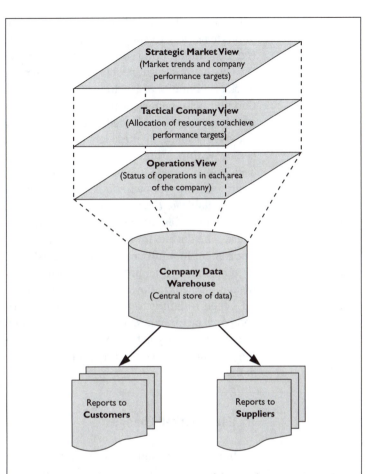

The data warehouse supports views of data at the strategic, tactical, and operational levels. This makes it easy for management and staff in a company to get quick access to the data they need to do their jobs. The data warehouse also supports the sharing of data with customers and suppliers needed to coordinate supply chain activities.

Figure 7-3. The data warehouse displays different views of data to different audiences.

SPOTLIGHTING PROBLEMS AND OPPORTUNITIES

Now we know that, depending on the type of markets a company serves, senior management must define a handful of key performance targets in the areas of customer service, internal efficiency, demand flexibility, and product development. The task then becomes one of figuring out how to manage operations to achieve the target numbers. The point of collecting performance data is to help monitor and control daily, weekly, and monthly operations.

For the most part, people can run their business or do their job by keeping track of a handful of key indicators that tell them where to direct their attention and help them steer through a complex and changing world. No matter how much data is collected, the system should be set up to provide succinct, one-page displays of these key indicators for each department, or even each person within a department. These snapshots are known as **dashboards** because—like the odometer, speedometer, and gauges on a vehicle—they are "right up front," showing a person at a glance the top-level, most important data available *for them*. As shown in Figure 7-4, the data displayed on a senior management dashboard will be different from an operating manager's dashboard. The dashboard of a salesperson in one department is different from a salesperson in another department. Dashboards generally show current performance as well as projected performance. This allows the person to see if what is happening now is on target with or falling short of goals.

When a data warehouse and software reporting tools are in place in a company, people can experiment with the design of their dashboard displays or reports. As they get better at using their dashboards to guide their actions, the company as a whole can become more efficient and more responsive to its markets.

Tracking Market Changes

Nothing stays the same, and the retail industry is living proof of that! Products and markets have life cycles, migrating from one quadrant to another. Over time, market forces are always pushing a market toward an equilibrium where supply meets demand. At the same time, other forces pull and push the market, causing it to fluctuate back and forth around the equilibrium point. Call it supply and demand, or just call it crazy! But put it on a chart and a life cycle usually resembles Figure 7-5 more closely than it would a flat, stable line.

Supply chain participants adjust their operations accordingly to remain competitive. Adaptability is now as important to survival and success as the four performance categories. Market evolution can often be measured in years—and sometimes, in months. Companies no longer have the luxury of being able to focus on optimizing any single mix of performance capabilities over the long term.

A company may become very skilled at internal efficiency and customer service as called for in a steady market; but as the market matures, the same company will have to add skills in the area of demand flexibility. The company may even need to deemphasize some of its internal efficiency policies in order

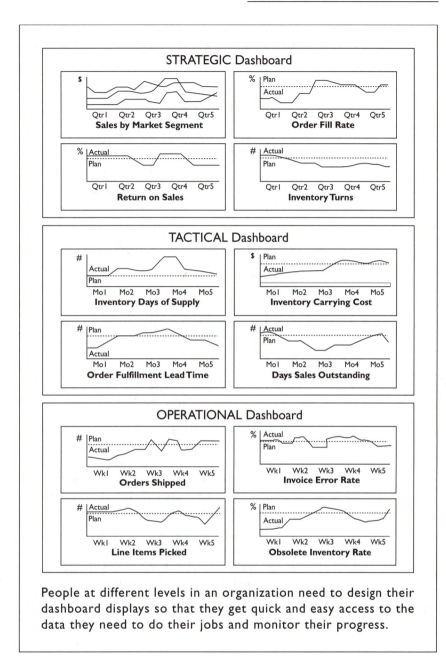

People at different levels in an organization need to design their dashboard displays so that they get quick and easy access to the data they need to do their jobs and monitor their progress.

Figure 7-4. Dashboard designs are different at each level.

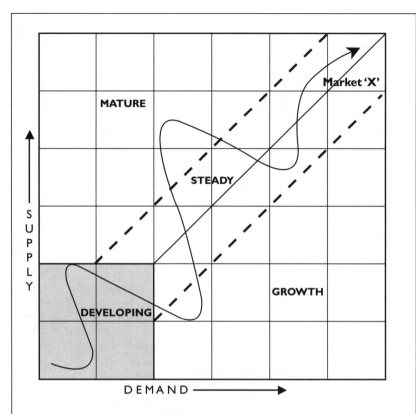

A market (call it Market "X") follows a life cycle. It develops and then it goes on to become a growth market that leads to a steady market and then a mature market and so on. Over time the forces of supply and demand are always pushing the market toward a steady state where supply and demand are equal yet at the same time other forces disrupt this balance.

The supply chains that support Market "X" need to be able to provide first one kind of performance and then another as the market moves through its life cycle. The companies that are most successful in supplying this market are those that can adapt their performance appropriately to follow the market as it changes.

Figure 7-5. Market conditions shift over time.

to ramp up its performance in product development so that it can participate in a promising developing market. The key here is that a company needs to know *when to shift its emphasis* from one mix of performance categories to another, just as a ship at sea adapts to the wind and waves and responds appropriately—and when it comes to necessary course corrections, the quicker, the better.

In the meantime, great demands are placed on the supply chains that support each retailer. In fact, sometimes the supply chain itself can push a market from one quadrant to another, as was illustrated by the "Beer Game" simulation described in Chapter 6. It showed how slight changes in demand by the end customer (or the market as a whole) can cause wildly escalating product demand forecasts to be sent to companies further down the supply chain. This bullwhip effect results in changes in production that outstrip the market's true demand for the product—pushing the market out of "steady" and into "mature." As excess inventory is finally used, the market swings back into the "steady" quadrant once again.

One cure for this wild ride known as the bullwhip effect is better sharing of data among all the companies in a supply chain, sometimes known as better **visibility**. Companies need to work through their concerns about sharing data that would otherwise be confidential. There are serious issues to be negotiated: Exactly what data is reasonable to share? How can privacy of critical data be maintained? What are the benefits of sharing data and how can they be quantified?

Hau Lee, director of the Stanford University Global Supply Chain Management Forum, envisions the supply chain as "an intricate network of suppliers, distributors and customers who share carefully managed information about demand, decisions and performance, and who recognize that success for one part of the supply chain means success for all."[2]

With this in mind, companies need to see demand information from their immediate customers, and also from the end customers of the supply chain—and not just the basics (like demand data), but information about any decisions they make with supply chain implications. In any chain, someone is bound to be "the last to know," and this lack of information—whether or not it is intentional—can impact product demand and sour supply chain relationships.

Companies are accustomed to sharing demand information with each other, but far less likely to share their decisions or performance metrics because they are afraid this information could wind up in the hands of competitors and be used against them. However, this has not reduced the need for sharing it, as customers continue to demand more and more from their supply chains. In an interview with *CIO* magazine, Professor Lee put it this way: "If you are late because your distributor is late, your customers will go to a competitor whose distributor isn't late. That is more than a company-to-company competition. We're going to see more supply-chain-to-supply-chain competition."[3]

Measuring Supply Chain Confidence

So how does a supply chain promote trust and confidence among its wary, business-savvy partner companies? And further, can trust and confidence actually be measured, since they are based on people's perceptions? Professor Lee and colleague Martin Christopher of Cranfield University in Bedfordshire,

TABLE 7-1 Lack of Confidence in Practice	
Business Area	*Lack of Confidence Outcomes*
Sales	• Over-order to hold buffer stocks for key customers • Over-quote on delivery times to customers—may lose the order • Misuse of samples to compensate for lack of stock
Customer service	• Cannot give accurate information on resolving supply issues • May order buffer stock to assist customers
Operations	• Can derive no patterns on sales due to lack of confidence in other areas; forecasting becomes inaccurate, and the trend continues • Likely to overproduce to compensate for other areas' lack of confidence
Marketing	• Delays in essential product launches due to uncertainty of supply
Raw material supplier	• Does not have accurate forecasting and has suffered from previous "emergency" requirements; starts to hold more stock and passes the cost on to their customer

Source: Martin Christopher and Hau L. Lee, "Supply Chain Confidence: The Key to Effective Supply Chains Through Improved Visibility and Reliability," for Vastera, Inc. (now JPMorgan Chase Vastera), Dulles, Virginia, November 6, 2001.

United Kingdom, collaborated on a 2001 study of this topic for Vastera, a global import/export consulting company (that has since been acquired by JPMorgan Chase). They write

> If we consider the supply chain to be, in effect, a chain of customers, then we should be seeking to measure the degree of confidence that each "customer" in the chain has with their upstream "suppliers." Because confidence is all about perceptions, it is perceptions that should be measured. As well as measuring this qualitative aspect of confidence, it should also be possible to find tangible measures of confidence. For example, how many days of inventory are carried at each step in the chain? Supply chain mapping is a helpful tool for highlighting those points where inventory is highest and therefore, presumably, where confidence is lowest.[4]

Table 7-1 summarizes their findings about how lack of confidence shows itself throughout the chain. Each of these symptoms signals a point that might be measured to determine confidence levels. As Christopher and Lee put it, a well-synchronized supply chain, in effect, "substitutes information for inventory"—that is, when the partners trust each other and communicate accurate and complete information openly, no one has to overproduce, overstock, or overpromise. There is no need to hedge their bets.

CHAPTER SUMMARY

Supply and demand can be used to create a simple model that consists of four market quadrants, into which every product fits at some point during its life cycle:

1. **Developing.** New markets and new products where both supply and demand are low and uncertain

2. **Growth.** Markets where demand is higher than supply and supply is uncertain

3. **Steady.** Established markets where supply is high and demand is high and both are stable and predictable

4. **Mature.** Markets where supply exceeds demand and where demand can be unpredictable

Each type of market has a unique set of performance requirements that are placed automatically on their supply chains: customer service, internal efficiency, demand flexibility, and product development.

Briefly, developing markets require performance in the areas of customer service and product development. Growth markets demand customer service above all else. Steady markets call for customer service and internal efficiency, and mature markets require customer service, internal efficiency, and demand flexibility. In order to succeed, companies and supply chains must excel in the performance areas that are required by the markets they serve.

Neither company nor supply chain can gauge its progress in these performance areas without taking measurements, and the chapter mentioned typical tasks or outcomes that may be measured for each. A data warehouse must be designed as the repository for this information. Most companies err on the side of collecting too much data, and a system was suggested for organizing it into tiers for use by different groups, including dashboards of concise, relevant information for individuals and departments. The most important thing about information is not the quantity of it, but whether it can be accessed and successfully used by the people who need it to do their jobs.

How much and what types of data to share among supply chain partners is an issue of continuing concern in the competitive retail industry, but companies that can learn to trust and share data effectively will be the ones to create the most efficient supply chains.

DISCUSSION QUESTIONS

1. What is the difference between gross profit and gross margin? To a retailer, why does this matter?
2. Of all the performance metrics described in this chapter, select one from each of the four "major categories" and explain how it might apply—not in a supply chain, but to your own life as a student.
3. What is the difference between upside flexibility, outside flexibility, and adaptability in a retail supply chain?
4. What items should be on the dashboard of a retail buyer? What items should be on the dashboard of a store manager in a multistore chain?
5. List the types of measurements that would be required to quantify each "lack-of-confidence outcome" in Table 7-1. Which of these would best be measured and studied by individual companies? Which would best be measured by the entire supply chain? Briefly explain your thoughts.

ENDNOTES

1. Warren H. Hausman, "Supply Chain Performance Metrics," Management Science & Engineering Department, Stanford University, Palo Alto, California, 2000.
2. Sarah D. Scalet, "The Cost of Secrecy," *CIO* magazine, © CXO Media, Inc., Framingham, Massachusetts, July 15, 2001.
3. *Ibid.*
4. Martin Christopher (Cranfield University, Bedfordshire, United Kingdom) and Hau L. Lee (Stanford University, Palo Alto, California), "Supply Chain Confidence: The Key to Effective Supply Chains Through Improved Visibility and Reliability," for Vastera, Inc. (now JPMorgan Chase Vastera), Dulles, Virginia, November 6, 2001.

THE INCREDIBLE JOURNEY

CONTINUES

SEPTEMBER 29—WHAT'S IN STORE

CVS store managers like Mike McGee, who manages a CVS in Framingham, Massachusetts, represent the next piece of the supply chain. As he does twice a week, McGee walks up and down the aisles of his store with a handheld computer from Telxon Corp. Underneath every product is a bar code label that tells McGee the minimum quantity of the item that should be kept on the shelf. He eyeballs the Cool Mint Listerine shelf and notices that several of the 500-milliliter bottles appear to be missing. Years of experience enable him to estimate that three bottles are gone instead of having to manually count them. He punches an order for three more into his handheld device. At the end of the day, he connects the machine to an IBM Corp. computer and downloads his full order via modem to (CVS headquarters in) Woonsocket.

CVS is in the process of installing a wireless network and new handheld computers from Symbol Technologies Inc. to automate ordering, says (Leo) Hartnett, the efficient consumer response vice president. Store managers will no longer have to manually figure out how much of an item to restock because the handheld will do all the calculations. Managers scan the shelf label with the handheld, which sends a query for information to CVS's Symbol Spectrum wireless network via the store computer. Within seconds, detailed item information and history, as well as the recommended quantity to order, travels back to the store computer and manager's handheld device. Hartnett would not reveal how much time and money the new system will save, but International Data Corp.'s Jill House, associate research analyst for smart handheld devices, says the savings will be significant.

"The use of handhelds has in past retail pilot trials seen as much as a 10 percent to 15 percent increase in worker productivity, and shipping and inventory accuracy nearing 95 percent to 100 percent," she says. "CVS should see comparable returns on investment."

DEFINING
SUPPLY CHAIN
OPPORTUNITIES

As companies such as Wal-Mart and Dell have so clearly shown, if a retailer can design and build a supply chain that is responsive to market
demands, it can grow from a small company to a world leader in its
niche or industry. Efficient supply chain operations are central to being able
to satisfy market demands and do so profitably. Where markets used to be
shaped by the availability of product, now they are shaped by the evolving
demands (some might say whims) of the end users or customers, who take
for granted that whatever they want will be available, where and when they
need it.

In this chapter, we take the market analysis framework created in Chapter 7 and use it to determine how and where a company can be successful in gaining market share based on identifying opportunities and risks. It also enables each company to focus on delivering value to the overall supply chain by providing "the right" goods and services with "the right" amount of flexibility. The chapter describes the following sequential steps:

- Determine the reasons to design, build, and/or improve a retail system.
- Create a strategy and the objectives needed to reach a goal.
- Estimate the budget needed for the system.
- Calculate the return on investment (ROI).
- Create a high-level project plan to guide the effort.

Now that technology enables conscious design and real-time management of a company's supply chain, how does a company use this ability to its competitive advantage? A well-designed and -managed supply chain should enable the store to offer high levels of customer service while at the same time holding its inventories and cost of sales to levels lower than its competitors—in other words, it should be taking full advantage of the opportunities the supply chain offers. This chapter introduces a process to use for defining these opportunities within a supply chain.

IDENTIFYING OPPORTUNITIES

Supply chains that deliver the best value to their end use customers generate a strong demand for their products and services. They are good places for producers, logistics providers, distributors, and retailers to do business. The efficiency of the entire supply chain greatly affects each company's ability to prosper, so standards of performance evolve in these supply chains over time. Typically, new companies cannot enter the chain unless they can meet these standards. This means that companies who are good at their core supply chain operations work together in self-selecting supply chain partners that can help deliver the greatest value to the consumer.

Retailers can benefit greatly from systems that include stronger technological links in their supply chains. *Retail Merchandiser* magazine and its sister publication, *Apparel,* have identified a few key segments of the clothing industry that are excellent examples of areas in which retailers and suppliers can improve their visibility to each other, lower costs, get products to market more quickly, and/or improve their decision-making abilities:

- **Design and product development.** Systems for product data management (PDM) or product life cycle management (PLM) allow users to save and manage ideas, materials, and data in one place so that they may be accessed by everyone involved in the creation of new products.
- **Color development and management.** Any type of product that comes in a range of colors (cosmetics, apparel, and many others) must ensure that the selected hues are clear and correct throughout the supply chain, from initial design to raw materials to finished product. Sears is one company that does spectral evaluations of submissions and saves results in a database so they can be tracked exactly.
- **Logistics.** In the garment trade, different items within the same designer's collection may be coming from different countries. Good third-party logistics (3PL) providers are prized for their ability to track items from origin all the way to the store.
- **Product identification.** This includes label information in multiple languages: care instructions, vendor and style numbers, and accurate packing information on cases and cartons that will not cause slowdowns in Customs.
- **Warehouse management.** The biggest buzz in retail warehouses is the fast-growing use of **radio frequency identification (RFID)**, which we'll discuss in greater detail in Chapter 10. But any system that allows greater visibility into the supply chain by automating processes like cross-docking, picking, packing, shipping, returns, and damage control in a warehouse has the potential for substantial savings of time and money.[1]

What do these pursuits have in common? They are all systems, created and deployed within a supply chain with goals of making the chain more efficient.

Supply chain opportunities generally fall into two categories, and the type of opportunity determines the way the company should go about accomplishing its goal:

- The first category is to fix or improve something already in place. If you are pursuing an opportunity that is in the "fix or improve something already existing" category, then use Goldratt's Theory of Constraints (introduced in Chapter 6) as the guidelines for taking action.
- The second category is to create or build something new. If you are going after an opportunity in the "build something new" category, then use the process outlined in this chapter.

First, what is the goal? The key areas mentioned for the apparel industry, for example, didn't become "key" overnight. Someone in a supply chain decided they were areas worth improving by creating new, better systems. A market creates a demand for a bundle of products and services to support it, and companies step up to provide them. So there are plenty of questions to be asked when a retailer decides to actively seek new (or greater) opportunity within the supply chain: What are the markets the company serves and who are the end use customers? Who are the producers in these markets? Who are the distributors, logistics providers, and other partners? What are the products and services demanded by this market?

What is the supply and demand situation in these markets? Use the market analysis framework in Chapter 7 to determine which market quadrants the company deals with—not just today but two years from now. Then, compare the organization with its major competitors in the market. Who leads the pack, equals, or lags behind in the four categories of performance: customer service, internal efficiency, demand flexibility, and product development? Should this particular retailer be trying to lead, equal, or excel in each of these areas? The answer is not necessarily to excel at all four—realistically, it is almost impossible to do so. But a position *can be identified* in each of the four areas, depending on the demands of the markets the retailer serves.

For example, as we mentioned in Chapter 7, a company must lead in flexibility if its target markets are mature, or it must lead in customer service if its markets are growing, and so on. The performance targets of Chapter 7 define the goals here in Chapter 8. They become the measures of success.

Creating a Strategy

Once a business goal is defined and the performance targets are set, the next step is to create a strategy to move forward. Simply defined, strategy is "the use of means to achieve ends." In other words, a strategy uses the business operations (means) of an organization to achieve its goals (ends).

To define each strategy, begin by looking at the five basic supply chain operations that are performed in the company—plan, source, make, deliver, and return. Achieving the performance targets will require improvements in one or more of these operations.

Now it's time for the fun part. Brainstorm to generate ideas for each of the five categories. Ask the question, "What seems impossible to do—but if it *could* be done, would dramatically change the way this company does business?"

Look for ways to change the business landscape, to give a retailer a significant competitive advantage by doing something new and different. If nothing absolutely "new" comes to mind, look for ways to significantly improve existing operations to get greater performance and better cost savings from them. Better efficiencies in existing operations will rarely provide huge business wins, but they will certainly help ensure the company's survival.

These ideas are the raw material from which the business strategy will emerge—and the longer the list, the better. Review the finished lists for each operation, and select three to six of them that seem to have the most impact, either because they promise the greatest payback or have the highest likelihood of success without too much complexity. These are the ideas that must now receive further attention. They will be the foundation upon which the strategy is based. See Figure 8-1 for a look at how the company of one of this book's coauthors set its goals using this system.

BUSINESS OPERATIONS / PERFORMANCE CATEGORIES	CUSTOMER SERVICE — As measured by: Fill Rate; On-Time Delivery; Product Returns	INTERNAL EFFICIENCY — As measured by: Inventory Turns; Return on Sales; Cash-to-Cash	DEMAND FLEXIBILITY — As measured by: Cycle Times; Upside Flex; Outside Flex	PRODUCT DEVELOPMENT — As measured by: New Prod Sales; % Revenue; Cycle Time
PLAN — Demand Forecast	(X)	X	(X)	
PLAN — Product Pricing	(X)	X		
PLAN — Inventory Management	X	X	X	
SOURCE — Procurement		X	X	
SOURCE — Credit and Collections	(X)	X		
MAKE — Product Design	X			X
MAKE — Production Scheduling		X	X	
MAKE — Facility Management	X	X		
DELIVER — Order Management	(X)	X		X
DELIVER — Delivery Scheduling	X	X		
RETURN — Timing		(X)		
RETURN — Refund and Replacement Policies	(X)			
RETURN — Satisfactory Complaint Resolutions	X	X		

Network Services set a goal and performance targets that called for improvements in the categories of customer service and demand flexibility. To excel in these two categories, Network Services Co. had earlier made major improvements in its credit and collections operations. Next, it decided to improve its demand forecasting, product pricing, and order management operations.

Figure 8-1. Improve selected business operations to meet performance targets.

The team must examine this handful of promising ideas that have been selected, and a little more brainstorming is in order:

- How will these ideas play out over the next few years? How do these ideas work together to help take the organization from where it is now to where it wants to go?
- What tasks must be assigned, and what new operating procedures and information systems must be created, in order to carry out these ideas? What's the best guess for how much time this will take?
- Look to see how these ideas relate to each other. Does the implementation of one idea build upon the implementation of a previous idea? What sequence should be followed in the implementation of these ideas?
- What kind of changes in operations, technology, and staffing are called for to implement each idea, and how can these changes be done in a manageable way?
- How can the implementation of these ideas be broken up into phases that can each be completed in three to nine months? A phase needs to create deliverables that provide value in their own right and that can be put to use as soon as the phase is completed. Figure 8-2 shows the two-year plan for Network Services' development strategy as an example.

It is important to see the big picture that stretches over a period of several years but also to segment the big picture into smaller phases, so the company is able to begin receiving tangible benefits from its work in a relatively short time period. It can also respond to new developments in the business environment in a timely manner by adjusting its strategy as necessary as each phase is completed. There is a saying that sums up this approach very nicely: "Think big, start small, and deliver quickly."

Designing Systems

The strategy to achieve the business goals is expressed in a **conceptual design**, which is a fairly simple diagram of a system or set of systems. Several different conceptual designs should be created for systems that will meet the desired performance criteria, using simple shapes (like cubes, cylinders, and spheres) to represent different components of the design. Connect these shapes with lines and arrows to show the direction of data flow and activity.

The point with a conceptual design is to illustrate a high-level concept. There's no need to get too technical or detailed in these diagrams; their purpose is to quickly communicate the basic structure of the proposed design. And, like any other "artist's rendition," there is an order to creating a useful design. Follow along on Figure 8-3.

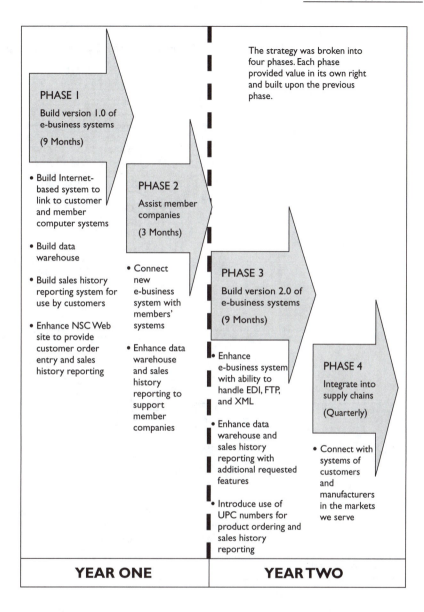

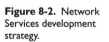

Figure 8-2. Network Services development strategy.

- First, approach it from the perspective of the business processes that are supported. Sketch out the different operations that are performed, and note the kind of information that is required by, and created by, each operation.
- Then add further definition to these process flows by specifying the data flows into and out of each operation. In each case, estimate the volume and frequency of the data flow, as well as the source and destination of each data flow. In addition, for each operation, define the types of people (if any)

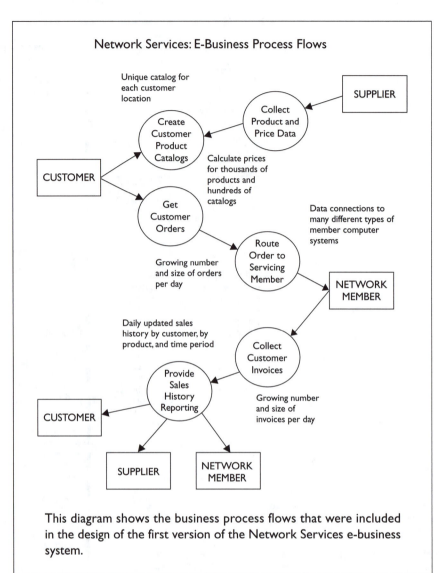

This diagram shows the business process flows that were included in the design of the first version of the Network Services e-business system.

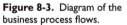

Figure 8-3. Diagram of the business process flows.

who will perform this work. How many people will there be? What are the skill levels of the different types of people?

- Next, decide which operation will be automated, which will be manual, and which will be part automated and part manual. As a rule, people like systems that automate the routine and repetitive tasks, thereby empowering the people to do the problem-solving and decision-making tasks more effectively.

People really are the most valuable resource of any company, so design systems that make maximum use of their skills. Technology's role is to support the people who use it, not the other way around.

However, be sure to evaluate the existing computer system's infrastructure in place in your organization and look for ways to build on it. The most cost-effective systems are those that deliver valuable new capabilities to an organization, quickly and with a minimum of effort. Select the simplest combinations of technology and business processes that meet the specified performance criteria. Balance the need for simplicity with the ability to increase the capacity of the system to handle greater volumes of data and to add new functionality as the business operations grow in volume. Keep the focus on building a supply chain infrastructure that is flexible enough to adapt to the needs of the markets the company serves as they change. Do not design a system that locks the company into one way of operating and that is not capable of evolving to support new operations.

The conceptual design diagrams are invaluable in communicating the features of the different designs clearly and simply to a wide audience of people. Reviews and comments should be sought from people who will use the new system, people who will pay for it, and people who will build it. Thoughtful input from a variety of sources is very helpful in selecting the best design, and adjusting it based on the feedback to increase the likelihood that it will succeed.

An Example of a Conceptual Design

Network Services Company selected a conceptual design for its e-business systems infrastructure to allow the company to meet its performance targets. This design was one of several presented to an audience that ranged from the board of directors to senior management, to the people who would build the systems infrastructure, and to the people who would use the systems. Feedback from each group contributed to the final design, shown here as Figure 8-4.

In this schematic, four main components work together to provide a flexible and cost-effective infrastructure that can change as business conditions evolve and can handle greater volumes of data as business operations grow. The four main components are as follows:

- **The extranet.** A high-speed, Internet-based network to provide all member companies with a secure environment in which to exchange information and work together to serve national accounts.
- **Web-based eCommerce systems.** A suite of systems accessed via the Network Services Web site. A packaged system from an application service provider (ASP) is used to provide order entry, inventory, and order status. Network Services provides the sales history reporting system. This suite of

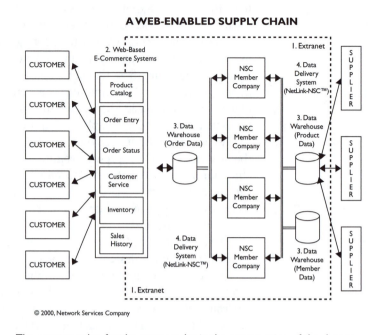

A WEB-ENABLED SUPPLY CHAIN

© 2000, Network Services Company

The greatest value for the company lay in the construction of the data ware-house to house the databases and in building the data delivery system called "NetLink-NSC.™" Those components working together would best meet the performance criteria defined by the company. In order to meet the financial performance criteria and reduce project risk, Network Services decided to lease the use of an existing Web-based product catalog and order entry system instead of building its own.

Figure 8-4. A sample conceptual design.

eCommerce systems is also available to member companies to serve their local customers.

- **NSC data warehouse.** A collection of databases to support the Web-based eCommerce operations and internal NSC operations, such as proposal development, price file maintenance, account book creation, and sales reporting.

- **Data delivery system (NetLink-NSC™).** A two-way, Internet-based data transfer system to allow each member company's internal systems to read and write data in a common format to support delivery of seamless and consistent national account service. This component incorporated and reused software from an earlier system that provided for receipt and error checking of invoice data from member companies.

COMBINING SYSTEM DESIGN AND STRATEGY

Designing supply chain systems, or any other kind of in-store system, can quickly become a very complex undertaking. The business manager can feel overwhelmed by the choices and be tempted to leave this activity to the technical experts. Our advice is this: Do not give in to this temptation! Retail managers need to remain actively involved with the technical people in creating the conceptual design for the system—it's the only way to truly ensure that the system aligns with the strategy that the company requires to accomplish its goal. The retail manager's input is needed to think through the steps required for the process; the technical staff then should be able to provide the technical expertise to design and build it. Together, the initial high-level design may be sketched out and fine-tuned.

In fact, it is wise for retailers and their IT staff to generate a number of possible conceptual designs. Some will eventually "fly," and others will be discarded. There are some simple, reliable guidelines for determining the quality of a new system design. A design that respects *all seven* of these guidelines is the best. It may still be a workable design if one or two of these guidelines are violated (as long as it is not # 1). But if guidelines are violated, there must be very good reasons for doing so, and specific compensations must be made to cover those violations.

If three or more guidelines are broken, then the conceptual design is seriously flawed and it is very unlikely that the design can be successfully built. The seven system design guidelines are as follows:

1. Closely align system designs with the business goals and performance targets they are intended to accomplish. For any systems development project to be a success, it must directly support the organization to achieve one or more of its goals. No new system can be effective until a business opportunity is clear that makes the system worth building. And no new system will bring a sustained benefit to a company unless it supports the efficient exploitation of the business opportunity it was built to address.

2. Use systems to change the competitive landscape. Here's that key question again: "What seems impossible to do today, but if it could be done, would make positive, fundamental changes in what the company does?" Put yourself in your customers' shoes or, as Nordstrom puts it, decide what would "surprise and delight" the customers. Look for opportunities to create a transformation or value shift in the market. Find ways to do things that provide dramatic cost savings or productivity increases. Then place yourself in a competitor's shoes and think of what course you could take that would be the least likely to be foreseen, quickly countered, or copied. In retail, as long as you are able to do something of value that your competitors cannot, you have an advantage. If you are going to take

bigger risks and incur larger costs to develop a system, make sure it is a system that will change the competitive landscape. In reality, it's the only kind of system that can deliver benefits to justify the greater risks and costs.

3. Leverage the strengths of the existing system's infrastructure. When existing systems have proven over time to be stable and responsive, find ways to incorporate them into the design of new systems. Part of good strategy is using the means available to the organization to best accomplish its goals, and the design of a system is the embodiment of the strategy being used. Think of it as a type of evolution, building new systems on the strengths of older systems. New systems provide value only insofar as they provide new business capabilities. Time spent replacing old systems with new systems that do essentially the same things will not, as a general rule, provide enough value to justify the cost.

4. Use the simplest possible combination of technology and business procedures to achieve the maximum number of performance targets. From a practical standpoint, this increases the probability that at least some performance targets can actually be achieved. Simple combinations of technology and business process reduce the complexity and the risk associated with the systems. If you use the same technology to achieve several different objectives, it is also much easier to shift people from one objective to another as needed because the skill sets used are the same. There is no need for a completely separate system to meet each performance goal.

5. Break the system design into separate components or objectives, and as much as possible, run the work on individual objectives in parallel. Try not to make the achievement of one objective dependent on the prior achievement of another objective, to avoid bottlenecks and slowdowns in the development process. Use people on the project who have the skills to achieve a variety of different objectives. Your project plan should foresee and provide for an alternative plan in case of failure or delays in achieving objectives as scheduled. The design should be flexible enough to delete some system features if needed and still be able to deliver solid value to the business.

6. Do not try to build a system whose complexity exceeds the organization's capabilities. When defining business goals and the systems to reach those goals, aim for things that are within your reach. Set challenging goals— not hopeless goals. Don't exhaust the confidence of your team as they strive to meet a goal that is, in fact, unrealistic.

7. Do not renew a project using the same people or the same system design if it has already failed once. Redoubling effort is not reason enough to take another run at it. The new approach must clearly reflect what was learned from the previous failure and offer a better way to achieve the business goal and performance targets.

Define the Project Objectives

You may have observed that defining the high-level components in a conceptual design is a somewhat subjective process, because there are many possible ways to design a system—some better than others. What makes for an outstanding design is to define high-level components that are highly cohesive in the functions they perform. This means each component performs a set of tasks that are all closely related to a single, well-defined activity.

For instance, a highly cohesive component in a conceptual design could be an order entry system. It does all the things that are required for a customer to enter an order. And that's all it does—nothing more. A component that is *not* cohesive would, for example, do order entry and also manage a database of sales information and route orders to different business locations. Showing all those activities as one component in a schematic design does not provide enough *definition of the design* to enable people to evaluate it effectively. In fact, it could be confusing. In this case, it should be broken down into three separate components—one for order entry, one for database management, and one for data transmission.

The building of each high-level component means defining a set of specific, measurable activities or objectives that must be achieved in order to create a system. There are generally somewhere between three and nine high-level components, and all other components will resolve into subcomponents of these high-level components. Why only three to nine high-level components? Because most of us are just regular folks and it would be difficult to remember or follow more than seven (plus or minus two) things at a time. A clear, simple system design goes a long way toward ensuring the success of the project because the people involved with it can understand it.

Without a clear conceptual design, the people involved with building, using, and paying for the system will all have different ideas about what the company is trying to accomplish. People working on the different parts of the system will find it increasingly difficult to coordinate their actions. The levels of tension and misunderstanding may increase as the work continues.

The development of each component in the system design becomes an objective in the project to build the system. Similar to the way that a long-term strategy is broken down into self-sufficient phases that each provide value in their own right, the building of a new system should be broken down into a set of objectives that each provide value in their own right. An objective should not be just an intermediate step along the way that depends on the completion of some future step to be of value. Each objective should each be achievable within a timeline of three to nine months—or less, in some cases. The more quickly an objective can be achieved, the faster it will begin providing value (and repaying the cost of the project) before it is even entirely finished.

Also be careful not to define objectives that lock the project into some rigid sequence of development activities. The world rarely goes according to plan, so the plan must be flexible in order to adapt as reality unfolds. Begin work on as many objectives as possible simultaneously. As much as possible, make the tasks needed to achieve each objective independent of the tasks needed to achieve the other objectives. The reason for this is maximum flexibility—if one objective is delayed, it will not also delay the completion of others. Resources can then be shifted from one objective to another as needed to respond to situations that arise.

INITIAL PROJECT PLANS AND BUDGETS

It is always a challenge to create a project plan early in the game, when there are so many things that are not entirely known. There will be much agonizing and grumbling about the plan, so be prepared for it. People will gripe that they are being asked to commit to something they know very little about, or they worry that whatever they say will come back to haunt them. In an attempt to give themselves as much "wiggle room" as possible, some will create plans that are so high level and vague they are little more than smoke screens. Others will plunge into the task with determination and produce a plan showing minute detail—about things that can hardly be defined yet! These plans amount to wishful thinking about a future that will probably be nothing like what is shown.

How can these natural tendencies be avoided? Let's start with a definition. Simply stated, a plan is a sequence of nonrepetitive tasks that lead to the achievement of one or more predefined objectives that do not yet exist. A plan should not be confused with an operating schedule, which is a repetitive sequence of tasks that perpetuate an already existing state of affairs. This means that the plan should focus on laying out the tasks that need to be performed to achieve each objective that was identified in the conceptual system design. Do not clutter the project plan with repetitive tasks related to ongoing administrative or business operations.

Create a section of the overall project plan for each objective, listing the major tasks needed to achieve that objective. There will be tasks related to designing, and then building, the deliverables necessary for each objective. Show the dependencies between the tasks related to an objective, and show the dependencies between the objectives.

When estimating how long each task will take, remember the old saying that "any job will expand to fill the time available." Use a technique called **time boxing** to define the time limits for each task, a type of trade-off between the work involved in carrying out a task and the time that is available. Realistic and adequate time periods must be assigned to each task, and then it is up to the people doing the work to tailor the job to fit the time that is allocated. When setting these time boxes, get input from the people who will be asked to do the work. In a good plan, the time boxes for each task are aggressive. They require people to work hard and stay focused, but they should not be so aggressive as to make them feel they have no chance of getting the work done.

A useful way to think about the work on a project is to divide time spent on it into three main steps and assign an overall time box to each of the main steps. Then, within each step, subdivide the time available to accommodate the tasks involved. The three steps and their durations are as follows:

1. Define what will be done—the goal and the objectives. (2 to 6 weeks)
2. Design how it will be done—the detailed specifications. (1 to 3 months)
3. Build what is specified. (2 to 6 months)

For each objective, set a time box for the design step and the build step. Don't worry about the define step—that's what you are doing right now, and showing it on the plan is not necessary. Look at the tasks required to achieve each objective. For example, let's say that Objective A has a one-month time box for design and a two-month time box for build. Decide which tasks fall into the design step and which tasks are in the build step. Allocate the time available in design among the tasks involved, and do the same for the tasks in the build step. You have now subdivided the larger design and build time boxes for Objective A into smaller time boxes for the tasks that are involved.

Figure 8-5 is a sample based on the Network Services' project plan.

Assigning time boxes is an iterative process. It involves adjusting both the time allocations and the scope of the work to be done. It will probably take several passes through the plan before you have something that seems reasonable—that is, aggressive and yet still doable.

Estimate the Budget and ROI

At this point, the team must answer one of the most fundamental questions about the project: "Is this worth doing?" At first glance, you'd assume it was worth doing or you wouldn't have gotten this far . . . right? However, only after the design and plan have been constructed can the budget be created. And only the budget can estimate the true "worth," financially speaking, of what seems to be a pretty good idea.

Project plans and budgets are just two sides of the same coin. Plans show the time, people, and materials needed to get things done. Budgets show the cost of the people and materials over the time frames involved. In many cases, the cost and benefits related to a project cannot be defined with absolute certainty, but it is still valuable to get as accurate an estimate as possible.

The value of budgeting comes in two areas. The first is an opportunity to create a consensus among the people who have to pay for the system. Everyone whose budget will be affected by the project should have an opportunity to review the costs and benefits of the project. It is often hard to assign specific monetary values to the benefits, but it must be done. When in doubt, understate the

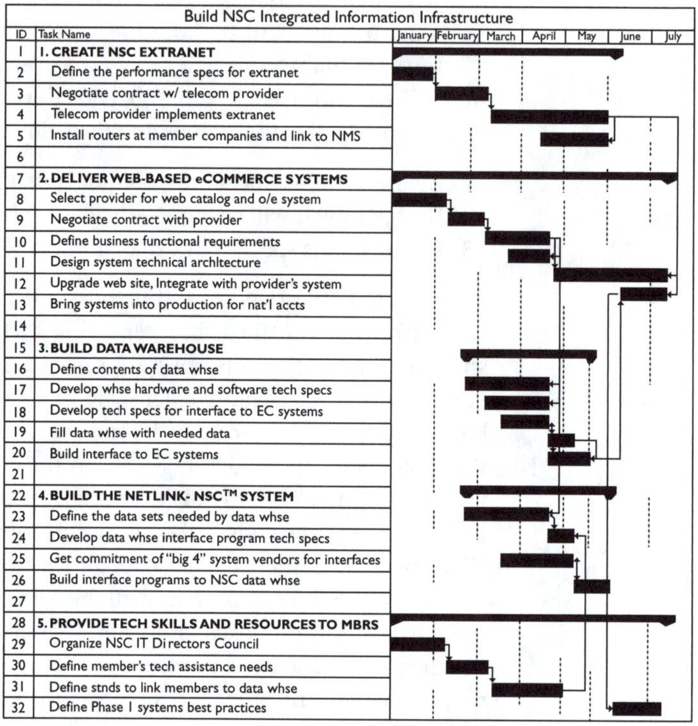
Build NSC Integrated Information Infrastructure
ID Task Name
January February March April May June July
1 1. CREATE NSC EXTRANET
2 Define the performance specs for extranet
3 Negotiate contract w/ telecom provider
4 Telecom provider implements extranet
5 Install routers at member companies and link to NMS
6
7 2. DELIVER WEB-BASED eCOMMERCE SYSTEMS
8 Select provider for web catalog and o/e system
9 Negotiate contract with provider
10 Define business functional requirements
11 Design system technical architecture
12 Upgrade web site, Integrate with provider's system
13 Bring systems into production for nat'l accts
14
15 3. BUILD DATA WAREHOUSE
16 Define contents of data whse
17 Develop whse hardware and software tech specs
18 Develop tech specs for interface to EC systems
19 Fill data whse with needed data
20 Build interface to EC systems
21
22 4. BUILD THE NETLINK- NSC™ SYSTEM
23 Define the data sets needed by data whse
24 Develop data whse interface program tech specs
25 Get commitment of "big 4" system vendors for interfaces
26 Build interface programs to NSC data whse
27
28 5. PROVIDE TECH SKILLS AND RESOURCES TO MBRS
29 Organize NSC IT Directors Council
30 Define member's tech assistance needs
31 Define stnds to link members to data whse
32 Define Phase 1 systems best practices

The Network Services Co. e-business project objectives were defined by the conceptual system design. The conceptual design had four components:

1. The Extranet
2. Web-Based eCommerce Systems
3. The Data Warehouse
4. The NetLink-NSC™ Data Delivery System

Thus, the creation of each of these four components became a project objective. There was also a fifth objective to address the strategy of providing technical skills and resources to member companies. This initial project plan laid out the time boxes for the effort needed to achieve each objective. These time boxes defined the amount of time available for each activity. Work was then tailored to fit the times available.

Figure 8-5. How to create an initial project plan.

benefits—just make sure that the benefit numbers are ones that people can understand and support. The sum of these benefit numbers is the value of the project, and it is very important to have agreement on the value of a project.

The value of the project is the main reference point to keep in mind when evaluating the rest of the project. The value of the system is what tells you how

SUPPLY CHAIN SKILLS—REALISTIC COST-BENEFIT ANALYSIS

Analysis of any project's costs and benefits calls for a company's financial executives to exercise judgment based on experience and industry norms. Network Services' CFO Bob Mitchum shared his thoughts about the costs and benefits of his company's e-business system design, seen in Figure 8-4: "First of all, I use a 12- to 18-month time frame for the analysis and I need to see an attractive payback in that time. If you accept a three- to five-year payback period, you are probably using the analysis to justify what is really an emotional decision. Beyond 18 months, the world changes in ways you cannot predict and I don't think you can effectively estimate numbers that far out."

Mitchum says costs are usually easier to estimate than benefits, but a realistic estimate of benefits is very important nonetheless. "Look at the tangible benefits and try to assign some numbers over a period of time. Then look at other intangible benefits, such as reputation and relationships with customers and suppliers. Look at employee productivity and leveraging their talents. Who are the stakeholders? What are the alternatives to doing the project and getting the same benefits?

"When I looked at the design and the cost benefit analysis for the e-business systems infrastructure for Network Services, I saw a couple of things. We knew that not many national accounts were going to use our order entry system to key in orders—they have their own systems. But unless we could check off a box on a checklist that said, yes, we have a Web-based ordering system, we wouldn't make it past the first cut in their screening process. So in the system design, we proposed to use an application service provider to deliver that feature on a pay-as-you-go basis.

"The real benefits came from electronic communications between us and the members, and that was where the bulk of the proposed budget was going to be spent. These communication links would make us stronger as a core group. The investment would strengthen the organization. The conceptual design met our basic needs and provided the most cost-efficient way to do so. The price tag was much lower than the price of the other options that were presented."

much can be spent to build the system. If the costs to develop a system add up to more than the benefits that will be produced, there are two choices: Find a less expensive way to produce these benefits or don't move forward with the project. Businesses exist to make a profit, and that is a discipline that all businesspeople must live with.

Defining Specific Costs and Benefits

From a financial perspective, a system generates a stream of costs and benefits over the length of time in which it is built and used. As a rule, a system should

---

ITEM PRICING SYSTEM—TOTAL ESTIMATED COSTS AND BENEFITS

Project Description

Build system to assist staff of account development group to more quickly create contract proposals and explore impact of different product cost and pricing structures. Monitor status of existing contracts and provide notice before cost supports expire.

Project Cost and Benefits (Dollars in Thousands)

	Qtr 1	Qtr 2	Qtr 3	Qtr 4	Qtr 5	Totals
Hardware and Software	(7.0)					(7.0)
Development Costs	(68.5)					(68.5)
Operating Costs	0.0	(1.2)	(1.2)	(1.2)	(1.2)	(4.8)
Total Costs	(75.5)	(1.2)	(1.2)	(1.2)	(1.2)	(80.3)
Direct Benefits	0.0	8.4	8.4	8.4	8.4	33.6
Incremental Benefits	0.0	30.0	30.0	30.0	30.0	120.0
Cost Avoidance Benefits	0.0	18.2	18.2	18.2	18.2	72.8
Total Benefits	0.0	56.6	56.6	56.6	56.6	226.4
Net Benefits	($75.5)	$55.4	$55.4	$55.4	$55.4	$146.1
Cumulative Benefits	($75.5)	($20.1)	$35.3	$90.7	$146.1	
Discount Rate	5%	(5% per Qtr. = 20% Annual Discount Rate)				
Net Present Value	60.6					

Figure 8-6. Sample cost-benefit analysis.

pay for itself and return an appropriate profit within one to three years. Generally after that, the system will require major enhancements, from routine upgrades to complete redesign. Specific benefits, and their dollar values, must be identified.

Measure system costs and benefits on a quarterly basis. Subtract costs from benefits to arrive at the quarterly cash flow generated by the system. Calculate the value of that cash flow using whatever method the financial decision makers in the company would like (net present value, internal rate of return, etc.). The higher the risk involved in building and operating the system, the higher the profit that it should generate.

Detailed Schedule of Costs

Cost of Hardware and Software (Dollars in Thousands)

Item	Description	Cost
Application Server	Server to run the system—allocate 1/3 of server cost	3.0
Personal Computers	PCs for use by staff—allocate 1/3 of cost	3.0
Visual Basic language	Allocated cost of VB programming language and tools	0.5
SQL Server database	Allocated cost of SQL Server and tools	0.5
Total		**$7.0**

Cost of Development (Dollars in Thousands)

Task	Description	Cost
Define Phase	5 days at average cost of $900 per day	4.5
Design Phase	15 days at average cost of $900 per day	13.5
Build Phase—Coding	30 days at average cost of $900 per day	27.0
Build Phase—Test and Train	30 days at average cost of $650 per day	19.5
Build Phase—Roll Out	5 days at average cost of $800 per day	4.0
Total		**$68.5**

Cost of Operation (Dollars in Thousands)

Activity	Description	Cost
Qtr 1		
Qtr 2	Incremental costs of operating the system	1.2
Qtr 3	Incremental costs of operating the system	1.2
Qtr 4	Incremental costs of operating the system	1.2
Qtr 5	Incremental costs of operating the system	1.2
Total		**$4.8**

Figure 8-6. Continued

Detailed Schedule of Benefits

DIRECT BENEFITS (revenue and cost savings due to productivity improvements)

Direct Benefit 1   Save staff time on proposal creation; 10 proposals per Qtr.; 20 Hrs. per proposal; $35/Hr.

Direct Benefit 2   Do 2 additional proposals per Qtr.; 20 Hrs./proposal; $35/Hr.

Value of Productivity Improvement (Dollars in Thousands)

	Qtr 1	Qtr 2	Qtr 3	Qtr 4	Qtr 5
Save time on proposals		7.0	7.0	7.0	7.0
Do 2 additional proposals		1.4	1.4	1.4	1.4
Total Direct Benefit	$0.0	$8.4	$8.4	$8.4	$8.4

INCREMENTAL BENEFITS (benefits due in part to new system, e.g., attract new customers, make better decisions, etc.)

Incremental Benefit 1   Win more proposals due to better pricing decisions; $30,000 per Qtr. in additional profits

Incremental Benefit 2   —

Value of Incremental Benefits (Dollars in Thousands)

	Qtr 1	Qtr 2	Qtr 3	Qtr 4	Qtr 5
Win more proposals		30.0	30.0	30.0	30.0
Incremental Benefit 2	—	—	—	—	
Total Incr Benefit	$0.0	$30.0	$30.0	$30.0	$30.0

Figure 8-6. Continued

System Costs

In a system development project, there are three types of costs:

1. Hardware and software costs for the technical and communications network components to be purchased from vendors for the new system design.
2. Development costs as estimated by the time and cost needed to achieve each project objective. Each task that is part of the work plan for an objective will

COST AVOIDANCE BENEFITS (savings related to growing business without needing to add new staff or incurring other expenses)

Cost Avoidance 1   Avoid hiring more staff as business grows; half a person per year; $35/Hr.

Cost Avoidance 2   —

Value of Cost Avoidance (Dollars in Thousands)

	Qtr 1	Qtr 2	Qtr 3	Qtr 4	Qtr 5
Avoid hiring more staff		18.2	18.2	18.2	18.2
Cost Avoidance 2		—	—	—	—
Total CA Benefit	$0.0	$18.2	$18.2	$18.2	$18.2

INTANGIBLE BENEFITS (benefits that are hard to quantify in dollar amounts but that should be identified and listed)

Maintain Competitive Advantages

- Item Pricing system should be a competitive benefit for next 2 yrs.
- After that, it will simply become a necessary tool to do business

Provide Superior Service Levels

- Provide customers and prospects with timely and accurate proposals

Increase Job Satisfaction

- Release staff from tedious and time-consuming pricing calculations
- Allow staff to focus on more valuable and interesting work

Figure 8-6. Continued

require some number of people with certain skills for some period of time. Each task will also require certain technology and perhaps other expenses, such as travel for some employees. Set a standard cost for each type of labor involved, and estimate the related expenses for each type of labor, for each step in the system development process: the "define" step, the "design" step, and the "build" step.

3. Operating costs have a number of components. Estimate labor expenses for the types of jobs to be filled for the ongoing operation and support of the new system. Estimate the line charges and usage fees for the communications network and technical architecture used by the system. Obtain yearly licensing and technical support costs from vendors of the hardware and software components used by the new system.

System Benefits

There are four types of benefits provided by a new system:

1. *Direct benefits* are productivity increases and cost savings due to the capacity increases brought about by a new system. Define the new functions the system provides that the company does not now have. Estimate the productivity increases and labor savings that these new features provide.
2. *Incremental benefits* are monetary benefits that may not be solely a result of the new system but are measurable and due in some significant degree to

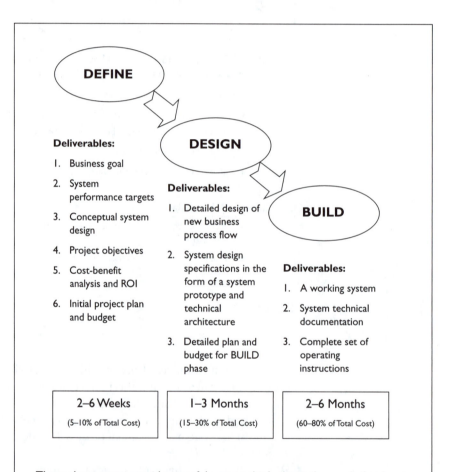

Figure 8-7. System development sequence.

the capabilities of the new system. This may be an increased ability to attract and retain new customers and the extra revenue that generates. It may be the new system's ability to help the company avoid bad decisions, or to manage and plan for certain business expenses and the reduced costs that result.

3. *Cost avoidance benefits* are savings related to the increased capacity provided by the new system and the company's ability to grow the business without having to hire new staff, or hiring fewer new people than would otherwise be the case.

4. *Intangible benefits* are hard to quantify monetarily but should be identified and listed nonetheless. These benefits include such things as a competitive advantage through better intelligence and adaptability, superior service levels that solidify customer relationships, and leveraging the abilities of talented employees and increasing their job satisfaction.

On paper or on a spreadsheet, a cost-benefit analysis can be intimidating until you understand the reasons for the figures—assigning a monetary value to each and every step of the process to create a new system. Take a look at the sample analysis in this chapter (Figure 8-7), and follow it through based on the steps we've discussed. In the real world, the senior business executive or management group responsible for accomplishing the business goal that the system will address must confirm that the cost-benefit analysis is valid.

CHAPTER SUMMARY

Companies should always be looking for ways to improve how they do things, but making good ideas into goals, and then successfully executing plans to get there, requires a great deal of thought. This chapter introduces a step-by-step process to create opportunities for improvement, and it will work within a company or across a supply chain. The process includes five deliverables:

1. A clear statement of the business goal to be accomplished.

2. The performance criteria required from the system. These criteria fall into four measurement categories: internal efficiency, customer service, demand flexibility, and product development. These are the conditions of success that the system must meet.

3. A conceptual design for a system to accomplish the business goal and meet the performance criteria. The system design is composed of people, process, and technology. The conceptual design is the embodiment of the strategy being used to attain the goal.

4. A definition of the project objectives needed to build the system. The objectives are the things that must be built to create the system outlined in the conceptual design.

5. A cost-benefit analysis that verifies the project is worth carrying out.

In formulating supply chain improvement projects, it is a far better approach to successfully carry out a sequence of small steps than to attempt to make a great leap forward and risk falling short. In an approach that involves taking a sequence of smaller steps, the stakes at each step are modest and the work is more manageable so success is easier to achieve. In the approach of taking a great leap forward, the stakes are high—the work is enormous, success is harder to achieve, and the cost of failure is high.

DISCUSSION QUESTIONS

1. Using the list of possible retail opportunities at the beginning of this chapter, brainstorm one of your own. What is not being done, or could be done better, in a store with which you are familiar? How would your idea improve it?

2. From the information in this chapter, do computer software and Internet access always have to be part of a system? Why or why not?

3. Since the system development process focuses more on an individual company, how would you modify or adapt it for use among several companies in a supply chain? How should the various responsibilities be divided up among several teams working together?

4. Why do the authors say the risk of failure is greater by not following this system? What about a team that has a "good hunch" and feels they must act on it quickly in order to take advantage of market conditions? Would it be okay *not* to follow the development process, or to skip a step?

5. Which of the four types of benefits of system development do you think is the most important to a retail business? Explain your choice.

ENDNOTE

1. Jordan K. Speer, "Supply Chain Links," *Retail Merchandiser*, a publication of Schofield Media Ltd., Chicago, Illinois, May 2004.

THE
INCREDIBLE
JOURNEY

CONTINUES

SEPTEMBER 29—TAKING ORDERS

McGee's order and those of the 4,054 store managers are transmitted to CVS's E3 system for replenishment and the warehouse management system for fulfillment. (As mentioned earlier, E3 collects and analyzes data from Category Map, the warehouse management system and from the stores to gain a comprehensive view of what CVS needs to order and when.) The warehouse management system creates an optimized schedule for picking, packing, and shipping orders to the individual stores.

Why CVS managers check inventory levels instead of relying on POS data

Why do CVS store managers check inventory levels before ordering when the cash registers collect POS data that could be used for automatic replenishment? The plan is that someday they won't have to. Certainly, many other companies already have automatic replenishment systems in place. But in 1998 CVS was in no hurry to implement a system that could diminish customer service and quality levels without first addressing the political and logistical issues that go along with it, says Senior Vice President for MIS and CIO Howard Edels. "A lot of companies say they have such a system . . . but when you're talking about something where the computer takes over the responsibility of individuals, you want to make sure everyone buys into that program. CVS is known for its excellent customer service because the store managers are empowered. If they make a mistake [by forgetting to place an order, for example], it's their mistake; they treat you nicely and say, 'I'm sorry, I'll take care of it.' But if they see the computer as having control, the answer becomes, 'I don't know why your order isn't here, the stupid computer didn't bring it.' It changes the whole relationship with customers. So we want to make sure that the store folks really understand that it's helping them. That's why we've been slower than some companies."

This careful, conscientious management style is a hallmark of the "CIO-100" winners, says Andersen Consulting's Gregory J. Owens.

DEVELOPING
SUPPLY CHAIN
SYSTEMS

Much of the future success of retailers depends on their (and their supply chains') ability to adapt to technological advances. Apparently, they are catching on. The demand for information technology (IT) staff members in the retail industry grew 25 percent in the first six months of 2004, with no letup in sight.

As Jon Butterfield, managing director of IT Business for Spring (a British-based recruitment consulting company), told *Computer Weekly* magazine: "There is good job security in the retail sector, with an exciting range of technologies to manage."[1]

How often do you hear *that* about *any* type of employment nowadays? Luckily, you don't have to be in an IT position with a major global retailer to be part of the excitement—you could lead, or be a member of, a project team that implements a new system.

Chapter 8 introduced a three-step process to create new systems to improve either a business or a supply chain of businesses using computer technology. The three steps are define, design, and build. The first step (define) was also discussed in Chapter 8; this chapter presents the last two steps in the process, which include the following tasks:

- Organize a systems development project for a new supply chain computer system.
- Investigate supply chain processes and document the findings.
- Produce detailed specifications for a conceptual system design.
- Test the design and/or other vendors' applications.
- Create accurate project plans and budgets based on the detailed system specifications.
- Evaluate progress on projects and recognize problems as they emerge.

The basic structure of this planning process, especially the portion introduced in Chapter 8, can be adapted for many different kinds of projects. But this chapter deals with designing and/or upgrading a store's computer systems. Often, to do what a store needs done or to work with its partners in a supply chain, an existing computer system must be enhanced or a new system needs to be built. This chapter presents a process to follow to create more detailed system designs, and to build those systems if necessary.

By "build," we don't mean you *have* to program your own computers from scratch! A business will frequently employ the help of consultants and software vendors to do this work. However, no company can delegate the work entirely to outsiders and expect that its best interests will be served. The retail project team must be able to show the programmers or software developers, step by step, exactly what they need the system to do, and when, and why. Or, if the store is considering purchasing a packaged software application—sometimes at the insistence of another supply chain member—this basic background knowledge will help the store's management team decide if the system features and price tag are really worth it. This is why it is important even for non-IT professionals to understand how systems development works.

ORGANIZING A SYSTEMS DEVELOPMENT PROJECT

A simple three-step process may be used to organize the project. For each step, a certain amount of time and a budget must be allocated. This provides a framework of regular deadlines, through which each step is completed within the boundaries of its time and budget limits.

Before we introduce the three-step process, there is a short list of six principles that should be used to run a project. Just as there are guidelines for conceptual design, which were listed in Chapter 8, if these six principles are consistently applied, the probability of success for the project is high. However, if any one of these principles is ignored, then special precautions must be taken to compensate for it; and if two or more principles are violated, then the project is almost sure to fail.

SUPPLY CHAIN SKILLS—SIX PRINCIPLES OF PROJECT MANAGEMENT

- Every project needs a full-time leader with overall responsibility and authority.

- Define a set of measurable and nonoverlapping objectives that are necessary and sufficient to accomplish the project goal or mission.

- Assign project objectives to teams of two to seven people with hands-on team leaders and the appropriate mix of business and technical skills.

- Tell the teams *what* to do but not *how* to do it.

- Break project work into tasks that are each a week or less in duration, and produce something of value to the business every 30 to 90 days.

- Provide project office staff to work with the project leader and team leaders to update plans and budgets.

1. **Every project needs a full-time project leader with overall responsibility and the appropriate authority.** There must be an individual who is responsible for the project's success and totally focused on getting the job done. This person must also have the authority to make decisions and delegate responsibilities. It is wise to have a steering committee or management oversight group in place to whom the project leader reports, but a committee cannot generally make decisions in a timely manner. If there is no one person in this role, then the project progress and cost will reflect it. Progress will be slower, and costs will be higher.

2. **A set of measurable and nonoverlapping objectives must be defined that are necessary and sufficient to accomplish the project goal or mission.** It is crucial that clear project objectives be defined so that the people who are assigned responsibility to achieve the objectives know exactly what is expected of them. We mention "nonoverlapping" because overlapping objectives cause confusion and conflict between the teams assigned to work on them. Who does what? Who's usurping whose authority? Whose job is this, anyway? Minimize these conflicts by being specific about the objectives.

   Along the same lines, make sure that each objective is absolutely necessary to the accomplishment of the project goal. Do not pursue an objective just because it seems like a good idea. And the list of objectives must "add up" to a final result—that is, if each objective is achieved, then the mission or goal has been accomplished. The objectives must cover *everything* that needs to happen.

3. **Assign project objectives to teams of two to seven people with the appropriate mix of business and technical skills, and assign hands-on team leaders.** If you're in a position to select the project team members, choose the people who, in your judgment, have among them the necessary business and technical skills and the experience to address the issues that will arise in the work that is being delegated to them. A team is a group of people with complementary skills who organize themselves so that all members can contribute their strengths and not be penalized for their weaknesses.

   Each member of the team concentrates on the aspects of designing and building the system that they are good at and/or most interested in. For the most part, no one is required to do things they are not interested in or not good at. Within a team, the operative word is "we," not "me." The whole team is rewarded for successes and takes responsibility for mistakes. Singling out superstars or scapegoats undermines team morale and performance.

4. **Tell the teams *what* to do—but not *how* to do it.** Point a project team in the right direction by giving it a well-defined project goal and clearly identifying the project objectives the team is responsible for. If the project goal is "the game," and the objectives are "what the team must do to be successful in the game," then the team itself must make "the game plan" for meeting the objectives.

   The famous U.S. military general George Patton said, "Tell people what you want but don't tell them how to do it—you will be surprised by their resourcefulness in accomplishing their tasks." The teams can make changes or additions to the objectives they are given, as long as the project leader agrees that the modified objectives are still necessary and sufficient to accomplish the project goal.

5. **Break project work into tasks that are each a week or less in duration and that produce something of value to the business every 30 to 90 days.** This kind of schedule allows the project team to keep an eye on the prize. Each task must have a well-defined deliverable and can be tracked: in progress, delayed, or completed. Do not fall into the trap of tracking tasks by a percentage of completion, because it is often unclear what "percent complete" really means. What matters is whether the task deliverable has been produced—and if not, when it will be produced. The project leader must be able to track progress at this level of detail in order to understand what's really going on week to week, and to keep accurate projections of the time and cost to complete each of the project's objectives.

Multiweek tasks make progress hard to measure, and they are the ones that inevitably cause cost overruns and confusion, which compounds when they are reported by "percent complete." They seem to be making good progress—and then in the last week, they suddenly turn out to be nowhere near completion and the team members ask for several more weeks to complete them. To avoid this problem, break big tasks into a set of subtasks, each of which require a week or less to complete.

These tasks should combine to produce *something that is of value to the business* every 30 to 90 days. This provides the opportunity for the business to verify that the project is on the right track. It also provides deliverables that the business can perhaps begin to use even before the entire project is complete. In this way, the company may start to recoup the cost of the project.

6. **Every project needs an office staff, dedicated to this particular project, to work with the project leader and team leaders to update plans and budgets.** The project plan and budget are analogous to the profit and loss statements of a business. They must be updated continuously and accurately in order to provide the people running the project with the information they need to make good decisions. There is a common but misguided notion that the project leader and team leaders should be the ones who keep the plans updated, which is like saying the president of a company and its managers should spend their time keeping the company's books! The project leader and the team leaders are responsible for creating the initial plan and budget. After that, their time, attention, and energy are better spent making the plan a reality.

Just as there is an accounting department to keep a company's books, there should be administrative staff members assigned to each project to keep that project's plans and budgets. This staff reports to the project leader and works with the team leaders on a weekly basis to review and update the plans and budgets. In this way the project leader can accurately monitor project progress, and the team leaders are able to focus on running their teams—and not on filling out reports.

SUPPLY CHAIN SKILLS—TYPES OF SYSTEMS IN RETAIL

If you think your little corner of the retail world has hardly been touched by technology, think again! Here's just a partial list of the types of technology that store managers and employees may have to deal with daily. And, remember, each of them has its own hardware, software, and system requirements. Most involve the storage and sharing of data on demand.

Bar code readers	Handheld inventory terminals	Point-of-sale terminals (cash wraps, electronic cash registers)
Cash drawers	Internet ordering capabilities	Printers
Checkout lanes (self-service)	Kiosks (self-service)	Security systems
Credit card readers	Labeling and tagging systems	Touch screens
Data warehouses	Laptops	Uninterruptible power supplies (UPS)
Electronic article surveillance	Line (queue) management	Visual merchandising systems
Electronic scales	Local area networks	
E-mail systems	Pin pad devices	

DESIGNING A SUPPLY CHAIN SYSTEM

In Chapter 8, we went through the process of creating a conceptual system design—the high-level framework or skeleton of the project. Now it's time to put some meat on the bones, so to speak, by creating more detailed system specifications. In so doing, we will create a detailed project plan and budget, which are the last steps before actually building the system.

This is the point at which the people who will work on the project get to take a look at what senior management wants and figure out how they will do it. In a system used by multiple companies in a supply chain, cross-functional teams from different companies may divide up the work and share the results. This is also where adjustments and refinements are made to the project objectives, as the people who will build the system consider the realities of the job before them.

By the end of the design step, it is usually possible to predict the success or failure of any project. If the people on the project finish this phase with a clear set of system design specifications and confidence in their ability to build a system to these specifications, then the project will succeed. If the opposite occurs—the design specifications are vague, incomplete, or hard to understand and if people are ambivalent about their chances for success or uncertain about the accuracy of their cost estimates—then the project will likely fail.

The phase begins with the project leader reviewing the project goal, the conceptual system design, and the objectives with the project work group. The work group is composed of business and technical people who have the necessary mix of business and technical skills and experience needed to do the detailed system design. It is important for the people to understand senior management's intentions and the project's goal. Specific issues relating to the project objectives and budget can be investigated during this phase. This is the time when the work group should make adjustments, if necessary—before starting on the design details.

Once the people on the project work group understand the goal and the objectives, they (and their project leader) lay out a work plan for this phase, in which two major steps are accomplished:

1. Create detailed process flow diagrams for the new system.
2. Build and test the system prototype (i.e., the user interface and technical architecture).

The technique called **time boxing** introduced in Chapter 8 may be used to create a work schedule and stick to it, by breaking each activity into a set of tasks and assigning times to complete them. (Avoid the temptation here to spend extra time doing excessive amounts of analysis and checking and rechecking the results that come out of each activity.)

These two steps should take somewhere from one to three months to complete. For the most part, work on each of the two activities can proceed simultaneously. In some cases this phase could be finished in less than one month, but in no case should it drag on any longer than three months. If it does, this indicates a lack of clear focus or of effective organization (or both) on the project.

CREATING A SYSTEM PROTOTYPE

The project team should review the system performance criteria as described in the "define" phase. The criteria will be some mix of performance targets from the four categories, which should be familiar by now: customer service, internal efficiency, demand flexibility, and product development.

It's almost time to sketch process flows again, an activity known as **process mapping**. But before doing so, the project leader must brainstorm with the teams on ways to meet the criteria, encouraging a free flow of ideas. It is important to guide the group away from the common trap of premature criticism and dwelling on why things cannot be done and instead shift the focus to how things *might* be done. Generate as many ideas as possible, since these are the raw material to be blended together to create the designs for the new system process flows. Then, start mapping, much as we discussed in Chapter 8.

Once the process flows have been sketched out, the design sessions can begin to focus on how technology will be used to support this process. The design team must envision how people who use the system will interact with the technology supporting it. In this area, look for ways to automate the rote and repetitive work, and to empower the problem-solving and decision-making tasks. People (and those using computers are no exception) usually don't like to do the rote, repetitive work because it is boring; but they do like problem solving and decision making because it is creative and interactive.

Remember that people are the spark that animates a business process, not computers. Design systems that will be a rewarding experience for people—where they feel they are in control, not the computers. A good system—a retail Web site, for example—empowers people with access to information so that they can find things faster and make better decisions.

A **system prototype** is the model or sample system that the team believes will effectively support these new processes. The **process decomposition diagrams** (the fancy term for the maps or flowcharts) provide the processing logic and sequences to be used and indicate the kinds and volumes of data that the new system needs to handle.

There are two kinds of system prototypes: user interface prototypes and technical architecture prototypes. You might compare it to designing a building—you'd have to create two kinds of designs:

- The first is the floor plan and façade of the building to show what the building will look like.
- The second is the design of the structural, electrical, and plumbing components needed to support the specified floor plan and façade. This design shows how the building will be built.

In system design, the **user interface** can be thought of as the floor plan and façade. It shows what the system will look like and how a person would move through the system. The structural engineering for a building is called the **technical architecture** of a system—the hardware, operating system, and database software that will be used to support the user interface.

Both the user interface and the technical architecture designs are created in parallel. It is an iterative process that makes trade-offs among the user interface, the system functionality, and the underlying technical architecture. The aim is to find an overall design that provides a good balance between system functionality and ease of use, minimizing the complexity of the underlying technical architecture. The key is to find ways to use relatively simple technical architectures to creatively support a wide variety of user interfaces and system features.

Prototype the User Interface

Entire books have written about the design of user interfaces for computer systems. One of the most basic but important concepts is that the user interface should be "intuitively obvious." This means a person who already knows how to do the activity for which the system was designed should be able to figure out the basics of the new system within about 20 minutes of playing around with it, just trying things out. The better a system interface design, the less the amount of training is required to teach a person to use it.

The process flows become the model for the prototype of the user interface, as shown in the diagram. The process decomposition diagram (Figure 9-1) shows what activities are performed in what sequence and what data is needed to support these activities. The sequence that leads a person from one computer screen to another should be designed to map closely to the process flows and should allow the user to manipulate the data involved in the process.

Prototype the Technical Architecture

As the user interface design is progressing, a parallel design effort is under way to select and test the technical components that will be used to build the system. Decisions should be made on the computer hardware and software to be used. How will remote users be able to connect to the system? How secure

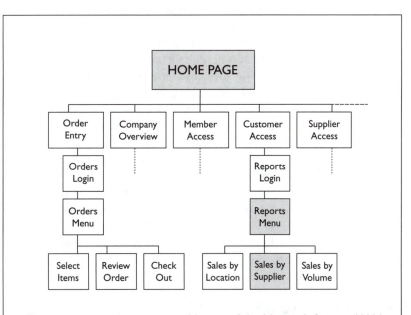

This screen map shows a partial layout of the Network Services' Web site. The shaded screens are shown in greater detail with screen layouts below

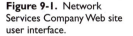

Figure 9-1. Network Services Company Web site user interface.

must the data be to satisfy the users? The database and other packages must be specified and a programming language chosen if there is custom coding to be done. All of these components must be assembled in a test environment and tried out to see if they work as advertised. Sometimes it's as simple as connecting the pieces and making sure they actually do work the way the vendors said they would.

If there's one thing you will notice in the IT end of retail, it is that everyone is trying to sell new technology to stores—systems that are faster, bigger, more convenient—and of course, *brand-new*, probably on sale, and so on. (You're retailers, so you know the buy-now-or-miss-out-forever sales pitch!) But until a technical component has been in use for at least two years, it is not wise to take any of the vendors' published performance statistics at face value. There's just not a wide enough base of experience with it to provide a well-balanced assessment, and it will be unclear just how the performance statistics were derived. There is no substitute for running various performance tests to generate benchmarking data. The technical design team cannot be shy about changing the component, or the technical architecture design itself, if certain components prove to be incapable of performing as desired.

The database package must be installed on the hardware and operating system platform on which it is intended to run. Any packaged application software that will be used must be installed. Then test data needs to be loaded into the database and performance trials conducted to test the operation of the whole architecture. Simple code should be written to pass data from one component to the next, to test out the data interfaces and the speed of LAN, WAN, and Internet connections. By the end of the prototyping activities, the technical architecture must be shown to perform up to the requirements of the new system that it will support. If a prototype cannot be created that performs well, then there is no sense in trying to build the real "production version" of the system using this same technical architecture.

If the decision is made to purchase a packaged software application developed by an outside vendor, it should be brought in and installed in a test environment. Realistic usage scenarios need to be scripted out, including loading the databases used by the package with a sampling of real data. Security concerns about who can and cannot obtain access to the data should be addressed. People who will both use and support the package need to evaluate it by working through the usage scenarios.

FINAL PLANNING AND BUDGETING

Toward the end of the design phase, as the detailed design specifications are produced, everyone involved will have a clear idea of the work they need to do and how long the tasks will take in the "build" phase. The project leader is now able to oversee the creation of a detailed project plan and budget for building the system.

Project teams are assigned responsibility for specific objectives, and the people on these teams can then lay out the sequence of tasks they will perform to achieve each objective assigned to them. Working with project office staff, each team lays out the plan for its work. Each task has time and resource requirements assigned to it so a cost for each task can be calculated. Respect the seven guidelines for running projects that were introduced in Chapter 8.

As the project teams are each creating their specific task plans to achieve the objectives assigned to them, the project leader is combining these plans into the overall project plan. It's smart to segment the "big" project plan by objective. Devote one section of the project plan to each objective. The project leader determines the necessary sequence for achieving the objectives and arranges them in this order on the plan. He or she looks for opportunities to run activities in parallel, which will allow the flexibility to, when one activity is finished, perhaps shift manpower or other resources over to help with another activity that was delayed.

Delays are inevitable on a project. A plan that does not account for them or provide the flexibility needed to effectively respond to them will almost surely have its timetable and budget thrown into unnecessary disarray and confusion.

When the project plans are in place, a detailed project budget can be derived, which is a fine-tuning of the cost/benefit analysis shown in Figure 8.6. If the project tasks have undergone a lot of change in the planning process, the budget should be adjusted accordingly. The bottom line on this budget document should be the final, accurate cost of the project.

The Decision to Proceed . . . or Not

One of the things that may be hardest for beginning management students to grasp is that, even after all the intensive designing, planning, and budgeting activities described in Chapters 8 and 9, the project team is still not absolutely certain the project will move forward. Theirs is still an exercise in patience. In most companies (and/or supply chains), the detailed system design and prototype, as well as the updated project plan and budget, are presented to a senior management steering committee or an executive sponsor of the project. If there are doubts about the viability of the project or if the revised budget has gotten too big, some tough decisions must be made—like whether to reduce the scope of the project or cancel it altogether.

At this point, the company or partners have already spent between 20 and 40 percent of the total project cost! How could they not move forward? In most businesses this is one of the accepted norms of research and development. Sometimes it is best to drop a project rather than commit further funds to it if its prospects for success do not seem clear.

And why now? Because once the project moves into the "build" phase, it will be very hard to make significant design changes without negative impact on the budget, the completion date, and the organization of the project. That commitment of effort and funds must not be made if there are continuing questions and changes in the basic design of the system that will throw the whole project into confusion.

How does this happen? We may be dealing with computer systems here, but we are also dealing with human nature. It is all too common for companies to run the design phase as a poorly defined research project. Much time is spent in detailed analysis of what already exists, but only sketchy design work is done on the specifics of the new system. Debates ensue about various aspects of the system design, but nobody sees them through to a clear conclusion. Excitement about the idea obscures the tough questions. Preliminary design flaws are brushed aside, and people figure they'll fix them in the "build" phase. Senior managers who conceived of the project in the "define" phase may still be enthusiastic about it, but the folks who actually have to build the system have their doubts. Rumors and grumbling begin and disillusionment sets in.

The design phase is the opportunity for a company to reduce the risk on a project before committing large amounts of time and money to it. The more detailed the design specifications, the better the chances for building or refurbishing the system on time and on budget. The broader the understanding of and support for the system among both business and technical people, the greater the likelihood that it will be used effectively and produce the desired results.

So at the end of the design phase, the executive sponsor and the project leader must pause and take stock of the project. Is there an air of understanding and confidence among the team members? Are they "good to go"? The answers will be evident, for those who want to hear them.

If the design phase has not produced clear design specifications, if the strategic design guidelines have been ignored, and if people on the project team seem to have doubts about their abilities or the eventual outcome, then there will be no success. The project leader can only fail in these situations, no matter how sincere or heroic the use of leadership skills.

The biggest eye-opener here is the 75 percent failure rate on IT system development projects. It's not so high because we are incapable as people. It is because we make fundamental mistakes in our system designs and our plans for building them.

THE BUILD PHASE

This is the "go for it!" phase. If the project has gotten this far, the project leader should be sure everyone sticks to the aim and resists the temptation to change direction. There is a time frame that, at this point, should be realistic. Activity must be tightly focused on the completion of specific sequences of tasks. This is the step where good design and planning pay off handsomely.

In this phase, the project effort really ramps up. The full complement of people is brought on to fill out the project teams. Because of this, the weekly cost or "burn rate" on the project also rises significantly in the "build" phase. So, unlike the previous two phases, the cost of false starts and wrong turns now adds up very quickly.

The Project Office

The project leader and the team leaders are fully engaged in leading the project, and they must depend on the office or administrative staff to keep up on the planning and budgeting updates as milestones are approached, reached, and passed. It is startling how quickly the plan and budget can become outdated as coordinating and decision-making tools, and keeping them up-to-date to reflect reality is in itself a full-time job. The plan is the map of where the project is going and the progress made to date.

That said, there is a pervasive tendency for people to hide bad news such as delays and cost overruns. Unless the project leader takes active steps to counter this tendency, the project will run into trouble. People need to see that they will not be penalized for reporting bad news. On the contrary, they must be shown that by reporting delays and potential cost overruns as soon as they detect them, they can improve their chances of success. Early reporting gives everyone more time to respond effectively.

The team members must also understand that the project office staff is there to help them keep track of what is really going on and make timely decisions based on realistic data. If bad news is hidden on a project, when the truth finally does come out, there is usually very little (if any) time to respond effectively to the situation.

System Test and Rollout

The first step in taking a system from development into production is to perform a system test with all the system components in place. If competent load and volume testing was done on the system prototype during the design phase, then there should be no surprises about whether the system technically works and can handle the workload expected of it. The purpose of system testing is to work through a series of test scripts that subject the system to the kinds of uses it is designed for and to exercise various features and logic of the system. Some embarrassing logic mistakes may well emerge during system test, and this is okay. That's what a test is for, to flush out and fix these kinds of errors before the system goes into **beta test**.

The beta test is the second system test—this time with a pilot group of business users, typically a few long-term customers or other members of the supply chain. The pilot group should have been involved in some way in the design phase of the project, so they already have a basic understanding and acceptance of the need for the new system and are ready to help the test team work out the bugs. Many minor adjustments are made, both to system architecture and the user interface, during the beta test, as the operating parameters are fine-tuned to get the best response time and stability from the system. The people who designed the user interface spend time with the pilot group of business users, listening to their ideas for improvements.

The business user who works with a system day in and day out will have a different perspective on the system's features than the people who designed and built the system. Minor inconveniences in the system's operation can become major irritants to the people who have to use the system on a daily basis. No matter how "minor," these inconveniences should be fixed.

As the pilot group makes suggestions for adjustments, some will emerge as advocates for the system. They feel a personal connection to the success of the system, especially if it has taken on a "look and feel" that was influenced by their suggestions. These are the people who will sell the benefits of the system to the rest of their company, and who may even be the ones who train their coworkers in the use of the system.

One of the deliverables that is key to the success of a system in the field is documentation. The people who operate a system need to know how to boot the system up, bring it down, and do performance tuning, troubleshooting, and operating maintenance. The project team is responsible for documenting these procedures clearly and understandably, and like the system itself, these documents will undergo a lot of fine-tuning.

When the system first goes into production, the rollout for a "big" system (one that affects more than one area of the business, or many people in a single area) may last a while, from six months to a year. There is not a lot of new development going on during this time, but a steady stream of minor enhancements and "bug fixes." The project team can be slimmed down, but the project leader needs to stay involved during this time to facilitate the rollout and respond quickly if some unexpected obstacle arises.

SUPPLY CHAIN SKILLS—CREATING A PROPRIETARY SYSTEM

Network Services Company built the first version of its "Web-enabled supply chain" in 2000. The system has been enhanced and new features added since then as market needs have evolved. Through the strategic planning process, Network saw the biggest benefit to be gained was from using Internet technology to electronically connect all the different computer systems of its member companies. This would allow passing files such as purchase orders, invoices, and product masters quickly and accurately among customers, members, and manufacturers. With this type of system, Network would be able to plug into whatever electronic trading networks were evolving in the markets it served. The system to connect Network with its members, customers, and manufacturers was named NetLink-NSC.™

The second opportunity the company saw and acted on was to make sales history data available via its Web site. Since Network is the hub of the NetLink-NSC™ system, a handy by-product is that Network gathers a lot of valuable information that can be used by customers, members, and manufacturers. The company decided to build a data warehouse that could be accessed through report generation screens on its Web site.

Many of Network's customers already had, or were building, their own order entry systems. They wanted to send the company purchase orders directly from their systems using either EDI or the Internet. Network decided to lease the use of a Web-based order entry package from a supply chain service provider named Tibersoft.

As Network's CIO, I was given the responsibility for building this e-business systems infrastructure. It was very important to develop it quickly and cost-effectively, so I used the time-boxing guidelines suggested in the define-design-build process. A team of business and technical people was assembled; they identified the company's most pressing business issues and ideas for how technology could help. These ideas were translated into a conceptual system design (shown as Figure 8-4 in Chapter 8). Within six weeks, the define phase was complete. The conceptual design and a proposed budget to develop the infrastructure were presented to the board of directors. They gave their approval to proceed with development.

Even before the define phase was finished, work began on a design-and-build sequence to produce a beta test version of the data warehouse that stored sales history data. This was completed quickly and provided the business with a valuable tool as well as proof that the technical architecture was viable. It also gave everyone a clear indication that the system development effort was off to a good start and would live up to expectations.

A select group of consultants was brought in to work with company IT staff. Four project teams were created—one team to design and build each of the four components of the e-business

Continued

infrastructure. Two of the project team leaders were from the Network IT staff, and two were consultants. There was also a two-person project office team headed by one of Network's IT managers.

The hardware and software components chosen for the systems architecture were assembled and tested by the teams that would use them. Data was passed between the components to make sure they could work together. Response times were tested under different data volumes to verify that the system could handle the expected amounts of data. When testing was finished, we had a solid design and there wasn't any talk of, "We'll figure this out after we get into the build phase . . ."

As each team finished the design phase of its work, it was well positioned to launch into the build phase. Each team had a clear set of design specifications and had been able to test and verify that the hardware and software would meet their expectations. This allowed each team leader to work confidently with the project office manager to create very accurate project plans and budgets for the build phase.

The first versions of all the system components were finished within nine months and demonstrated to member companies and suppliers at the Network annual trade show. The systems were well received by Network members, and some members asked if they could use these systems to support their own local business as well as to handle national account customers. So a set of enhancements to NetLink-NSC™ and the data warehouse were quickly designed and built to let members use them for their local customers. In the last three months of 2000, the project team worked with Network members to roll out version 1.0 of these systems.

Going into 2001, Network assessed its business situation and the market conditions, and defined a set of major enhancements to add to the systems it had just rolled out. These enhancements were again designed and built within nine months and were demonstrated in the fall at the annual trade show. Every Friday afternoon, the team leaders and I met to discuss the project. We spent several hours and reviewed the progress and the issues as each team encountered them. The project office staff provided accurate and updated plans and budgets for these meetings. We could all see the most current time and cost estimates to finish each objective. We could see if work on an objective threatened to push beyond its time box or if it was likely to overrun its budget.

The development sequence was focused and tightly time-boxed. Work ran in parallel during the design and build phases, requiring good planning and coordination. Version 1.0 of the e-business systems infrastructure was created in nine months! Based on positive reception and feedback from version 1.0, enhancements for version 1.1 were created. Further assessment of business needs led to the definition of the next round of major enhancements that created version 2.0 of the e-business infrastructure . . . and so on.

Source: This was written by coauthor Michael Hugos about his own computer design experience as CIO of Network Services Company, Mt. Prospect, Illinois.

CHAPTER SUMMARY

Designing a computer system for a company to enable data synchronization with others in the supply chain is one of the most collaborative and intensive efforts employees and managers will undertake. After the basic planning process (which was covered in Chapter 8), the designing and building of the system can be broken down into these steps:

"Design" Deliverables

1. A detailed design for the business process flow of the system. Also, agreement among the people who will have to work with the system that it will meet the performance criteria expected of it.
2. A system prototype that specifies both the technical architecture and user interface. The technical architecture must be capable of handling the projected data volumes and user demands that are expected. There must be a complete set of screen layouts, report formats, and specifications for all aspects of the user interface.
3. A detailed project plan and budget that accurately reflects the time, cost, and resources needed to build the system.

"Build" Deliverables

1. A working system that matches the design specifications and meets performance criteria. The building of the system should be scheduled so something of value is delivered to the business every 30 to 90 days. This means certain pieces of the system must be finished and put into use before the entire system is completed.
2. A complete and updated set of technical design documents. The design documentation is analogous to the floor plans and infrastructure plans of a building.
3. A complete set of operating instructions. The people who operate and maintain a system are different from the people who build systems, and they require clear, concise instructions about everything from how to boot up the system to troubleshooting and operating maintenance.

No one in business today works in a vacuum. The design or upgrading of any company's computer system requires extensive input from other supply chain members to ensure that the systems can work together, as well as the companies themselves manage to do so. In retail, business would be impossible without this type of coordination.

DISCUSSION QUESTIONS

1. List the basic technology-related information you believe a retail employee should be familiar with in order to advance in a midsize to large store chain today.

2. Explain the difference between the types of process sketches required in Chapter 8 (the plan phase) and the ones required in Chapter 9 (the design phase).

3. Why do costs for each task in a system development project have to be calculated? How would you counter a staff member's assertion that this is "micromanaging"?

4. Describe one "bug" or shortcoming of a computer system you now work with that drives you crazy—you'd change it if you could! Knowing now how a system is designed, why do you think the project team didn't fix it?

5. What should a project manager do when, in beta testing of a system, the critics outnumber the advocates?

ENDNOTE

1. Antony Savvas, "Drive to roll out new technologies makes retail a hotspot for IT job opportunities," *Computer Weekly*, June 8, 2004.

THE INCREDIBLE JOURNEY

OCTOBER 1—PRODUCT MEETS STAFF

In the wee hours of the morning, a CVS truck appears at McGee's store with his order. McGee unloads the tote in the back room and, voilà, there is the bottle of Listerine that originated in the Australian eucalyptus grove back in May. He displays it on the shelf according to the dictates of the store presentation managers at Woonsocket who determine ideal store layouts and product placement.

OCTOBER 2—THE PURCHASE

Now for the last step of our journey—the customer. A man walks into McGee's store to pick up aftershave and a box of chocolates for the date he's planned for the evening. On impulse, he decides to buy a bottle of Listerine. His purchase is recorded by the cash register and sent to E3 and Category Map that night for future forecasting. In a few days, McGee will place an order for a replacement bottle of Listerine. And so begins the cycle again.

How do store managers know how much product to stock?

CVS management frowns upon stores keeping extra inventory in the back room because it ties up capital. So instead of having each store manager project demand, once a year, category managers at headquarters analyze annual point-of-sale data generated in each store and calculate the weekly sales rate for every product by store. Then they multiply that number by 4 to get the minimum shelf quantity (MSQ). In other words, at any given time, CVS carries four weeks' worth of supplies on the shelves. At Mike McGee's store in Framingham, Massachusetts, the MSQ for the 500-milliliter bottle of the best-selling Listerine flavor, Cool Mint, is 20 because the store sells an average of five bottles per week.

10

THE REAL-TIME SUPPLY CHAIN AND BEYOND

The pace of business change and creativity today is both exciting and re-lentless. Innovative retailers in different market segments have learned to design and deploy their supply chains to improve their competitive positions in the markets they serve. They create supply chains that enable them to develop and deliver products, and provide levels of service at price points that their competitors cannot match.

What tools do they use to accomplish this? This chapter explains the importance of some of the current trends in retail supply chain management, including:

- The "always-on" connection and its impact on supply chain partners
- A realistic look at global sourcing
- Inventory management and product identification technology
- Strategic thinking for supply chain success
- The concepts of emergent behavior and adaptive behavior

We all sense that something profound has happened in the world since the invention of online communication. But it's about a lot more than the Internet or eCommerce, as you'll see in this chapter. It is about combining various types of technology with people skills—fine-tuning our abilities to cooperate and observe and learn from other business partners in a supply chain.

POWER ON DEMAND

As an historical analogy, let's consider what happened some 200 years ago at the beginning of a time period that came to be known as the Industrial Age. The people of the time sensed that powerful potential had been released with the invention and growing popularity of the steam engine. For the first time, this invention provided a movable source of power that could be generated on demand and efficiently harnessed to perform a wide variety of tasks.

The Industrial Age was not so much about the steam engine as it was about the possibilities it opened up with the power and convenience that it created in business. Of course, as the era continued, technology outgrew the steam engine as more advanced engine capabilities evolved: internal combustion, jet engines, electric motors, and even atomic power.

In much the same way, the Internet has created a new kind of "power on demand" that has changed the way business is done. Today, even the tiniest specialty firms work as part of a global, multidirectional communications network that is "always on." As more and more companies use the Internet, EDI, and other communications networks to create always-on connections, they find ways to share data that enable them to better coordinate their interactions. They also learn and adapt to changing conditions more quickly. These capabilities clearly result in efficiencies that can be turned into business profits.

The always-on connection is a new light that sheds steady illumination on a landscape that, before real-time connections, could be seen only in periodic snapshots. The effect is a lot like seeing a sequence of still photos turn into a moving picture. As more pictures are taken at shorter intervals, you cease to see a sequence of still photos and instead come to see a continuous, moving image. This continuous, moving image is what we see as we move from the snapshot or batch-time world into the real-time world.

Supply chain management is a process of coordination between companies. Those companies that learn to coordinate comfortably in real time will become incrementally more efficient. They will become more profitable and perhaps see new opportunities more quickly than their competitors who are still working in a batch-time world of business snapshots.

The Challenges of Technology

As beneficial as all this sounds, it is not easy to automate a supply chain. There are many challenges to be faced by companies and their supply chain partners, who must commit to sharing data and keeping up with the technology once they've embarked on the course together. As *Advanced Manufacturing* magazine's online columnist Predrag Jakovljevic correctly observed, "Neither planning nor execution tools can fix a dysfunctional supply chain, but planners need to analyze and optimize both areas."[1]

Here are a few examples of issues that commonly create tension:

- It is often difficult to get suppliers on board. Mega-retailers like Wal-Mart, Albertsons, and Target can mandate the adoption of certain systems or technologies, but not everyone has this kind of clout. Deciding to automate a supply chain means not only your employees but other key players in the chain have to learn how to work with the new system. When automation means less work for the distributors, or layoffs of pickers and packers in the warehouses, not everyone is going to cooperate cheerfully.
- Most supply chains are made up of companies large and small, and not all of them can afford to make similar investments in technology. Better-funded partners in the chain must decide if their less prosperous partners' participation is important enough to step in and assist with the initial costs and/or system upgrades to allow the necessary interface.
- Retail is an intensely people-oriented business, and people throughout the supply chain may protest the lack of human contact in a highly automated system. Distributors' representatives may be more comfortable with phone calls and sales visits. Store managers pride themselves in knowing their inventory inside and out. They may balk at using a system that places automatic reorders or that stocks each store with exactly the same items and quantities. A balance must be struck between using technology and maintaining the uniqueness and camaraderie of the business relationships.
- "If you can't convince people that using the software will be worth their time, they will easily find ways to work around it," wrote Lee Pender in a 2001 article for *CIO* magazine. Forecasters and planners will soon decide the data is "useless" if they don't realize it takes a while to get the bugs worked out of a new implementation, and to input enough historical data to

the system to ensure accurate output. Retailers must also be confident about the security and reliability of their own systems, as well as those of their supply chain partners.

- The same *CIO* article mentioned the dilemma of companies that buy software and customize it. Customization is expensive, and often the original developer of the software or hardware will not support the altered system. In other words, companies can inadvertently lock themselves into using "homegrown" systems that may not provide the agility required to react to market changes or multichannel demands.[2]

- Multiple distribution channels require multiple supply chains. Office Depot is an example of a retailer with two separate supply chains—one for retail and store shipments, the other for corporate accounts that buy online or through its office supply catalogs—both under the purview of an executive vice president of supply chain to help avoid duplication of efforts.[3]

GLOBAL SOURCING

Another major supply chain trend today is a by-product of technology. Global sourcing is the ability of a company to get what it needs from anywhere on the planet, a trend that has skyrocketed in the last 50 years. The primary reasons companies look outside their traditional regions for manufacturing capacity are to take advantage of lower-cost materials and labor, or that they have discovered a more favorable climate for their type of business—more tax advantages, familiarity with certain types of industries, perhaps fewer environmental restrictions, and so forth. Many nations have, in turn, scrambled to make these foreign investment arrangements even more appealing.

There are two types of technology that have allowed global sourcing to blossom. One is the use of communications technology, such as the Internet, cellular phones, wireless technology, and the like. The other is that international freight companies have developed larger and more sophisticated vessels, more than double the size of "traditional" cargo ships. They can now carry so much more freight per load that they have significantly reduced shipping costs—by some estimates, up to 70 percent less than in past decades.

While the cost impacts of these developments may be impressive, they also increase the complexity—and literally stretch the length—of the retail supply chain. A 2003 study by Maersk Logistics, the giant Danish-based shipping company, showed that compared to a domestic supply chain, there may be as many as seven additional partners in a global supply chain—from customs departments to compliance authorities to the freight companies themselves. The long overseas manufacturing and shipping journey may add only 2 to 5 percent to the final cost of the item but may account for 30 to 50 percent of the item's total time in the supply chain.[4]

More partners and more distance between them also mean more room for error. Back in 1988, professors Constantinos Markides and Norman Berg criticized some of the first efforts to move American manufacturing operations offshore in a report published in the *Harvard Business Review*. Alan Braithwaite, executive chairman of LCP Consulting in the United Kingdom, says their initial points ring true almost 20 years later:

- There are risks that the total acquisition cost may be greater than anticipated and erode the net benefits that the initial purchase cost implies. When all factors including transportation, handling, duty, obsolescence, inventory, lost sales, and "market blocking" are factored in, the total cost may not be as attractive as the headline advantage—labor costs are typically as little as 7 to 10 percent of the total product costs, and even less on the selling price (of most items).
- The extended chain cannot be as responsive to demand variations as local sourcing; hence, there may be opportunity costs of lost sales.
- There may be risks with quality and execution due to the long-distance relationships and the many handoffs in the process to move the product to its destination. Inaccuracies cause service failure and hence (increase) cost.
- Valuable know-how may be given away to vendors, allowing others to enter markets and for product and engineering skills to be lost.
- The long-term impact on supply and demand is less clear and may distort markets, both in terms of the benefits gained and also for the risks of secure supply.[5]

Markides and Berg did not take into account another reasonable assumption that has come to light more recently—that unstable governments and terrorist threats can disrupt commerce just about anywhere in the world today. In addition, the glut of containers entering the United States—at least 7 million of them per year—has caused enormous backlogs at seaports, in Customs, and with Homeland Security's efforts to screen the incoming merchandise in antidrug and antiterrorism efforts.[6]

Braithwaite, working with England's Cranfield School of Management, has charted the types of supply chain risks companies face (as seen in Figure 10-1), in three external and three internal categories. The external categories include the following:

- *Demand risks* are potential or actual disturbances to the flow of product, information, and/or cash that begin in one company and impact other companies and customers "downstream" in the supply chain.
- *Supply risks* are the upstream equivalent of demand risk; they relate to potential or actual disturbances to the flow or product or information that disrupt companies "upstream" in the supply chain.
- *Environmental risks* are external, uncontrollable events that can impact a company directly or through its suppliers or customers, upstream or downstream.

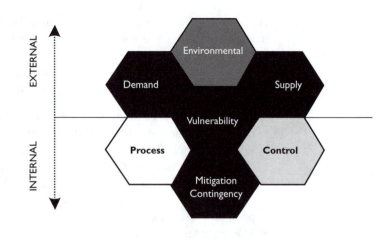

Figure 10-1. The drivers of supply chain risk. (The use of global sourcing increases supply chain risks, making companies vulnerable in a number of areas.) (Source: Alan Braithwaite, LCP Consulting, Ltd., Berkhamsetd, United Kingdom and Cranfield School of Management, Bedfordshire, United Kingdom. Used with permission of Alan Braithwaite.)

The internal risks can be categorized as follows:

- *Process risks* are disruptions to the managerial or value-adding activities undertaken by a company, which are likely to be dependent on internally owned or managed assets and a functioning infrastructure.
- *Control risks* occur when the rules, systems, and procedures used by a company are applied or misapplied, either way with incorrect results. They include anything from safety stock policies to order quantities to the way assets are managed in a company.
- *Mitigation* is a hedge against risk built into the operations; hence, the lack of mitigation can itself be a risk. *Contingency* is the existence of a plan, and resources that can be mobilized to carry it out, in case a risk is identified.

In short, retailers must consider all aspects of their global partnerships to accurately quantify the risks as well as the benefits, and even when cost savings are evident, they must still plan much further in advance in order to take advantage of them. Every company's senior management team deals with potential risk factors differently, and Braithwaite's conclusion is that "global sourcing is not a consistent proxy for higher sustained profits."[7]

RETAIL TECHNOLOGY TRENDS

The types of technology most likely to impact retail supply chain partners in the coming years are as follows.

In inventory management, order pickers who pull and group products to prepare them for shipment in a traditional warehouse generally start at an assignment desk, where they are given their orders on papers known as **picking labels**. They refer to the labels as they go through the warehouse and select the merchandise that corresponds with the labels.

Using **voice-activated technology**, the picker wears a headset and microphone, and a wireless terminal on his or her belt that links to the software of a warehouse management system (WMS). The system tells the person what to pick (and perhaps where it is located); the worker responds by speaking to the system through the microphone. The system is sophisticated enough to recognize human speech, and it can be programmed to trigger inventory counts and restocking activities. Voice-directed picking is 10 to 20 percent more accurate than the old system and has the side benefit of keeping the warehouse cleaner with the elimination of paper labels.[8]

Universal Product Codes, more commonly known as *UPCs* or **bar codes**, have been in existence for more than 30 years. The original idea behind this system of instant product identification by a computerized reader or scanner was to speed up checkout time at stores and improve the accuracy of prices, and for these aims it has been a huge hit. There are literally trillions of bar codes printed and placed on products worldwide every year! But technology will certainly change—and perhaps eventually eliminate—bar codes in the coming decades, for several reasons.

First, the plethora of new products demands the constant creation of new codes, and with only 12 digits in the United States and 13 digits in Europe's Electronic Article Numbering (EAN) bar code system, these systems are reaching their practical limits. Second, the global nature of business also makes a single code system a smarter idea. The Uniform Code Council (UCC) suggests adopting a 14-digit code system called **Global Trade Identification Numbers (GTIN)**. Third, there are limits to the amount of information that can be contained in a single bar code—hence, the development of two- and three-dimensional (2-D and 3-D) bar codes. They require special bar code readers. All three of these developments in bar code technology require significant additional investment on the part of supply chain members.[9]

Some businesses are hesitant to make bar code investments because they believe the future of product identification is in **radio frequency identification (RFID)**. RFID tags are small computer chips placed on products. The chip transmits a large volume of information about the product to a wireless reading device, far more than a bar code can contain. The device does not have to make contact with the chip, or even be in its line of sight, in order to "read" it. RFID allows for an amazing amount of precision and accuracy in inventory management, giving companies the capability to literally track a shipment's exact whereabouts in the supply chain.

Wal-Mart made headlines when it mandated its Top 100 suppliers to be RFID-compliant by January 2005, which sent them scrambling. The problem has been that this new technology is expensive. The chips themselves cost far more to manufacture—now and in the foreseeable future—than the much simpler bar code label, and they require new, more sophisticated types of readers and software. Thus far, most companies are experimenting with RFID tags on

SUPPLY CHAIN SKILLS—HOME DEPOT'S SELF-CHECKOUT PAYS OFF

In 2003, Home Depot announced plans to increase capital spending 21 percent (to $4 billion) for store remodeling and using technology to improve customer service. The list of projects included the creation of digital dashboards to monitor store operations, reengineering business processes to focus employees' efforts on the sales floor, upgrading point-of-sale equipment, speeding up replenishment at stores, and implementing SAP (the leading ERP software system).

The company decided its best move would be to use technology to up-sell goods and services. Self-checkout aisles allow Home Depot to deploy an average of two cashiers to the floor instead of standing behind the checkout counter. These people can restock shelves or sell big-ticket items like appliances and kitchen cabinets. If one former cashier sells just one customer on a home installation in every Home Depot store, that equates to $1 billion in additional revenue per year! Kiosks can be used to handle special orders when products such as window treatments aren't in-store.

The result: a steady increase in average tickets (sales totals). The retailer closed 2004 with an average ticket of $54.89, up 7.3 percent from fiscal 2003's tally of $51.15.

On the back end of the store, Home Depot is rolling out an automated inventory replenishment system. Its pilot project with the new system showed 20 percent fewer out-of-stocks. The 2005 goal is to have auto-replenishment systems for 20 percent of the SKUs carried in Home Depot stores.

caseloads or containers rather than individual products. RFID-related expenditures are expected to approach $27 billion by 2015, compared to $2 billion in 2005.[10]

THINKING STRATEGICALLY

In addition to linking to other members of a supply chain, companies that are competitors are learning to link up for procurement purposes in collaborative **trade exchanges**. Six major airlines, for example, have joined forces to buy at least some goods together. The trade association Grocery Manufacturers of America has spearheaded one of the largest trade exchange efforts with more than a dozen major consumer goods companies. The idea is still fairly new, but member companies of the GMA trade exchange can purchase materials, supplies, and services from each other, and even share cargo space jointly to increase efficiency. Companies that regularly order electronic components can do so on iSuppli, an online trade exchange for manufacturers.[11] All of this collaboration is enabled by technology and aimed at reducing costs and improving supply chain efficiencies.

Many of the global supply chain risks outlined earlier in this chapter can be managed with strategic thinking. Companies can design products using generic materials or components that can be used in a number of products instead of just one. Orders can be filled based on a forecast made just before the order is placed, improving accuracy. RFID technology will allow products to be correctly identified and tracked at every moment during their journey through the supply chain.

The Self-Adjusting Feedback Loop

Tracking performance and making adjustments accordingly is sometimes called a **self-adjusting feedback loop**, and it is another useful tool in the supply chain arsenal. A simple example of the principle is the cruise control in an automobile, which constantly compares the vehicle's actual speed to the speed it was set for and responds to bring the actual speed in line with the desired speed. This causes the engine to either accelerate or decelerate accordingly. You might say the cruise control is operating the engine in order to achieve its goal.

Other examples of self-adjusting feedback loops are a thermostat that controls the temperature in a room and a guided missile that zeros in on a heat source or radar emission source. Self-adjusting feedback loops use negative feedback to continuously correct their behavior—and that does not mean "negative" in the sense of criticism. This type of negative feedback occurs when a system compares its current state with its desired state (or goal) and takes *corrective action* to move it in the direction that minimizes the difference between the two states. A continuous stream of negative feedback guides a system through a changing environment toward its goal.

How can the self-adjusting feedback loop be used in a supply chain? As companies link up using always-on communication networks to conduct business, they begin to collect useful data as a by-product of their interactions: electronic purchase orders, order status, order receipts, invoices, payment histories, and so on. It is no longer a huge administrative chore to regularly track performance in the "big four" areas of customer service, internal efficiency, demand flexibility, and product development.

Performance can also be tracked by individual store or sales associates. For example, Home Depot receives more than 200 customer comments per store, per week—and it's not because they fill out and mail in customer comment cards. Every sales receipt has a code number printed on it, with instructions prompting consumers to rank their sales experience in a simple format on the company's Web site.[12]

Similarly, corporate customers can use supply chain "report cards" to grade the performance of their suppliers and to ask for suppliers' critiques in return. The next step is for companies to move beyond using these report cards as merely convenient tools for "beating up" their suppliers, looking instead for ways to work together to meet mutually beneficial performance targets. A dominant company in the chain can set the performance targets, or groups of companies can negotiate among themselves to set targets. The important things are that all participating companies in a supply chain believe the targets are achievable—and that when they are achieved, there will be rewards as a result.

The natural desire to receive these rewards is what brings the self-adjusting feedback loop to life. If companies and people in a supply chain have real-time access to the data they need, then for the most part, they will steer toward their targets. If they are rewarded when they achieve these targets, then they will learn to hit them more often than not, allowing companies to realize the profit potential of the feedback loop.

SCM as a Strategy Game

Supply chain management is often such serious business that perhaps it would be helpful to think of it for a moment as a game of strategy. From childhood, most of us learn and improve our skills by playing games. Companies such as Wal-Mart and Dell and their supply chain partners have, in many ways, created evolving games of managing their supply chains. They have steadily learned and developed supply chain organizations that are better than those of their competitors, and that clearly hold business advantages for them.

There are only a few things required to start a game. In the early 1990s, SRC Holdings Group (formerly Springfield Remanufacturing Group) President and CEO Jack Stack wrote a popular business book, *The Great Game of Business*. In it, Stack laid out the four conditions that are needed (in this case, for a business pursuit) to qualify as a "game":

1. People must understand the rules of the game and how it is played. They must know what is fair, what is not fair, and how to score points.
2. People must be able to pick the roles or positions they want to play in the game. They must also get the training and experience necessary to keep developing the skills required to succeed in their positions.
3. All players must know what the score is at all times. They need to know if they are winning or losing, and they need to see the results of their actions.
4. All players must have a personal stake in the outcome of the game. There must be some important reward, either monetary or psychological, that provides a reason for each player to strive to succeed.[13]

Seen in these terms, the "game" of supply chain management is not quite as complex as today's business experts would have one believe. In fact, the game is relatively simple, like soccer or basketball or golf—which is not to say that any of these pursuits can be mastered without years of practice and play! The main techniques and operations of supply chain management are well enough understood to be taught to a wide range of people in different supply chain positions. Online, real-time access is the way for everyone to know the score at all times and see the results of their actions. Profits generated by operating efficiencies provide people with rewards and reasons to strive to succeed.

In supply chain management, everyone can acquire and install technology, so technology alone cannot constitute a significant competitive advantage. The advantage, then, must lie in the way the game is played. Let's rethink the example of Alexander the Great in Chapter 1. Remember, his army did not have any type of technology that was not also available to his opponents—in fact, Alexander deliberately used less technology. He simplified his army's operations and equipment in order to make it more mobile and more efficient, and, therefore, his army could travel faster and lighter than his adversaries' forces.

Advantage goes to those players who learn to use simple technology and simple tactics extremely well. Alexander's soldiers were well trained in how to use their technology. Further, the simplicity of their tactics allowed the soldiers to remember and use them effectively in the heat of the moment, when it really counted.

Even today, supply chain success is often just a matter of consistent performance and making fewer errors than the competition.

Recognizing Emergent Behavior

In the workings of a free market system, we witness **emergent behavior**—an interconnected system of relatively simple elements, which begins to self-organize to form a more intelligent and adaptive higher-level system. The famous British economist Adam Smith referred to it as the "invisible hand" of the market, which "emerges" to set product prices so that available supplies are best allocated to meet market demands. Local interactions between large numbers of agents, governed by simple rules of mutual feedback, produce a macro effect that results in emergent behavior of the system as a whole.

If we begin to think of supply chain management as a game between companies and people who are motivated to achieve certain performance targets, we see emergent behavior in supply chains. Good "players" in the supply chains of particular markets seek each other out because by playing together they can create more efficient supply chains and generate better profits. Modern supply chains form like sports teams, who compete with each other for market share. Just as the games of basketball or soccer evolve over time, so too does the game of supply chain management. New tactics, techniques, and

SUPPLY CHAIN SKILLS—EMERGENT BEHAVIOR IN SUPPLY CHAINS

Steven Johnson is a "techie" and former magazine editor who authored the book *Emergence: The Connected Lives of Ants, Brains, Cities, and Software* (Scribner, 2002). Michael Hugos asked Johnson to share his insights, including how companies can organize their supply chains to encourage and benefit from emergent behavior.

Q: What is an "emergent system"? How is an emergent system different from, say, an assembly line?

A: The catchphrase I sometimes use is that an emergent system is "smarter" than the sum of its parts. They tend to be systems made up of many interacting agents, each of which is following relatively simple rules governing its encounters with other agents. Somehow, out of all these local interactions, a higher-level, global intelligence "emerges." The extraordinary thing about these systems is that there's no master planner or executive branch—the overall group creates the intelligence and adaptability; it's not something passed down from the leadership. An ant colony is a great example of this: Colonies manage to pull off extraordinary feats of resource management and engineering and task allocation, all by following remarkably simple rules of interaction, using a simple chemical language to communicate. There's a queen ant in the colony, but she's only called that because she's the chief reproductive engine for the colony. She doesn't have any actual command authority. The ordinary ants just do the thinking collectively, without a leader.

A key difference between an emergent system and an assembly line lies in the fluidity of the emergent system: Randomness is a key component of the way an ant colony will explore a given environment—take the random element out, and the colony gets much less interesting, much less capable of stumbling across new ideas. Assembly lines are all about setting fixed patterns and eliminating randomness; emergence is all about stumbling across new patterns that work better than the old ones.

Q: You refer to emergent systems as "bottom up," not "top down," because they solve problems by drawing on masses of simple elements instead of relying on a single, intelligent "executive branch." What does this mean for people who are trying to design and build emergent systems?

A: One of the central lessons, I think, is that emergent systems are always slightly out of control. Their unpredictability is part of their charm—and their power—but it can be threatening to engineers and planners who have been trained to eliminate unpredictability at every turn. Some of the systems that I've looked at combine emergent properties and evolutionary ones: The emergent system generates lots of new configurations and ideas, and then there's a kind of natural selection that weeds out the bad ideas and encourages the good ones. That's largely what a designer of emergent systems should think about doing; it's closer to growing a garden than it is to building a factory.

Q: What do you mean when you say that emergent systems display "complex adaptive behavior"?

A: The complexity refers to the number of interacting parts, like the thousands of ants in a colony, or the pedestrians on a street in a busy city. Adaptive behavior is what happens when all those component parts create useful higher-level structures or patterns of behavior with their group interactions, when they create something, usually unwittingly, that benefits the members of the group. When an ant colony determines the shortest route to a new source of food and quickly assembles a line of ants to transport the food back to the nest; when thousands of urbanites create a neighborhood with a distinct personality that helps organize and give shape to an otherwise overwhelming city—these are examples of adaptive behavior.

Q: What is negative feedback, as opposed to positive feedback? What role does negative feedback play in the ability of a system to exhibit adaptive behavior?

A: Negative feedback is crucial, and it's not at all negative in a value-judgment sense. Positive feedback is what we generally mean when we talk about feedback, as in the "guitar effect" that we first started to hear as music in the 60s—music is played through a speaker, which is picked up by a microphone, which then broadcasts it out though the speaker, creating a sound that the microphone picks up, and so on until you get a howling noise that sounds nothing like the original music.

So positive feedback is a kind of self-perpetuating, additive effect: plug output A into input B, which is plugged into input A. Negative feedback is what you use when you need to dampen down a chain like this, when there's a danger of a kind of runaway effect, or when you're trying to home in on a specific target. Think of a thermostat trying to reach a preset temperature: It samples the air, and if the air's too cold, it turns the heat on, then samples it again. Without negative feedback, the room would just keep getting hotter, but the thermostat has been designed to turn the heat off when the air reaches the target temperature.

Ants use a comparable technique to achieve the right balance of task allocation throughout the colony. An individual ant who happens to be on foraging duty will sample the number of ants also on foraging duty that she stumbles across over the course of an hour. If she encounters a certain number, she'll switch over to another task (nest building, say) in order to keep the colony from becoming overrun with foragers.

Q: In your book, you mention a designer who has proposed building a learning network of traffic lights that will find an optimal solution to continually changing traffic conditions. You observe that, "You can conquer gridlock by making the grid itself smart." What is it that would make the grid smart, and would this grid be an example of an emergent system?

A: The idea proposed in the traffic model is not to take the traditional engineering, top-down approach and say: "Let's look at the entire city and figure out where all the problems are, and try to design the roads and the light system to eliminate the problems." The smart grid

Continued

approach is to give each light a local perspective with a little bit of information, and give it the goal of minimizing delays at its own little corner. So the light would be able to register the number of cars stacked up at the intersection, and it would be able to experiment with different rhythms of red and green, with some feedback from its near neighbors. When it stumbles across a pattern that reduces delays, it sticks to that pattern; if the delays start piling up again, it starts experimenting again. The problem with this sort of approach is that on Day One, it's a terrible, terrible system, because it doesn't yet know anything about traffic flows! You'd have to teach it quite a bit before you could actually implement it. But it would learn very quickly, and most importantly, it would be capable of responding to changing conditions in a way that the traditionally engineered approach would not. That's a hallmark of adaptability.

Q: Okay, let's apply these ideas to a system composed of many different companies—a supply chain, whose goal is to provide a market with the highest levels of responsiveness at the lowest cost to themselves. High levels of responsiveness require that these companies work together to design, make, and deliver the right products at the right price at the right time in the right amounts. What could these companies do to organize themselves into an emergent system?

A: There's a telltale term in supply chain systems, which may well be unavoidable—the term "chain" itself. Almost all emergent systems are networks or grids; they tend to be flatter and more horizontal, with interaction possible between all the various agents. The problem that supply chains have with positive feedback revolves around the distance between the consumer and those suppliers further down the chain; because the information has to pass through so many intermediaries, you get distortion in the message. Most emergent systems that I've looked at have a great diversity of potential routes that information can follow. The more chainlike they become, the less adaptive they are.

The other key here is experimentation: letting the system evolve new patterns of interaction on its own, since these can often be more useful and efficient than the preplanned ones. Of course, you don't want to waste a few economic quarters experimenting with different supply chains, most of which are a disaster. But that's where some of the wonderful new modeling systems for complex behavior can be very handy—you can do the experimenting on the computer and then pick the best solutions to implement in real life.

technology will continue to be introduced. Market demands and the desire for competitive advantage will drive companies to collaborate and innovate with each other to win at this game. Some chains (and retailers) will remain at the forefront; others will lag behind.

Computers are best used to automate the rote, repetitive activities that humans consider boring—the routine and/or mundane activities of recording and monitoring supply chain operations. Computers do these tasks very well.

SUPPLY CHAIN SKILLS—FUTURE BUSINESS TRENDS

In February 2005, Robert J. Bowman, senior editor of *Global Logistics & Supply Chain Strategies* magazine, shared his choices of 10 business trends that make supply chain management, in his words, "more complex than ever before." These are most definitely the areas to watch in retail as well as many other industries.

Look on the Web site SupplyChainBrain.com for the current issue of *Global Logistics & Supply Chain Strategies,* as well as archives of past issues and many case studies involving specific companies and how they are meeting these "top 10" challenges.

1. **Globalization.** In a relentless push for cost-cutting, companies large and small are sourcing product far from their markets. China is the location of the new gold rush for cheap manufacturing. Recent surveys by Deloitte Research found that more than 80 percent of manufacturers are either buying, or plan to buy over the next three years, components from other countries. Nearly half engineer products outside their home regions. In this regard, don't think of a supply "chain," forged from links of steel. Visualize a rubber band: stretch it too far, and it snaps.

2. **The need for supply chain agility, coupled with lower inventories.** Customers want it yesterday. Just-in-time is the new executive mantra. And products are getting to market with unprecedented speed. According to Deloitte, manufacturers over the last three years have cut product-development cycles by an average of 12 percent, to 16 months. By 2006, that span will have shrunk to 13 months. At the same time, companies are struggling to slash inventory levels, even as they acknowledge the need for core safety stocks in the event of supply interruptions, labor unrest, natural disasters, terrorist attacks or unforeseen shifts in consumer demand.

3. **Mass customization and make-to-order.** In another form of supply-chain agility, manufacturers are looking to meet the needs of individual customers, configuring product in countless ways. Dell Computer led the way on the consumer side. Cisco Systems has long offered a universe of options to its high-tech manufacturing base. The technique calls for highly efficient postponement programs, where basic components are customized at the moment of sale. The impact on supply chains? More complexity, of course.

4. **New-product mania.** Increasingly rare is the consumer item that looks the same—or even continues to exist—a year or two later. Faced with a limited base of consumers, suppliers and retailers are forever shoving new items into the limelight. SKU proliferation is rampant; just walk down the toothpaste aisle of any superstore. In 2003, Deloitte said products introduced within the previous three years would generate 29 percent of manufacturers' total revenues for the year. That compares with 21 percent in 1998, and a projected 35 percent in 2006.

Continued

5. **Value-added services.** Manufacturers used to make product or components, then sell them. Not anymore. In a bid to cut overhead, buyers are demanding a raft of underlying services from suppliers. Vendor-managed inventory (VMI) programs delay the ownership of goods until the last possible moment—and saddle the supplier with the job of managing stocks. Even contract manufacturers are getting into the game, offering third-party logistics services and direct shipment to end users, bypassing original equipment manufacturers (OEMs).

6. **Outsourcing.** The rush to abandon links of the supply chain to outsiders continues. First, it was back-office processes like accounting and payroll. Then came logistics. Next, nominal manufacturers gave away their assembly work to contractors. Other functions ripe for outsourcing include information-systems management, call centers, service-parts-repair, product engineering and chief executive officers (well, maybe not that last one). The result is more partners in the chain—and more chances for failure.

7. **Security.** For contemporary society, September 11, 2001 was in many respects the dividing line between Before and After. For business, it meant a whole new universe of security concerns. Billions of dollars have been spent on additional security measures, documentation and oversight. And it's still not enough. Ports and airports remain highly vulnerable to attack, analysts say. Listen to Noha Tohamy of Forrester Research: "The next terrorist attack is likely to be staged through a supply chain."

8. **New rules on corporate governance.** The hijinks of executives at companies like Enron and WorldCom have given rise to a slew of regulations, including the Sarbanes-Oxley Act, requiring companies to keep a tight rein over operations. The new reporting and accounting laws will have a huge impact on day-to-day supply-chain management, which touches virtually every aspect of a company's operations.

9. **Mergers and acquisitions.** Whether it's hard goods, soft goods or software, big companies are gobbling up smaller ones and growing even bigger in the process. This unstoppable trend raises some new issues of scalability for the survivors. How does a typical supply chain handle massive, overnight growth in revenues, product mix and customers? In most cases, not very well.

10. **Technology.** Wasn't this supposed to make things simpler? On the contrary, with every new convenience offered by innovative software or hardware, new complications arise. On balance, the impact on supply chains is usually a positive one, but getting to that point may require lots of time, money and migraines.

Source: Robert J. Bowman, "Supply-Chain Complexity Masters: A Special Report," *Global Logistics & Supply Chain Strategies*, Keller International Publishing, Great Neck, New York, February 2005.

They do not fall asleep, they do not miss details, and they can handle enormous volumes of data without complaint.

Human skills are best suited to the creative and problem-solving activities, putting their minds to work on problems that do not have clear right or wrong answers. These are the types of pursuits that call for people to collaborate, to share information and try different approaches to see which ones work best. People are good at strategic activities, and they like doing them—so they learn and keep getting better at them.

At a macro level, this will give rise to supply chains that, in effect, learn and grow smarter. Computers will listen to the hum and crackle of data flowing through the real-time, always-on supply chain. They will employ pattern recognition algorithms to spot exceptions and events, and they'll be programmed to bring these to the attention of human beings. Like good pilots and navigators, people will learn to respond effectively to these developments as they happen. People will learn to keep steering their supply chain on a course toward its desired performance targets.

ADAPTIVE NETWORKS

Cynical consumers may assume that the closer companies in a supply chain work together, the more they are probably conspiring to boost profits at the expense of the "little guy," but that is both a limited—and limiting—viewpoint. Instead, technology and the cooperation it enables can give retailers and their business partners the ability to recognize and smooth out excessive swings in demand, prices, and productive capacity. If other companies in other areas of the economy do the same, it should create greater stability.

In industries ranging from electronics manufacturing to real estate development to telecommunications, the bullwhip effect and related boom-to-bust cycles have caused nothing but waste and disruption—and, of course, news headlines that unnerve consumers and investors. These cycles also bring with them all the related human hardships. Think of the wealth that was destroyed by the excessive investments that created more dot-com companies and more telecommunications capacity than were needed. Think of the shutdowns and job losses when these companies and their suppliers finally had to face the consequences of too much supply and not enough demand.

Adaptive supply chain networks using real-time information and "negative" feedback can effectively dampen excessive market swings. This ability alone will have a wealth creation effect that is even more powerful than what was created by the steam engine two centuries ago. Retailers should be excited to be part of it.

CHAPTER SUMMARY

The "always-on" connection of the Internet and other communications networks allows companies to see themselves and their supply chain partners' data in real time. This makes it possible to constantly adjust, week to week or even day to day, to gain significant new efficiencies in almost every aspect of business. At least, that's the ideal.

However, adapting to technology requires enormous flexibility and financial expenditures, and every company handles the changes differently. This chapter mentioned several of the most common challenges faced by supply chains trying to get all members "up and running" with compatible systems and software.

Global sourcing is so common as to not even be considered a trend anymore, but it is included in this chapter as a by-product of technology, and to prompt discussion of the inherent risks in "stretching" the supply chain across continents. Most of the risks can be grouped into one of six categories, and each must be mitigated to realize the full benefit of global business. Companies must see the risks realistically in order to decide whether the potential savings are worth using foreign suppliers and/or participating in trade exchanges.

Other types of technology mentioned in the chapter are employed to improve communication, increase supply chain efficiencies, and reduce costs—or all three.

The chapter ended by bringing the human elements of business back into the picture, because it is humans who will use the technology to make strategic decisions. The authors suggest seeing the basics of supply chain management as a sport or game to cut through the complexity. Everyone in the game needs to know how to play, how to score points, and how to get the skills they need to improve their performance. The self-adjusting feedback loop is harnessed to the supply chain through the daily actions of the people who carry out supply chain operations. They can be motivated by rewards for achieving predefined performance targets and armed with real-time information that shows them how to hit their targets more often than not.

The potential emergent behavior that can be created by this dynamic will create supply chains that are both highly responsive and very efficient. Real-time operation results in supply chains that can better adapt to business changes and deliver performance and profitability without compromising quality or service for the end users of retail products.

DISCUSSION QUESTIONS

1. Other than the obvious—steam engines, automobiles, airplanes, telephones, computers—name at least one other invention of past centuries that changed the way people and companies do business. Has it evolved into something that is still useful today?
2. Give a hypothetical example of each of the six types of risk to a global supply chain, as described in this chapter.
3. Is a supply chain a type of self-adjusting feedback loop? Why or why not?
4. How do you feel about competitor companies teaming up in trade exchanges? How much cooperation is "too much," in your opinion? How should companies avoid collusion or the appearance of unethical tactics?
5. In the "game" of supply chain management, name two of today's retailers that you believe have been left behind, so to speak. Explain the reasons for your choice. What could they do to catch up?

ENDNOTES

1. Predrag Jakovljevic, "It's One Thing to Plan, and Another to Execute," Advanced Manufacturing, © CLB Media, Inc., Aurora, Ontario, Canada, January 2005.
2. Lee Pender, "The 5 Keys to Supply Chain Success," *CIO* magazine, © CXO Media, Inc., Framingham, Massachusetts, July 15, 2001.
3. David Hannon, "Retailers Push the Logistics Learning Curve," *Purchasing* magazine, © Reed Business Information, Inc., New York, September 2, 2004.
4. Alan Braithwaite, "Making Global Networks that Maximize Net Margins," for Maersk Logistics, a division of A.P. Moller-Maersk Group, Esplanaden, Copenhagen, Denmark, 2003. Used with permission of the author.
5. Alan Braithwaite, "The Supply Chain Risks of Global Sourcing," © LCP Consulting, Berkhamsted, United Kingdom. Used with permission of the author.
6. 2004 estimate, Retail Industry Leaders Association, Arlington, Virginia.
7. See endnote 5.
8. "A Guide to Voice Technology in Warehousing," VoicePicking.com, © Information Technology Toolbox, Inc., Scottsdale, Arizona, April 2005.
9. "The UPC Bar Code at 30 Years of Age," Retail Insight, newsletter of LakeWest Group, LLC, Cleveland, Ohio, April 2004.
10. Evan Schurman, "RFID Market In for Major Shakeup, Report Shows," eWeek.com, © 2005, Ziff Davis Publishing Holdings, Inc., New York, April 7, 2005. All rights reserved.
11. Daniel Lord, "B2B eCommerce," © Business Insights, Ltd., London, United Kingdom, 2001.
12. "Home Depot Self-Checkout Boosts Sales, Satisfaction," eWeek.com, © Ziff Davis Media, Inc., New York, April 10, 2005.
13. Jack Stack, *The Great Game of Business* (New York: Doubleday/Currency Publishing, 1992).

GLOSSARY

B

bar code   See *Universal Product Code (UPC)*.

beta test   A test of a new computer system with a group of business users to get feedback and make adjustments before the system is finalized.

boom-to-bust business cycle   A phenomenon in trendy or emerging markets in which sudden bursts of demand for a product prompt overproduction and excess inventory buildup to avoid shortages; then when the demand drops (sometimes just as suddenly), companies are left carrying too much unsold inventory.

build-to-order (BTO)   The manufacturing practice of waiting until an order is placed to make or assemble the product, and only in sufficient quantities to fill the order with very little overage. This prevents having to store unsold items until needed. Also called *mass customization*.

build-to-stock (BTS)   The manufacturing method of making commodity-type products in advance and keeping them in stock until they are ordered or purchased.

bullwhip effect   A phenomenon in which small changes in consumer demand for a product cause a ripple of misinformation through the supply chain. The result is that demand is overstated to companies further removed from the consumer, creating behaviors like hoarding, over-ordering, and overproducing in anticipation of a demand that is not as great as expected.

C

carrying costs   The term for what it costs at various points in a supply chain to store, handle, and insure the inventory.

conceptual design   A high-level overview of a system, or set of systems, drawn using simple shapes to represent components of the design, and lines or arrows to show the direction of data flow and activity between them.

core competencies   The things a company specializes in or does best.

cross-docking (or crossdocking)   An inventory-minimizing process in which products are brought in large quantities to distribution centers, where they are off-loaded, recombined, and reloaded onto outbound vehicles for delivery based on needs of individual stores.

D

dashboard   A concise one-sheet (or one-screen) display of key metrics or indicators, which includes top-line information for the person or department that will use it to check the progress of a program, project, department, and so on.

data warehouse   A storage system for data. It consists of a database, appropriate software, and automated connections to other systems so that relevant data may be collected on a regular and timely basis and retrieved easily as needed.

distribution center (DC)   A large, regional warehouse where bulk shipments of products arrive from single product locations to be combined into smaller orders and quickly reloaded for reshipment, usually to individual stores.

E

economic lot size (ELS)   The calculation of what is the most cost-effective quantity of an item to make in a single lot or production run.

economic order quantity (EOQ)   The calculation of what the minimum order should be for a product to be considered cost-effective to produce or supply it.

Electronic Article Numbering (EAN)   The 13-digit *bar code* system used in Europe.

Electronic Data Interchange (EDI)   The capability to receive orders, send delivery notifications and invoices, receive payments, and so on by computer.

emergent behavior   An interconnected system of relatively simple elements (a group of individuals, company, or supply chain) that self-organizes naturally to form a more intelligent and adaptive higher-level system.

Enterprise Resource Planning (ERP)   A common type of computer system used in business to gather data from across multiple functions in a company. ERP systems monitor orders, production schedules, raw material purchases, and finished goods inventory. ERP systems are good at tracking data but generally do not have the more complex capability to analyze it.

e-procurement   The ability to complete purchasing functions online, usually on a secure Web site where vendors put their product catalogs, order forms, and other data for customers or supply chain partners to access.

eXtensible Markup Language (XML)   A technology that enables data transmission in flexible formats, which can be used to store any type of structured information and to encapsulate information to pass between computers that would otherwise be unable to communicate.

F

forward buying   The tendency of consumers to purchase an item sooner, or in greater quantity, than they normally would because it is on sale.

G

generalized assignment   A type of *milk run* delivery scheduling system in which trucks are assigned delivery routes based on the vehicle's capacity or total travel time.

global data synchronization   The ability of companies in a supply chain to use technology to synchronize its data with partner companies' data so they can work together to plan, forecast, produce, and deliver the right amounts of goods to their end users.

Global Trade Identification Number (GTIN)   A 14-digit *bar code* system for product identification being suggested by the Uniform Code Council as a universal replacement for UPC and EAN numbers.

J

job lot storage   A method of storing goods or parts together based on their use in or relationship to a particular job or for a particular type of customer.

M

mass customization   See *build-to-order.*

maverick spending   The purchase of items by employees or officers of a company without having a contract with the supplier, or using an unapproved vendor.

metrics   Measurements of performance.

milk run   Slang term for a delivery schedule that is routed to bring products from a single origin to multiple receiving locations, or to pick up products at a variety of locations and drop them at a single receiving site, such as a DC.

MRO   Abbreviation for "maintenance, repair, and operations," some of the indirect purchases companies make to service their own needs.

multiple sourcing   Purchasing quantities of the same item from a number of suppliers.

O

order batching   The practice of ordering large amounts of product to minimize shipping or production costs. When done without regard to the actual demand for the product, order batching can become a factor that causes a bullwhip effect in a supply chain.

out-of-stocks (OOS)   Industry slang for products that would normally be sold but are unavailable, often (but not always) due to a supply chain malfunction.

outside flexibility   The ability of a company to quickly provide customers with additional products that enhance other items the customer normally purchases.

P

postponement   A technique in which generic subassemblies are prepared and stored by supply chain partners and only assembled as needed in order to minimize the risk of holding large parts inventories that may become obsolete. Also known as *variability pooling.*

process decomposition diagrams   Process maps or flowcharts that provide the processing logic and sequences to be used, indicating the types and volumes of data that a new system will handle. Also see *process mapping*.

process mapping   Drawing a diagram to show the steps in a process or system. Also see *conceptual design*.

procurement   The range of activities a company undertakes to select and qualify suppliers, negotiate prices, and engage in other pursuits related to the purchasing of goods and services.

R

radio frequency identification (RFID)   A product identification system that uses tiny computer chips placed on products. The chips contain and can transmit large volumes of information about the product to a wireless reading device without physical contact or close proximity.

relational database technology   The most common type of computer database, in which related groups of data are stored in individual tables and retrieved as needed with the use of a standard programming language.

reverse logistics   The system of handling items that are returned to a supply chain for any reason—damaged goods, defective merchandise, customer returns, and so on.

run-out time   A manufacturing term for estimating the number of days or weeks it will take to deplete product inventory on hand based on its expected demand.

S

savings matrix   A system for scheduling *milk run* deliveries in which each vehicle and delivery driver has certain customers and orders to fill within delivery time windows.

self-adjusting feedback loop   The practice of using real-time data to monitor business activity and make adjustments quickly and efficiently.

shortage gaming   Retailers or distributors' over-ordering when they know that a product is in short supply and/or being rationed, to ensure that they get as much of it as they want.

single sourcing   A company's decision to purchase exclusively from one supplier of a product, even though there are other potential suppliers.

sole sourcing   The use of a single supplier of a raw material, product, or component because there is no other supplier that can provide it.

stock-keeping unit (SKU) storage   A style of storing goods based on their SKU numbers so that all of a given type of product is stored together.

supply chain   A combination of the companies and their business activities needed to design, make, deliver, and use a product or service.

supply chain integration   The ability of companies in a supply chain to share data and synchronize business functions using technology, in order to perform more efficiently or cost-effectively.

system prototype A model or sample system, usually of a technology-based deliverable such as a Web site or computer program.

T

T&E Slang for "turn and earn," a calculation of the profitability of inventory by tracking the speed with which it is sold ("turned over") during a particular time period.

technical architecture The hardware, operating system, and database software of a computer system that supports or allows the *user interface.*

third-party logistics (3PL) A type of outsourcing; the use of a separate company to handle another company's logistics functions, such as delivery, usually under contract.

throughput In a supply chain, the rate at which sales to the customer or end user occur.

time boxing A method for defining the time limits and/or setting deadlines for each task in a long-term project. A realistic time box or time period is presented to the people doing the work, who must then figure out how to do the job within that time period.

trade exchange Alliances between companies that may typically be competitors in order to make cheaper, bulk-quantity purchases of some goods or services.

U

Universal Product Code (UPC) A product identification label. The code consists of up to 12 numbers and black lines and white spaces of varying widths, which can be read by a computerized scanner. Also called a *bar code.*

upside flexibility The ability of a company or supply chain to respond quickly to additional order volume for the products they carry.

user interface The way a person uses a particular computer program; a step-by-step process map for what the screens will look like and how a person negotiates or "moves through" the system.

V

variability pooling See *postponement.*

vendor-managed inventory (VMI) A replenishment system in which the vendor (supplier) is responsible for checking the product quantities in stores and filling as needed to prevent out-of-stocks.

vertical integration A traditional supply chain system in which a company owns or manages as many parts of its supply chain as possible, in order to gain maximum efficiency through economies of scale.

virtual integration The linking by computer companies in a supply chain that all perform different, complementary activities in the chain with maximum efficiency because they are able to share real-time information.

visibility A term for the sharing of data and other information among all the companies in a supply chain for their mutual benefit; sometimes referred to as "transparency."

voice-activated technology   Computer software that can recognize human voices. In inventory management, it is used in wireless communication systems to instruct order pickers by headset. Also known as *voice-directed picking*.

INDEX